AF321643

Luminos is the Open Access monograph publishing program from UC Press. Luminos provides a framework for preserving and reinvigorating monograph publishing for the future and increases the reach and visibility of important scholarly work. Titles published in the UC Press Luminos model are published with the same high standards for selection, peer review, production, and marketing as those in our traditional program. www.luminosoa.org

RACE, LABOR MIGRATION, AND THE LAW

Robyn Rodriguez and Leticia Saucedo, editors

This series publishes works that foreground race and the development of labor arrangements and the ways in which employers continue to rationalize treatment of foreign workers through processes of dehumanization that depend on logics of white supremacy, anti-Blackness, and other forms of racialized difference production. Importantly, the series explores the ways in which law shapes conditions of unfreedom, given that the law is deeply implicated in structures of global capitalism.

1. *Constructed Movements: Extraction and Resistance in Mexican Migrant Communities*, by Ragini Shah

Constructed Movements

Constructed Movements

Extraction and Resistance in Mexican Migrant Communities

Ragini Shah

UNIVERSITY OF CALIFORNIA PRESS

University of California Press
Oakland, California

© 2025 by Ragini Shah

This work is licensed under a Creative Commons (CC BY-NC-ND) license. To view a copy of the license, visit http://creativecommons.org/licenses.

Cover art: "Puentes," by Cecilia Sánchez Duarte

Suggested citation: Shah, R. *Constructed Movements: Extraction and Resistance in Mexican Migrant Communities*. Oakland: University of California Press, 2025. DOI: https://doi.org/10.1525/luminos.214

Library of Congress Cataloging-in-Publication Data

Names: Shah, Ragini, author.
Title: Constructed movements : extraction and resistance in Mexican migrant communities / Ragini Shah.
Description: Oakland : University of California Press, 2025. | Series: Race, labor migration, and the law ; vol 1 | Includes bibliographical references and index.
Identifiers: LCCN 2024026588 (print) | LCCN 2024026589 (ebook) | ISBN 9780520404472 (paperback) | ISBN 9780520404489 (ebook)
Subjects: LCSH: Foreign workers, Mexican—Legal status, laws, etc.—United States. | Migrant labor—Legal status, laws, etc.—United States. | United States—Emigration and immigration—Government policy. | Compensation (Law)—United States. | Compensation (Law)—Mexico. | Forced migration—Mexico. | Mexico—Emigration and immigration. | Quality of life—Mexico.
Classification: LCC KF4848.M48 S53 2025 (print) | LCC KF4848.M48 (ebook) | DDC 342.7308/2—dc23/eng/20240614

LC record available at https://lccn.loc.gov/2024026588
LC ebook record available at https://lccn.loc.gov/2024026589

34 33 32 31 30 29 28 27 26 25
10 9 8 7 6 5 4 3 2 1

*To my parents, Navin and Rohini Shah, whose life and stories have always
been the inspiration for my work, including the work on this book*

CONTENTS

ILLUSTRATIONS

FIGURES

TABLES

Writing is both a solitary and a community activity. In this project, I was fortunate to be accompanied by the many migrant community members in Mexico who shared their time, homes, meals, experiences, hopes, and fears with me. Their stories have continued to move and inspire me through many secluded hours of drafting, redrafting, editing, and reorganizing. This book would not be possible without the contributions of dozens of people who confided their truths and exposed me to their work. I am particularly grateful to Norma, Itzel, Bernardo, and Rosa, who shepherded my work in many of the communities profiled here and offered their insights. Thanks also to Celeste, Bruno, and the other student researchers of the Mexican Migration Project, who allowed me to accompany and learn from them on their survey of towns in Tabasco. I was humbled to receive a Carlos Robles Fulbright award to engage in the ethnographic portion of my research and am thankful to Jorge Durand and the Departamento de Estudios sobre los Movimientos Sociales (Department of Social Movement Studies) at the University of Guadalajara for acting as my host institution.

Over the many trips to Mexico, I was supported by a generous community of organizers, lawyers, and scholars, including Ben Cokelet, Jorge Durand, Ariadna Estévez, Enrique Guerra Manzo, Agustin Hernandez Ceja, Arturo Lomeli, and Ofelia Woo. Ariadna patiently supported my work through its earliest phases and was sure that I had something unique to contribute. I was also fortunate to be part of a greater community of U.S.-based scholars working in Mexico, including Richard Mines, Adam Goodman, Jen Tyburczy, and the late Maria-Elena Martinez. Holly and Richard Mines were particularly crucial to helping me adjust to work and life in Guadalajara, along with Jennifer, Ignacio ("Nacho"), Bill, Mathilde, and Mathieu.

In the United States, I am extremely fortunate to be part of a collaborative, generous, and thoughtful community at Suffolk University. I am especially appreciative that former Suffolk Law School dean, Camille Nelson, and former director of clinical programs, Jeff Pokorak, enthusiastically supported my request for a year's leave to engage in nonlegal research for a book project. Suffolk University continued this support by agreeing to fund my follow-up research trip through its Faculty Initiatives Fund. Over the years, many colleagues have offered support and advice for which I am grateful. They include Sarah Boonin, Frank Cooper, Rebecca Curtin, Lolita Darden, Nicole Friederichs, Jonathan Haughton, Christina Miller, Kim McLaurin, Jeff Pokorak, Ilene Seidman, Pat Shin, Jessica Silbey, Elizabeth Trujillo, and Liz Valentin.

Early research for this book began as an examination of the connection between neoliberal economic adjustment in Mexico and migration from that country to the United States. I am indebted to my first research assistant, Melissa Bruynell, who obtained hundreds of International Monetary Fund (IMF) documents and helped analyze them over the course of almost two years. Those documents formed a significant part of the research for chapter 1 and for the overall theory I put forward in this book. I am also indebted to three other research assistants, Tristan James Smith and Jemmie Tejeda Martinez, who looked into several specific US immigration enforcement initiatives; and Hope Olsen, whose work contributed to the economically based tables in chapter 1.

Outside of my immediate institution, I am extremely grateful for the support of an incredible community of patient, generous, and brilliant scholars from across disciplines who gave of their time and intellectual energy to push my analysis forward. I am particularly fortunate to be part of "immprof," an extraordinarily engaged, kind, and supportive community of academics analyzing the law's impact on international migrants. Several of them, including Hemant Gundavaram, Karla McKanders, Rachel Rosenbloom, and Yolanda Vazquez, read almost every word of the manuscript, providing invaluable encouragement and kind, incisive feedback on the earliest and roughest drafts and continuing to patiently comment again on sections and chapters until the end. Karla was also the brains behind the legal ethnography roundtable, and I was buoyed by her input and that of Susan Biber-Coutin, Tanya Cooper, and Roslyn Satchel on our intersecting methodologies. Karla's and Tanya's input in particular helped me concretize connections that were hard to translate on paper. Another set of superb immprof/immprof-adjacent women—Sherley Cruz Elenny, Carmen Gonzalez, Laila Hlass, Carrie Rosenbaum, and Anita Sinha—offered their insights on key arguments, pushing me to sharpen and refine my analysis. I am humbled that Tanya Golash-Boza, Ruth Gomberg Muñoz, and Douglas Massey lent their expertise and critical eyes to important portions of the work and contributed to its overall lucidity. I gained valuable insights at several conferences, including from Ariadna Estevez, Jennifer Lee, Elisa Ortega-Velazquez at Law and Society and Valeria Gomez, Jayesh Rathod, Fatma Marouf, and Faiza Sayed at the Clinical Law Review Writer's Workshop. Clinicians, like immprofers, are a generous group. In particular, Wendy Bach provided key early encouragement and ongoing inspiration through her prolific writing and commitment to social justice. And just as I was honing my arguments, Nadine Naber provided valuable insights and concrete steps for finding my scholarly voice.

I am also grateful to the two anonymous reviewers whose comments and suggestions helped sharpen the analysis and make the arguments more precise. I am humbled to be part of any series edited by Leticia Saucedo and Robyn Rodriguez, particularly Race, Labor Migration, and the Law. Leti and Robyn, thank you for your insights and encouragement. To my editor, Maura Roessner, thank you for early enthusiasm and connecting me to this amazing series. And much gratitude to the UC Press team, including Maura, Sheila Berg, Teresa Iafolla, Emily Park, and Sam Warren for all your work shepherding and refining the manuscript and publicizing the book.

As a legal scholar, I am keenly aware that framing justice is more elusive than naming injustice. I am fortunate to have friends who imagine what is just and are committed to the intellectual, political, and day-to-day *work* it will take to get there. In this vein, I have been carried through the gloom and despair of relentless injustice to inspiration and hope by the exceptional and fierce lawyer-writers Sunu Chandy, Palyn Hung, Chaumtoli Huq, Jennifer J. Lee, Ranjana Natarajan, Robin Thorner, and Denise Tomasini-Joshi and visionaries of all trades: Toyin Ajayi, Anjali Kamat, Ronak Kapadia, Biju Matthew, Pooja Mehta, Ali Mir, Tejasvi Nagaraja, Rupal Oza, Prachi Patankar, Vijay Ramalingam, Prerana Reddy, Ashwini Rao, Smita Rawoot, Rakshi Saleem, Christian Schutz, Silky Shah, Svati Shah, Michael Shonle, Amita Swadhin, Saadia Toor, and Shalini Vallabhan. Thank you all for your friendship and courage. Being in your orbits has given me faith even during the darkest moments in our world. Thank you in particular to Rupal Oza and Svati Shah, who took my calls across oceans and time zones. Your wisdom and clarity cut through the muddy writing process at exactly the right moments.

I have also been fortunate to work with many immigrants' rights organizers in the United States, including Sabrina, Natalia, Lily, Renata, Kathy, Valeria, Conrado, Carlos, Isabel, and Reina, who have steadfastly and powerfully envisioned immigrant justice. Your work, commitment, and persistence has built so much power and yielded inspiring results in the face of steep challenges. I am honored to know and work with you.

My vast extended family is a source of great joy. There are, quite literally, too many to name, but their wisdom, humor, and love have buoyed me over the years. From the eldest grand-uncle to my littlest great-niece, I am lucky to have such warm, loving, and funny relatives. To my parents, Navin and Rohini Shah, to whom this book is dedicated, thank you for the sacrifices you made so that I never wanted and for your belief that I could do anything. Yours were the first immigrant stories that I heard and watched, and, in a very real way, being your daughter has inspired my career and this book. I am also fortunate to have been welcomed into the Lobo/D'Souza brood, whose warmth, love, and compassion for others has been a source of inspiration and delight. So too have I benefited from the love and support of the Indian community in Charlotte, North Carolina, a kind of extended family in its own right, including lifelong friends, Sadhana Char, Kruti Desai, Amita Patel, and Shimul Vasa, and adopted second parents, Shruti and Arun Shah and Charu and Kirit Shukla.

And finally, to my partner, Sanjay D'Souza, my life has been incalculably enriched by sharing it with you. I could not have engaged in the years of research and writing for this book without your unwavering support. Thank you for putting up with my long absences and weekends of furious editing with your characteristic cheerfulness. Your optimism and encouragement, including while you were reading the first draft, lifted me through my moments of doubt in this writing project, as it does in our daily life. Thank you for your light, love, humor, and companionship. I am absolutely the better for it.

Introduction

In the hills of San Martín Duraznos, Oaxaca, Elfego was tending to his harvest of *setas* (oyster mushrooms). The mushrooms were placed in paper bags and stored in a partially constructed house belonging to Elfego's son. The setas harvest was part of Elfego's and other returned migrants' efforts to create sustainable employment in the pueblo. Elfego met the other migrants and received technical support for his setas project from the Frente Indígena de Organizaciones Binacionales (FIOB; Indigenous Front of Binational Organizations). FIOB's and Elfego's goal was to create sustainable, locally based employment to serve as an alternative to migration.

Elfego himself was a returned migrant, having spent nearly thirty years traveling back and forth to the United States. Elfego's trips were not authorized by the U.S. government, but he found ways to enter the country. He described his first trip in 1985 as "easy," because at that time there were few U.S. law enforcement agents patrolling the area close to Tijuana–San Diego where he crossed. Even after the United States heightened its border enforcement efforts, his trips were successful. Like many of his compatriots, Elfego adjusted to U.S. enforcement efforts by moving his trips farther east and hiring a *coyote*, or guide. Though he was arrested by the U.S. Border Patrol on each of his trips, he was released each time and made subsequent trips. In all, he was able to successfully enter the United States half a dozen times. Moreover, each time he entered, he found work— picking strawberries and other produce in California and Oregon, gardening in Oregon, or building homes in Washington State. During his nearly thirty years in various parts of the United States, Elfego never encountered interior immigration enforcement officials.[1]

The reason for all these trips to the United States was straightforward, according to Elfego: "I left because in my town there was no work. Nothing else but farming only corn. There was no other activity in the town." Elfego took his first trip in 1985 when he was just sixteen years old. In subsequent years, he married and had four children. Once his children reached school age, he continued to migrate to provide his children with an education. As in other rural parts of Mexico, there was little access to public transportation, and the middle and high schools were located in far-off towns and charged fees that were difficult for families to pay. Elfego was able to educate his children through *secundaria* (middle school) but had to stop migrating before he could gather sufficient resources to pay for the more expensive *preparatoria* (high school). After nearly thirty years' working in some of the harshest labor conditions in the United States, Elfego's body gave out. He decided to return to Mexico permanently. Though he continued to work in agriculture when he returned to Mexico, he was now in better control of his working hours and conditions. When asked if he would consider going back to the United States, he said, "The body can only handle so much." He was in his mid-forties.

Elfego's eldest son, Jaime, benefited greatly from his father's migration. He was able to complete a higher level of education than either of his parents. However, work continued to be scarce in Mixteca in the late 1990s when he completed secundaria. As a result, Jaime gathered resources and paid a coyote to take him to California in 2006. Unlike his father, Jaime has not been able to return to San Martín Duraznos because the expense and danger of the journey has increased exponentially since his father's last trip. As we spoke in the house that Jaime was building for his family, Elfego was wistful about the fact that Jaime would likely not return for many more years, until his goal of finishing the house had been completed.

The story of Elfego and his family is not unusual. This book profiles eight migrant communities in the states of Oaxaca, Tabasco, Tlaxcala, and Puebla. By "migrant communities," I am referring to all of the people who live in communities from which migrants hail, including the migrants themselves and their family members, as well as community leaders and those who do not migrate. Two-thirds of the communities, like Elfego's, strongly identify as Indigenous. Unique to this book, the communities I discuss represent distinct Indigenous groups with very different histories in the context of Mexico and differing migration patterns to the United States. San Martín Duraznos and other migrant communities in Oaxaca that I discuss are Mixtec, whereas some of the towns in Tlaxcala and Puebla identify as Nahuatl. In contrast, the communities in Tabasco and one community in Tlaxcala did not report strong Indigenous group affiliations. Given this diversity, it was remarkable to find that most people living in these towns and villages face issues similar to Elfego's: lack of economic activity, insufficient public resources, industries pulling them to work in northern Mexico or the United States, and the inability to fully fill the community's economic gap with their earnings in the north.

The parallel economic gaps in the dusty hills of Oaxaca where Elfego lives, in the rich green tropical forests of Tabasco, and in the semiurban areas of Tlaxcala and Puebla are not naturally occurring. Rather, these gaps are the results of an economy constructed by economic elites in the United States and Mexico to enrich themselves. In order to benefit these elites, resources had to be divested and extracted, including the extraction of people dislocated by disinvestment. Once dislocated, people like Elfego were displaced into industries hungry for exploitable labor in the United States and in the northern borderlands of Mexico. While their earnings in these new spaces were higher than what they could earn at home, they were generally insufficient to allow their children and grandchildren to thrive in their home communities. Rather, a new generation began to move, seeking goals similar to their parents'. Moreover, the limited economic gains were outweighed in many families by the pain of family separation. Thus the overall experience of migration at the community level was one of dispossession, dismemberment of family relations, exploitation, and entrapment in a vicious cycle. Together, these interweaving experiences of migrants, their family members, and community leaders lead to an understanding of *migration as extraction*.

Considering migration as extraction may seem to discount the agency of migrants like Elfego by casting them as passive objects shuffled by large economic systems. Far from lacking agency, migrants discussed the choices they made in extremely limited and harsh circumstances. What is more, many migrants, like Elfego, participated in efforts to reverse extraction by fighting for self-determination rights for their communities, a return of resources, and investment in self-sustainability. This was particularly evident in Indigenous migrant communities. In Oaxaca, where Indigenous resistance to ongoing colonial efforts is particularly strong, community organizations like FIOB fight all of these battles as part of an effort to make migration more of a choice than the necessity that it currently is. Similarly, the Nahuatl communities in Tlaxcala and Puebla seek to reverse the effects of family separation and build sustainable economies. In Tabasco, where Indigenous identities and organizing are less apparent, individual migrants discussed the need to reinvest in their community's economic health. Thus agency in migrant communities is most clearly expressed in their resistance to migration.

MIGRATION AS EXTRACTION EXPLAINED

At the theoretical level, migration as extraction allows for an understanding of migration beyond the debates over what pushes migrants, what pulls them to certain industries or destinations, and whether migration can be a source of development. These debates generally treat questions about push, pull, and impact separately, implying that they function independently of each other. Elfego's story and those of others profiled in this book show that in fact these factors are closely connected. Migration as extraction seeks to represent these empirical connections in a theoretical frame. Thus, under migration as extraction, push, pull, and impact factors are treated as three phases of the same overall dynamic rather than three separate dynamics. These phases are not necessarily chronological as they can and do overlap temporally. However, sequentializing each phase helps clarify the contours of migration as extraction, including the actors, policies, and dynamics involved.

The first phase is *dislocation*, in which people are uprooted from their homes by their inability to make a sustainable living. The U.S. and Mexican governments have long colluded in colonial endeavors that move resources toward large corporate interests and foment dislocation. These endeavors reached a fever pitch under the neoliberal structural adjustment policies of the 1980s, which saw massive cuts to agricultural subsidies and spending on education and wage suppression. Of course, dislocation for Indigenous peoples, like the Mixtecs profiled in this book, began long before the twentieth century's neoliberal era, instigated at a large scale in the sixteenth century by the brutal Spanish conquest. For the Tlaxcaltecs, who collaborated with the Spanish conquistadors,[2] dislocation began more recently during the post-independence era of *mestizaje* (racial/cultural mixing) and other Mexican assimilationist policies. These cultural assimilation policies resulted in political and economic marginalization, which in turn brought on depictions of Indigenous peoples in Mexico as premodern peons who had to be uprooted in order to contribute to Mexico's growth.[3] Thus, calls for "modernizing" the Mexican peasantry in the 1960s during the era of the Bracero Accords with the United States and up to the 1980s neoliberal era are rooted in a much longer continuous thread of dislocations culminating with the migration of people like Elfego. Dislocation from the communities in Tabasco that identify less with any Indigenous group began much later, as neoliberal economic policies took hold across the country. In addition to its racial contours, these dislocations are gendered, with primarily male members of families migrating and most women experiencing either the "feminization of staying" or a highly feminized pattern of dislocation.[4]

These racialized and gendered scripts in Mexico were echoed in the United States, where Indigenous and non-Indigenous Mexican workers were characterized as both bestial and docile to justify their *displacement* into the U.S. agricultural industry. Gendered patterns of displacement brought mostly men into the fields and mostly women into food processing. As U.S. capital expanded to manufacturing and carceral operations, so too did the displacement of Mexican workers into a range of highly abusive labor markets that continued to include agribusiness in both Mexico and the United States but now also included *maquiladoras* (foreign-owned factories) that employed a highly feminized labor pool in Mexico, and the construction and service industries in the United States with often strict gender differentials. Alongside displacement into particular workplaces, Mexican men were used as the racialized fuel behind efforts to expand incarceration in the 1920s and justify expenditures on surveillance, deterrence, and detention beginning in

FIGURE 1. Three Phases of Migration as Extraction.

the 1950s.[5] These displacements are most clearly visible in U.S. agribusiness's continuous extreme reliance on Mexican labor and the consistently high percentage of Mexican migrants among those incarcerated for unlawful entry.[6] The twin policies of labor recruitment and incarceration resulted in making Mexican migrants into a "caste of illegals" who had to increasingly rely on coyotes to complete their displacement north.[7] *Coyotaje* then emerges as a third source of extraction in the form of ever-increasing fees charged to guide migrants to their constructed destinations. Migrants went from crossing the border on their own in the 1980s to paying up to US$8,000 in 2013.

Once in the United States, exploitation is not only situated in carceral spaces and places of employment, but also the economic extraction from migrants' efforts to improve conditions in their home communities and the emotional extraction of family separation. Formal and informal financial institutions and the Mexican treasury extract from migrant earnings and remittances, reducing migrant communities' ability to build self-sufficiency.[8] Migrants like Elfego attempt to leverage their earnings with programs like Tres por Uno (3x1, or Three for One) to improve conditions in their home communities and prevent their children from migrating. However, as was the case with Elfego's son, Jaime, the programs are not enough to overcome the gaps left by neoliberalism. Moreover, migrant families face a severance of family ties, what one interviewee called "family disintegration" and scholars have called "family dismemberment."[9] Women, specifically mothers, face the brunt of family separation as they navigate alienation from their partners, new roles within their family, and economic scarcity.[10] The result is an *entrenchment* of family separation and migration as a mode of economic stability. Entrenchment, in turn, leads to more migration, thus perpetuating the migration-as-extraction cycle.

As can be seen in figure 1, which shows the dynamics present in each phase of migration as extraction, migration is an integral part of a larger economic context of resource extraction and redistribution. This is qualitatively different from seeing

FIGURE 2. Traditional Theories of Migration and Extraction.

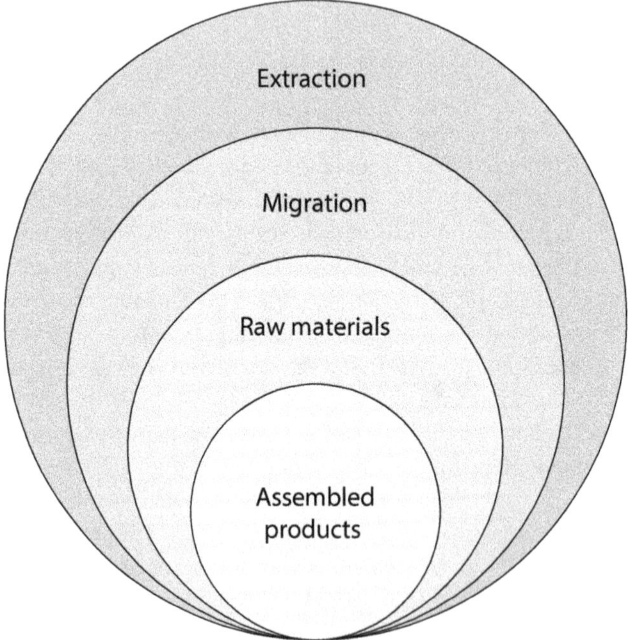

FIGURE 3. Migration as Extraction.

migration as impacted by extraction. Rather, it is more accurate to see migration as extraction itself (figures 2, 3).

MIGRATION AS EXTRACTION AND RESISTANCE IN COMMUNITIES

"Migration as extraction" refers to the structural nature of migration rather than the act of migrating by an individual or the particular experiences of one migrant family or even community. Thus the phrase was not explicitly used by migrant community members. Rather, it grew out of listening closely to the ways in which migrants, migrants' family members, and community organizers described their material conditions. In explaining both their decisions to migrate and the impacts that it had on their lives, migrants routinely referred to "the government [not] supporting us," with some Indigenous migrants going so far to say that "the government does not even make it to us." Returned migrants movingly described working until their bodies gave out, being injured, being *mal pagado* (badly paid), and, in the words of one Mixtec returned migrant, being "treated like slaves." Similarly, the stories that unfold in the ensuing chapters show that the impacts of migration are beneficial for individual family members of migrants, but, at the community level, migration cannot overcome the structural gaps created by decades—or even centuries, in the case of Indigenous migrant communities—of resource extraction and facilitation of highly exploitative industries. Community leaders explained the limits of remittances by saying that they "did nothing for the pueblo as a whole." And even individual family members who reported benefiting from remittances indicated that this was complicated by the "emotional loss" of family members that some referred to as "family disintegration." Thus, though the exact phrase "migration as extraction" was not used in migrant communities, their lived and reported realities lead to a structural understanding of migration as part of an overall extractive process rather than a form of resistance to it.

This does not mean that migrant communities are passively participating in the migration-as-extraction structure. To the contrary, within the Indigenous migrant communities in particular, extraction is being met by strong, organized resistance. Like the individual interviewees, the migrant community advocacy groups, like FIOB, do not explicitly use the terminology of extraction or extractivism. However, their efforts and arguments denote an understanding that the antidote to mass migration from their communities is a return of resources and the repair of relationships. Tellingly, one of the most advanced efforts, led by FIOB, is called a "right not to migrate," indicating the pernicious nature of migration and the desire, in these communities, to build a sustainable economy that does not require migration as part of its structure. The "right not to migrate" movement does not completely eschew migration as a strategy but rather seeks to make it a true choice, one that does not require a dangerous and expensive journey and that replaces the current exploitative employment relationship with robust employment rights. This movement and other efforts by FIOB to reverse the entrenchment of migration have been meticulously documented by FIOB members and academics alike.[11] In particular, these works have recognized the role that women have played in setting organizational agendas as well as the role the organization has played in transforming gender roles and family relationships.[12] This book builds on the insights into FIOB's organizational process, strategies, and demands by connecting those organizational dynamics to the processes they are resisting.

This book also offers insight into a less well-documented but equally powerful movement in Central Mexico. Like FIOB, the members of Centro de Atención de Familias Migrantes e Indígenas (CAFAMI; Indigenous Migrant Family Care Center) in Tlaxcala seek to build sustainable communities that allow migration to be a choice. In contrast to FIOB's membership of mostly returned migrants, CAFAMI's members are all family members of migrants and all are women. This provides critical insights into the ways in which women's leadership, virtually unhindered by male presence, informs the makeup, decision making, and demands of an organization. It is telling that one of the first projects that CAFAMI's membership took up was rebuilding family bonds eviscerated by migration. It is equally telling that the organization sought to reclaim language and community medicines and toiletries. Through these projects CAFAMI's members are resisting the extractive, separationist forces of family disintegration and capitalist consumption by rerooting their bonds with kin and land.[13]

Even in the absence of ties to Indigenous or other forms of organized resistance, returned migrant workers in Tabasco seek (re)investment by the Mexican state in their existing entrepreneurial efforts. Farmers (mostly men) seek the return of agricultural supports that made local production sustainable prior to the 1990s, and restauranteurs (mostly women) seek infrastructure improvements that would allow more customers to access their businesses. As part of these demands, returned migrant women discussed the need to share the resources extracted from the state by oil production occurring within view of their *locales* (small restaurants) on the *malecón* (boardwalk). These demands, like CAFAMI's, have not been documented previously and provide a powerful window into the ways in which local communities seek to resist the extractive force of migration and demand a return of resources extracted to enrich U.S. and Mexican elites. Figure 4 demonstrates the relationship between all of these forms of resistance and the phases of migration as extraction.

The resistance exemplified in these communities requires some rethinking of prevailing legal theories describing acts of migration as resistance, decolonization, or reparations for the economically and ecologically extractive policies of neocolonial states like the United States.[14] The international legal scholar Tendayi Achiume has argued that individual acts of migration should be viewed as "acts of decolonization at the personal level" because they are attempts to overcome the structural inequalities created by colonization and achieve better outcomes.[15] Approaching migration with a slightly different lens, the legal scholar Carmen Gonzalez argues that migration should be seen as one of several acts of reparations for "climate displaced peoples" to provide these persons with "compensation for climate change and for the North's colonial and post-colonial domination of the South."[16] Achiume's and Gonzalez's insights are both supported and challenged by the experience of migrant communities. While it is certainly true that migrants move to better their own situations and that of their families, the narratives in this book show that their choices (whether or not to migrate and where to move) are constrained by the political and economic structures created as a part of and to maintain the colonial relationship between the United States and Mexico. Thus, their acts are more accurately seen as being a part of colonial domination rather than resistance

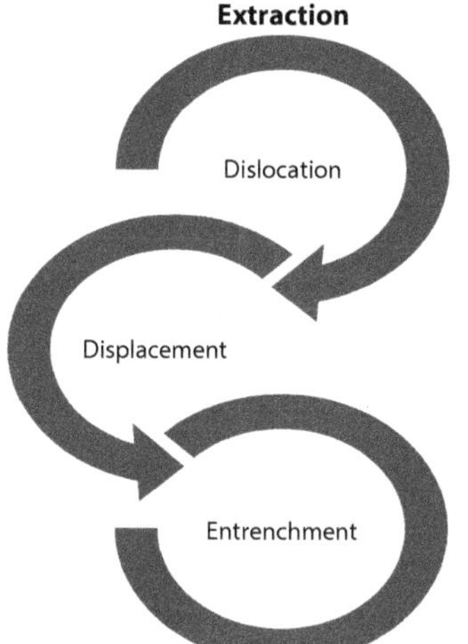

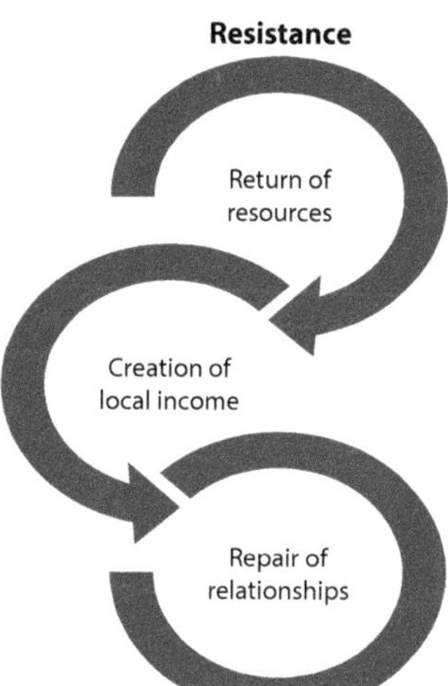

FIGURE 4. Extraction and Resistance.

to it. The resistance, exemplified by the work of Indigenous migrant organizations in particular, calls for a redistribution of resources that would lessen the need to migrate and convert migration into a more freely engaged in choice.

Migrant community members, while not specifically discussing U.S. immigration restrictions in terms of neocolonialism, did highlight the ways in which their labor contributed to the building of the U.S. economy. A number of migrants expressed frustration at being treated as illegal when their labor was what "built the country." Still others were more direct, stating that "the United States would be nothing without us." Thus, alongside demands for resources were demands for a more just immigration system that recognized the pivotal role Mexican workers in particular but also immigrant workers in general play in the development of the United States.

These demands overlap in some ways with Achiume's notion of the "co-sovereign" relationship between former colonies (which she calls "Third World states") and their colonizers ("First World states") built by the benefits of colonization to the colonizers and under which the "First World nation-state . . . has no more right to exclude Third World persons from its institutions of equal political membership than it has over its de jure citizens."[17] The demands correspond even more closely to Gonzalez's formulation of migration as reparations for the U.S. role in the "economic precarity that renders Central America particularly susceptible to climate change" and in the "conflict and poverty" resulting from "countless [U.S.] military, economic, and political interventions."[18] However, migrant community members placed much more emphasis on the ability to remain in their communities with their families and argued for migration only as a corollary to just resource distribution. Thus, they agreed with Gonzalez that migration was not a "magic bullet" but went further, by fighting for a return of state resources to make migration a much less dominant part of their everyday reality. This book seeks to amplify the demands of these groups for renewed state investment and safe pathways to migrate and to expand those demands to include the need for the U.S. government to funnel resources to these communities and to create more migrant-centered immigration policies.

MIGRATION AS EXTRACTION AS AN EVOLUTION OF EXISTING CRITIQUES OF RACIAL CAPITALISM AND NEOLIBERALISM

Migration as extraction builds on decades of work by scholars in a wide array of disciplines. Earlier work provided in-depth but functionally separate examinations of migration's push factors (dislocation), pull factors (displacement or transfer), enforcement mechanisms, and impacts (entrenchment). For example, Saskia Sassen, Douglas Massey, Jorge Durand, Dolores Acevedo and Thomas Espenshade, Bill Ong Hing, and Raul Fernández and Gilberto González have ably shown how U.S. interventions in the Mexican economy have created conditions pushing people to migrate to the United States.[19] Kelly Lytle Hernández, Deborah S. Kang, Joseph Nevins, Patrick Ettinger, Mae Ngai, Kitty Calavita, and Timothy Dunn have meticulously documented U.S. policies that displaced people from Mexico into certain industries in the United States.[20] Ngai and Calavita in particular have contributed to our understanding of Mexican workers, particularly agricultural workers, as colonized or captured labor that is simultaneously recruited and demonized.[21] Kevin Johnson, Yolanda Vazquez, Doug Keller, Tanya Golash-Boza, and Nicolas De Genova have more fully developed the demonization side of displacement, showing how racialized depictions of Latinos in general and Mexicans in particular are at the root of U.S. immigration enforcement policies.[22] Finally, the Mexico-based scholars Raúl Delgado Wise and Rodolfo Zamora and their collaborators have carefully and consistently demonstrated that the remittances of migrants, while potentially beneficial to individual families, cannot fill the structural gaps left by decades of disinvestment and resource redistribution and that migration results in a severe fracturing of family ties.[23]

Building on this foundation, scholars began to connect the various processes that make up what I call migration as extraction. Key to these connections was an understanding of migration as part of racial capitalism, particularly as expressed in the neoliberal policies beginning in the late 1970s. Coined by the historian Cedric Robinson, the term "racial capitalism" explicates capitalism as requiring the creation of new or the deployment of existing racialized categories to justify the exploitation required to sustain capitalist accumulation.[24] One of the key racialized categories that Robinson highlights in his exposition of the origins of capitalism is the migrant laborer who becomes "raced" as a natural worker by extracting states (i.e., as a "natural slave" in the case of the Slavs in England or the Tartars in Italy) in order to enrich the local elites.[25] Understanding the connections between racialization and capitalist accumulation proved fruitful in drawing parallels between what had seemed to be the separate policies of pulling resources out of marginalized communities and putting them into highly exploitative industries and policing/securitization practices. In the post-neoliberal era, scholars have expanded our understanding of the ways in which racial capitalism operates not only to naturalize the exploitation of workers but also to normalize economic disinvestment and the entrenchment of poverty and the creation and expansion of what Nicolas De Genova and Alfonso Gonzalez call the "homeland security state."[26] Sassen's notion of multiple logics of "expulsion," Golash Boza's articulation of the "neoliberal cycle," Jamie Longazel and Miranda Hallet's application of the concept "social death," and Cecilia Menjívar and Leisy Abrego's formulation of "legal violence" all connect the forces dislocating people from their homes with those that naturalize the displacement of migrants into highly racialized U.S. immigration enforcement methods, leading to ever increasing resources for the homeland security state.[27] A different portion of the displacement phase—that which pulls people into the United States—is combined with the dislocation phase in Raul Fernández and Gilberto González's "empire theory of migration."[28] And the Mexico-based social scientists Raúl Delgado Wise and Henry Veltmeyer have urged consideration of both the dislocation and entrenchment phases as part of a "development process" that includes forging a global labor market from the economically displaced and making those displaced laborers responsible for development in their home countries.[29]

In even more recent years, Latin American scholars have connected migration with "extractivism."[30] Like other foundational works, discussions of extractivism have evolved from considering one phase of migration as extraction to considering two or more together. For example, the work of the Mexican sociologist Mina Navarro encompasses what I call the dislocation phase when she posits that extractivism is "the forced separation and violent deprivation of people from their means of subsistence."[31] The Argentine social scientist and feminist scholar Veronica Gago connects the dislocation and displacement phases in her delineation of "extended extractivism" as acting to "loot, displace and redirect [people] into new exploitation dynamics."[32] The displacement phase is connected to entrenchment by the Mexican economists Rodolfo García Zamora and Juan Manuel Padilla, who write that "the extractivist model [in Zacatecas] has primacy in the economy of the state, first extracting massive resources in the form of the labor force, such as migrants headed towards the United States depleting entire populations"[33] Zamora and Padilla further find that depopulation leads to "family dismemberment," which then leads to divorce, domestic violence, and a host of other socially harmful behaviors.[34] These findings parallel those of Abrego and Deborah Boehm, whose ethnographic works show that migrant or "transnational" families experienced severe affective and economic consequences.[35]

These contributions have set critical groundwork by delineating the connections between two of the three phases of migration outlined here. This book builds on these contributions by providing a more comprehensive explanation that connects all three phases of migration as extraction. Such a comprehensive understanding is informed by the remarkable similarities in migrant community experiences despite their ethnic, economic, and geographic differences in Mexico. Grounded in these lived experiences, migration as extraction ties together the connecting theories, showing that the neoliberal cycle includes displacement of people into certain labor markets, that the empire theory of migration includes the displacement of people into carceral spaces, that both of these theories can be expanded to include the entrenchment of migration by what Delgado Wise and others call the "development process,"[36] and that the existing understandings of social death, legal violence, expulsion, and extractivism can be adapted to encompass the full tapestry of migration that consists of threads that dislocate people from their home communities and separate families; displace them into exploitative work, carceral systems, and indebtedness; and entrench patterns of disinvestment that reincarnate the cycle of migration and family disintegration. The argument that migration *is* extraction rather than that it is caused by or has an impact on extraction further erases the boundaries between acts of migration and the surrounding economic and political conditions. It situates migration as one of several incarnations of racial capitalist relations rather than as a product of these relations.

A BRIEF TIMELINE OF THE DIFFERENT PHASES OF MIGRATION AS EXTRACTION AND RESISTANCE

Migration as extraction stemmed first and foremost from the lived experiences in migrant communities. The ensuing chapters retell these experiences in community members' own words. But the narratives are bound by the time in which the interviews took place, expressing memories or experiences at that moment. Contextualizing these experiences in a broader economic and political context both contemporaneous with the stories and historically deepens the meaning of the narratives. The chapters detail the surrounding context, but a brief look into the larger pattern of resource extraction and resistance to it is necessary here to foreground the connectivity between the different phases of migration as extraction and resistance to it. In Mexico, as in large parts of the world, racial capitalist accumulation began in the form of colonialism by a foreign power. From the Indigenous perspective in Mexico, which is the perspective of about two-thirds of the contributors to this book, the process of racial capitalist accumulation through colonization moved from settler colonialism by Spain to political and economic control by Mexican *independistas* (ostensibly compatriots of Indigenous peoples) to a neocolonial relationship with the United States. Each of these three phases of colonization brought with it dislocation and forced movement for Indigenous peoples as well as movements to defend land and achieve self-determination. Beginning in 1521, Spain forced its way to political control by slaughtering or enslaving Indigenous populations, stealing the subjugated groups' land, and replacing the dislocated or murdered with settlers from Spain. The former inhabitants were often forced to work as serf laborers under Spain's strict hierarchal racial caste system. These colonial maneuvers played out differently in the different regions discussed in this book. In Tabasco, different Indigenous groups, including the Chontales, warded off Spanish invasion for some hundred years but were eventually almost completely annihilated. This may explain the current lack of identification with Indigenous groups in the Tabascan towns profiled. In Oaxaca, the Mixtec, along with many other Indigenous groups, resisted Spanish forces but were eventually forced off their land and made to adopt Spanish agricultural practices that led to massive erosion centuries later. In Puebla, the Mexica fought for years to allay the forces of Hernán Cortés but were eventually forced into labor for the new colonial government. The history in Tlaxcala is perhaps the most complex as the Tlaxcaltecs joined forces with Cortés to wipe out their common enemy, the Mexica Empire, leading to colonial subjugation of the entire area we now know as Mexico. In exchange for their assistance, the Tlaxcaltecs were able to keep their territory intact, but this did not stop extensive exploitation of their resources in the centuries to come.

Three hundred years later, the descendants of the Spanish conquistadors became independistas, seeking to control the land they settled without interference from Spain. After gaining autonomy from Spain in 1821, the newly formed Mexican government continued the caste system put in place by the Spanish in many ways, including exploitative and repressive policies toward Mexico's Indigenous populations. Elfego's ancestors in particular felt the brunt of these policies as they found themselves entrenched as peasant laborers on land they sowed freely prior to the Spanish conquest. But all of the communities profiled in this book were affected by policies seeking to erase indigeneity. The new government successfully imposed mestizaje, a uniquely "Mexican" race, on its inhabitants largely by outlawing Indigenous languages and cultural practices. Resistance to these laws was forced underground, but many groups like the Mixtecs and Nahuatl speakers of Central Mexico continued to preserve their language. Language preservation continues to the present day in Oaxaca, Tlaxcala, and other places as a form of resistance to colonial extraction.

Early in Mexico's life as an independent nation, it faced a new conquistador in the form of the United States. Under the philosophy of Manifest Destiny, the United States launched military operations in 1846 that forced the Mexican government to cede nearly half of its former territory in early 1848. The military conquest soon segued into neocolonialism, with the United States gaining financial control over various aspects of Mexico's economy. As the Chicano studies scholars Gilberto González and Raúl Fernandez remind us, building such financial control was a distinctly American version of empire construction.[37] The first sectors of the Mexican economy captured by U.S. financial elites under this new colonialism in the 1870s were mining, cattle farming, and cotton production. This capture was made possible by the willing participation of one of the first Mexican partners in extraction, President Porfirio Díaz (1877–80, 1884–1911). During Díaz's reign, company towns owned by U.S. business interests like Cananea, El Boleo, and Nacozari "sprang from virtual wilderness" in the northern Mexican states of Sonora and Baja California.[38] Díaz paved the way not only for U.S. companies to mine, farm, and produce cotton but also to build a railroad that would transport these goods more readily to the U.S. market.

The early twentieth century also saw the Mexican and U.S governments collude to bring "surplus" Mexican labor to U.S. agricultural areas to replace the now-outlawed slave labor and newly barred Asian immigrants. In Mexico, President Díaz was supportive of sending Mexican workers to the United States as part of his effort to maintain a good relationship with his northern neighbor at the expense of creating sustainable work in Mexico. These policies soon led to the Mexican Revolution, which lasted for ten years, overthrew the Díaz dictatorship, and brought about important land reforms for the benefit of peasant farmers, including Indigenous farmers. However, even after Díaz was overthrown in 1911, the post-revolutionary government continued to passively support emigration "as an escape valve for revolutionary unrest and political enemies."[39] During the 1910s and 1920s, the United States imported tens of thousands of Mexicans to perform grueling manual labor in U.S. fields, casting them as "perfect workers" and "docile birds of passage" uniquely suited to the role.[40] So powerful was this depiction that it overcame the strong eugenics movement to bar all migration except for that from northern Europe. However, Mexican migrants did not completely escape the eugenicists' exclusionary gaze. In addition to being cast as perfect workers, Mexican migrants were the basis for and targets of new laws criminalizing unlawful entry, setting the stage for the massive carceral system that would come to characterize U.S. immigration enforcement.[41] These new laws were passed in the context of the Great Depression in the United States and the first massive deportation of Mexican workers.[42]

By the mid-twentieth century, U.S. empire building in Mexico continued to involve cooperation with the Mexican state, including the Mexican public finance agency, Nacional Financiera (National Development Bank). U.S. investment banks like the U.S. Import-Export Bank, Chase Manhattan, and Bank of America began loaning money to Nacional Financiera to finance massive irrigation projects and manufacturing plants at the Mexico-U.S. border at the expense of smaller farming and industrial communities. These projects benefited many large Mexican corporations, including Ceuta Produce and Negocio Agrícola San Enrique, which would derive most of their wealth from trade with the United States. The irrigation projects also allowed large U.S. agribusinesses like Anderson Clayton to relocate their operations to northern Mexico, profiting from cotton produced on Mexican soil by the labor of Mexican workers.

The workers for these new ventures were migrants from other regions of Mexico. Mexican corporate interests actively recruit Indigenous workers from the southern part of the country, extracting their skills in agriculture, textile production, and so on, for great profit. These programs were met with resistance by groups that sought a more equitable distribution of resources. However, corporate bosses had much more sway in the Mexican government, resulting in little change.

On the U.S. side of the border, agribusinesses like Mastronardi Produce (various locations), Windset Farms (California), and Village Farms (Texas) continued their predecessors' long history of actively recruiting Mexican men and women to perform the dangerous and arduous work necessary to build wealth. U.S.-based agriculture successfully officialized their recruitment of Mexican labor through the Bracero Accords, a series of bilateral agreements between the governments of the United States and Mexico that created lawfully sanctioned pathways for large farms to induce and exploit Mexican workers. Like the early agricultural workers, braceros were simultaneously deemed necessary and demonized as illegal, naturally criminal, and, ironically, taking resources from the country they are coming to work in. Efforts to exert control over the large bracero workforce led to massive raids with racially demeaning monikers like Operation Wetback and continued targeting of Mexican migrants for criminal prosecution for unlawful entry. Eventually political pressure from both anti-immigrant forces and civil rights advocates concerned with widespread labor abuses caused the United States to pull out of the program in 1965.

For its part, the Mexican government was initially wary of entering into agreements given the abuses of Mexican workers during the 1920s program and the massive repatriation that followed. However, it eventually agreed to the program, marking the first proactive steps to promote emigration to the United States.[43] More than five million Mexican workers labored as braceros during the twenty-plus-year program. The Mexican government became so dependent on the safety valve of emigration that it sought to convince the United States to continue the program for ten years after it ended.[44] Its failure to do so resulted in a return to passively engaging migration in what became known as the "policy of having no policy."[45]

Faced with a large unemployed population returning to Mexico, President Gustavo Díaz Ordaz created the Programa Nacional Fronterizo (National Border Program) in 1965 in an attempt to create jobs. The program opened Mexico's northern border to foreign companies seeking to produce goods for export in a cheap labor market. The assembly plants, or maquiladoras, did create jobs but mostly benefited U.S. companies in search of cheap, exploitable labor and

Mexican officials seeking a new channel for surplus labor. The first maquiladoras were largely garment companies, but this expanded quickly to include the auto and electronics industries. Companies such as Chrysler, Fisher Price, and General Electric still have maquiladora operations in northern Mexico.

In the 1980s—the era in which the narratives in this book begin—racial capitalist accumulation began to be expressed as neoliberalism. Embraced by the U.S. and Mexican governments alike, the basic tenet of neoliberalism was that economies would grow faster with less state regulation. The three "pillars" of neoliberal policies were cuts to public spending, privatization of state-owned industries, and market liberalization. Mexico became one of the first Latin American states to agree to neoliberal reforms, known as structural adjustment after its debt crisis in 1982 forced it into a set of agreements with the International Monetary Fund (IMF) and the U.S. Treasury Department. The U.S.-educated elites governing Mexico—including Miguel de la Madrid and his minister of planning and budget turned president, Carlos Salinas de Gortari—embraced structural adjustment, which led to the widespread removal of social safety nets, drastic reductions in social spending, privatization of state-run price supports for agriculture, and active suppression of wages. It also led the Mexican government to enter into the North American Free Trade Agreement (NAFTA) in 1994, making Mexican producers the least protected workers in the world at the time.

While the rhetoric surrounding neoliberalism emphasized economic growth and efficiency, in truth neoliberal policies created vast inequalities. The number of new millionaires in Mexico soared in the years following neoliberal structural adjustment, as did the number of small farmers, assembly plant workers, and day laborers forced to abandon their land, families, and communities in search of sustainable work. This led to widespread movements against neoliberalism, particularly in places like Oaxaca where Indigenous organizers had helped launch labor strikes in the 1970s. However, these movements were only able to slow the march of neoliberal policies that would disinvest from agriculture, small business, and sustainable wages. Moreover, government officials justified the spending cuts by categorizing the work of "peasant"—largely Indigenous—farmers and other trades as inefficient and needing "modernization." Modernization meant implementing structural adjustment policies of dispossession, wage suppression, and service reduction. But it also meant displacing workers into industries at the Mexico-U.S. border or in the U.S. interior made thirsty for cheap exploitable labor by the same desire for capitalist accumulation that drove neoliberalism.

In the United States, Mexican migrants had by now been made illegal by the termination of the Bracero Program and the addition of quotas to migration from the western hemisphere. This ratcheted up justifications for expenditures on what Nicolas de Genova and others call the "homeland security state,"[46] increasing surveillance, incarceration, and other abuses of Mexican migrants by U.S. immigration officials. But even as immigration enforcement became more and more

structures of statehood and global capitalism may fully unleash the brutal forces of [racial capitalist] accumulation,"[51] including even more exploitative employment practices, wage suppression, and carceral structures. Alongside the potential to worsen the economic condition of migrants, right to migrate arguments ignore the very real emotional costs of migration that uproots people from their families and communities.

Policies aimed at addressing root causes of migration fail in different ways. These policies invest primarily in buttressing law enforcement efforts, exacerbating the extraction inflicted by these efforts and making marginal investments in human development programs. The focus on investing in security measures leaves intact and even magnifies the impacts of disinvestment that require people to leave their home communities. This book argues that investments must be directed at changing the structural relationship of migrant communities with those in power in both their home state (in this case, Mexico) and the destination state (in this case, the United States). In other words, rather than seek to prevent the migration their own policies fomented, Mexican and U.S. elites must replace investments in enforcement and security with those that support community development.

METHODOLOGY

The narratives that form the basis of understanding migration as extraction were obtained over the course of five years and were the result of a mixture of methods, including semistructured interviews; participant observation during group meetings, events, and outings; and focus groups that included study participants and nonparticipants. I originally set out to examine what was uprooting people from their communities of origin. I was particularly interested in what motivated people to migrate without authorization as debates about undocumented immigration raged around me in the early 2010s. From my position as a law professor running a legal clinic representing immigrants facing deportation, I was troubled by the narrow view of undocumented immigrant life in U.S. media and policy circles that began only after a person stepped foot in the United States. Analyses in these arenas seemed limited to the impact of undocumented immigrants on the U.S. economy and offered little insight into the relationship of the U.S. economy to these migrants. Increasingly, as I encountered more and more people whose reasons for departing their home communities sounded similar, I wondered what it would look like to examine immigration policies from the perspective of communities of origin. How similar were the conditions for people before (and after) they migrated to the United States? Legal rules required my students and I to focus on negative or harmful conditions in our clients' home communities *other than* economic harm.[52] But in getting to know clients, we all knew that the full story almost always included an economic component. I became interested in how to tell these stories outside the confines of legal argumentation. In my work with various immigrants' rights groups in the United States, I met numerous individuals and families that did not qualify for any immigration status largely because they failed to fit into one of several strict categories. Through their stories, I was beginning to understand the connections between U.S. policies and migration. This made me curious to see how visible these connections were in communities of origin. I also wondered how a different perspective might change the way my students—most of whom sought careers as immigration attorneys—and fellow immigrants' rights advocates thought about immigration issues.

Once I began to talk with people, I found that I had to broaden my research frame to include a more holistic picture of what migration is from the perspective of communities of origin. This included understanding what the journeys north looked like, how migrants fared in the United States, and what brought them back to their communities of origin. It required consideration of the stories of family members of migrants, including the emotional and economic impact of migration on them. It also included taking into account the efforts that returned migrants and others in migrant communities were making—either through community organizations or individually—to improve local conditions such that future generations would not need to migrate. The community organizations themselves became an additional topic of research as I learned more about their histories and vision for a more just future. And within all of these considerations, I had to carefully examine the impact that identification with indigeneity had on community conditions and community responses.

Access through Academic and Community Interlocutors

I chose communities in Mexico because I had previous experience living there during which time I had built networks of professionals who helped connect me with the various communities I visited. Fluency in Spanish allowed me to conduct all of my interviews without an interpreter, including those in Mixtec and Nahuatl-speaking communities. Though I did not rely on formal language interpretation, I was well aware that language fluency does not equate to understanding the syntax or context of the words being spoken. As a second-generation Indian American who is also fluent in my mother tongue, I have found that I needed my parents to "interpret" for me in many instances when spoken words hold hidden nuances of meanings that must be deciphered. And my work with clients from across Latin America has taught me that the same phrases or even words have very different meanings depending on where a person is from. I therefore sought out local interlocutors to help facilitate introductions to people to interview as well as to help me gain a deeper understanding of what my potential interviewees were saying beyond formal interpretation.

The first interlocutors were graduate students working under the direction of Jorge Durand with the Mexican Migration Project (MMP) at the University of Guadalajara (UDG). I was a Fulbright Scholar with UDG for the full academic year, allowing me to participate in MMP's well-regarded community survey in Soyataco and Chiltepec, Tabasco. Once in Tabasco, the ability to shadow graduate students as they engaged in the MMP's standard semistructured interviews allowed me to observe the kinds of questions asked, the phrasing, and the extent to which people were interested in answering questions. I then used these insights to edit the questions I had previously planned for migrants and family members. This served me well as I followed up with people the MMP researchers had identified as migrants and interviewed new people in Tabasco.

Once the research in Tabasco was completed, I looked for similar connections in other communities, this time with community organizations that could facilitate introductions and help interpret responses. In addition to an institutional connection, I looked for communities with differing levels of economic marginalization (poverty but also factors such as the presence of running water, fabricated flooring, and educational institutions), differing primary economic activity (primarily agricultural, industrial, or other), different rates of migration to the United States, differing levels of participation in formal community organizations, differing levels of investment of migrant remittances in community-based projects, and demographic differences such as the rate of women who migrate and whether community members identified as Indigenous. The reason that I sought out communities that varied along so many axes was to see whether, even with these levels of differentiation, patterns would emerge as to the reasons people migrated, the places where they ended up working in the United States, and the extent to which migration improved community-wide well-being. I was fortunate to be connected to CAFAMI in Tlaxcala and FIOB in Oaxaca, communities that had the kinds of differences with Tabasco that I sought. It became particularly significant that the communities I connected with through CAFAMI and FIOB identified strongly with two very distinct Indigenous groups, Tlaxcaltec and Mixtec. Their responses and history triggered important follow-up questions for all of the interviewees.

In Tlaxcala, Itzel Polo and Norma Mendieta gave generously of their time. Norma is responsible for introducing me to nearly every person I interviewed in Tetlanohcan and Sanctorum, Tlaxcala, as well as the interviews I conducted in Puebla when I returned to Mexico in 2017. She was present for some of the interviews and helped facilitate mutual understanding between the study participants and me. She also invited me to various CAFAMI meetings and outings where I was able to connect on a more personal level with many of the interviewees. At some of these events, I would conduct trainings on U.S. immigration law as a way of contributing to the community that was giving so generously of their time.

In Oaxaca, I was fortunate to connect with Bernardo Ramirez Bautista, the Oaxaca coordinator of FIOB. Bernardo spent hours explaining FIOB's organizing strategy and introduced me to other FIOB organizers, Cipriano and Rosa Mendez. Together, these three organizers facilitated introductions to potential interviewees and helped me interpret nuance. They also invited me to FIOB meetings, *encuentros* involving other academics and organizers, religious celebrations, and even a wedding. This allowed me to interact multiple times and in a variety of ways with potential study participants. It also allowed me to put what people were saying in context. FIOB members are particularly well versed in U.S. immigration law. Thus, I was less able to contribute to the community's knowledge base but contributed financially where it seemed appropriate and to help support the celebrations.

Participant Details

Through these various interlocutors, I connected with study participants using the purposive sampling method to interview people who had (1) a past migratory experience to the United States, (2) a family member who was currently or had in the past year been in the United States without authorization, or (3) experience as an organizer in the community. Within the first two categories, I sought a heterogeneous sample to ensure maximum variation along key characteristics of each group: age, gender, marital status, presence of children, ethnicity/language group,[53] hailing from a low/medium/high migrant-sending state, date of first migratory trip, and relative with migratory experience. In the states with formal community organizations, I also sought to interview and observe the staff of these organizations and people they identified as community leaders. And in all states, I sought to interview local political leaders. Drawing from such a varied group of migrants, family members, and community leaders allowed for comparison of responses from multiple angles and for common themes from these responses to emerge.

I conducted the research in two phases. The first phase lasted from August 2012 to May 2013. Over these months, I engaged in in-depth interviews, sat in on meetings, and accompanied individuals and groups of migrants, family members of migrants, and community organizers in six migrant communities. During this first phase, I interviewed a total of 70 people: 28 in Soyataco and Chiltepec, Tabasco; 25 in Tetlanohcan and Sanctorum, Tlaxcala; and 17 in the municipalities of the Mixteca region of Oaxaca. Of the 70 people interviewed, 43 were returned or current migrants, 20 were family members, and 7 were volunteers or staff at community-based organizations in Tlaxcala and Oaxaca. There were no community-based organizations in the two municipalities I visited in Tabasco. Of the 43 migrants, 13 were women and 30 were men. All 20 of the family members interviewed were women. Three of the seven organizational staff members were women, and four were men. All of those interviewed in Oaxaca and the municipality of San Francisco de Tetlanohcan, Tlaxcala, including all of the organizational staff, identified as Indigenous (33). In Oaxaca, the interviewees identified as Mixtec or Triqui, and in Tetlanohcan, they identified as Nahuatl. The 37 interviewees in Tabasco and the municipality of Sanctorum, Tlaxcala, identified as mestizo or ladino, as the Spanish-origin or mixed-race peoples are called in southern Mexico.

The second phase of my research was conducted in 2017. During this phase, I followed up with a subset of interviewees in all of the communities visited during

2012–13 and visited two new communities of Mexican migrants in Ozolco and San Pedro Cholula, Puebla. In this second phase, I conducted 21 new interviews; all interviewees had some experience migrating to the United States, and 3 had become involved as community leaders. Among these interviews, 4 were women and 17 were men.[54] All of the new interviewees in this second phase identified as Nahuatl. By the end of this second phase of the project, I had spoken with 91 people, 64 of whom were returned migrants, 20 of whom were family members of migrants, and 10 of whom were involved as staff or volunteer organizers with a community-based organization. (Three of the ten organizational workers were also returned migrants.) Demographically, the study had 54 participants who identified as belonging to an Indigenous group, 40 women, and 51 men.

In order to gain the most holistic insights from all of these groups, I used a mixture of interviews, participant observation, and focus groups to better understand what migration meant to people. Drawing on decades of experience interviewing clients and training students to do so, I began each conversation by building rapport. Building on clinical legal pedagogy's use of client centeredness and critical interviewing,[55] I then moved to broad, open-ended questions to continue to build trust and to allow interviewees to control the information they shared. To ensure some level of consistency in the information that I was getting from each group of interviews, I had checklists of the kinds of information I wanted from each person.

For migrants, the checklist consisted of information concerning the following:

- When they left and why.
- Whether they migrated with authorization or not. For those who migrated without authorization, whether they sought an authorized path.
- Whether they were recruited by an employer in the United States.
- How many trips they made to the United States and if the reasons for each subsequent trip evolved over time.
- How their journey was: What did they pay to cross? Where did they cross? Did they encounter Mexican or U.S. border officials?
- Experiences in the United States: How quickly did they find work? Did they encounter U.S. law enforcement?
- For those who returned, why they did so.
- For those involved in organizations: What brought them there? What activities were they a part of, and what did they think of the organization's efforts?
- For those still in United States, what kept them there.

For family members, the checklist was as follows:

- When their loved one(s) left and why.
- Their experience of their loved one being gone.
- How much the migrant contributed to the household financially and whether this was sufficient to cover their expenses.

- Whether they themselves considered migrating.
- For those involved in organizations: What brought them there? What activities were they part of? What did they think of these efforts?

For the organizers, I asked the following:

- How they organized.
- Why they did so.
- What programs they were part of.
- What the overall vision of the group was.
- What challenges they faced as a group.
- How the group developed over time.

In addition to the insights gained from talking with people individually, I was able to observe the answers to many of these questions as migrants, family members, and organizers participated in community meetings or focus groups. I held a number of follow-up meetings with people after these larger gatherings to ensure that I was correctly interpreting their comments.

In interpreting the responses to my questions and my observations, I looked for points of convergence and divergence in the stories. I was struck by the level of similarity in the various reasons for migrating; experiences in the United States, including with law enforcement; experiences of family members; and visions of the community organizations despite the deep differences in community makeup, location, and main economic activity. It is these similarities that I focus on in this book while still paying attention to the nuances of place, ethnic origin, and individual experience.

LANGUAGE AND TERMINOLOGY

All of the interviews were conducted in Spanish, a language in which I am fluent but not bilingual and the first or second language of all the interviewees. To convey the ways that the interviewees communicated and to give full respect to their analyses, some of the language in their stories has been left in the original Spanish. For example, terms are left in Spanish to reflect the ways in which people talk about migration both within a particular region and across states. Things like the way a person migrated, the name for the person they paid to be a guide, or the manner in which they found work in the United States are all left in Spanish to illustrate how similar concepts are talked about using different terminology in different places. In addition, the original Spanish is used to convey certain colloquialisms unique to a place outside the context of migration. Therefore, the way a farmer talks about working the land or the way a day laborer talks about basic necessities is left in Spanish. The original Spanish term is also used when there is not a direct translation into English or the term requires some explanation.

In addition to choice of language, I use honorifics like "Don" and "Doña" where they are used by migrant community members in referring to themselves or others. In some communities, like the Mixtec community in Oaxaca, these honorifics are used to signify a certain status in the community, regardless of age. Most Mixtec returned migrants have a relatively high status within their communities, so "Don" or "Doña" is used more frequently for these interviewees. In contrast, in the Tlaxcaltec and Nahuatl-speaking communities in Puebla and the largely non-Indigenous-identified communities in Tabasco, honorifics were used only to refer to those considered elders, so they are used much less frequently when referring to people from these areas. In order to avoid confusion regarding how people are named across chapters, an indication of the person's age is included in their narratives, as well as a short explanation of the use of Don/Doña in that person's region the first time it is described in the chapters. Though it might allow for less confusion to use Don and Doña in a more consistent manner, it would be a misrepresentation of the way in which these diverse communities are organized and therefore would provide a less than accurate picture of each place.

At the request of several of the interviewees, pseudonyms are used throughout this book. While the names have been changed, the honorifics match what the person is called, and all other details, including age, gender, indigeneity, dates of migration, and other details, remain intact. There are no composite narratives in this book.

In my analysis of the narratives, I use the term "migrant" to refer to people who moved across international borders and the term "unauthorized" to describe those who migrated without sanction of the destination states. I use "migrant" rather than "immigrant" as it is a more direct translation of the term *migrante* used by most of the people I interviewed to describe themselves or family members. "Migrant" also better captures the transnational nature of the narratives, including experiences moving back and forth across borders and family members who may never physically move but experience migration nonetheless. The term "unauthorized" is a descriptor of journeys that emphasizes the formal rules categorizing them.

Finally, another set of actors important to this book are policy makers, bureaucrats, and owners of private enterprises that set formal rules governing not just migration but also the distribution of resources. These actors are described with specificity and detail but are also collectively referred to as "elites" to reflect their relationship to migrant communities.

CHAPTER PREVIEW

This book is arranged in four chapters, with the first three chronicling one of the three different modes of migration as extraction and the fourth outlining migrant community resistance to migration as extraction. Chapter 1 highlights the highly localized ways in which migrant communities experienced the resource extraction policies of the United States and Mexican governments as dislocation from their homes and families and contextualizes this dislocation in the larger story of U.S.-Mexico relations. Chapter 2 moves to discuss how dislocated people from Mexico are then displaced into or relocated to highly exploitative labor markets in northern Mexico and the United States, to carceral spaces justified by the very movements that displace them into the United States, and by coyotes who profit from fees paid by migrants to circumvent ever increasing border controls. Chapter 3 demonstrates how extraction is entrenched at the municipal, family, and individual levels in migrant communities. Through stories of migrant families and entities that profit from migration, chapter 3 reveals how migrants' attempts to reverse the flow of resources to migrant communities is undermined by wealth extraction by U.S. and Mexican business and introduces the emotional layer of migration as extraction in the form of family disintegration. Chapter 4 outlines the resistance to migration as extraction, particularly in the Mixteca region of Oaxaca and the Nahuatl areas of Tlaxcala and Puebla. The resistance comes in many forms, from shifts in gender norms to movements for returning state resources to creating local sustainable sources of employment and earnings. The stories in chapter 4 chronicle the promise of collective action to address deep gaps in infrastructure and the limits to successfully addressing these gaps.

The conclusion connects the various aspects of migration as extraction exemplified in chapters 1 through 3 and builds on the arguments and strategies of migrant community organizations profiled in chapter 4 to argue that a reversal of the extractive nature of migration requires the United States and Mexico to divest from extractive policies such as immigration enforcement expenditures and employer-controlled immigration processes and invest in infrastructures of health, education, and work and employee-centered migration options. The conclusion situates the analytic and material shifts that need to occur in abolitionist and reparations frameworks, relating the demands and actions of migrant communities to these larger frames. As such, the conclusion seeks to concretize demands by Indigenous migrant groups like FIOB and CAFAMI and by non-Indigenous-identified migrants to make migration a choice.

1

———

Dislocation

What one earns only gets you to "mediovivir."
—ELIAS

*While . . . not[ing] the substantial drop [20%] in real income over the past
few years, success on the inflation front was likely to require continued firm
wage restraint.*
—IMF DIRECTOR N. WICKS, JULY 30, 1984

Near the entrance to Soyataco, Tabasco, a sleepy rural town ensconced in lush
tropical flora, Don Pablo speaks to me in front of the house he built from his earnings in the United States. Don Pablo made his first trip to the United States in 1961
and vividly described the conditions in Soyataco that pushed him to leave.

> In that time, Tabasco was very backward. To get to Jalpa from Soyataco you had to
> walk. It took about four hours. Also, there was no work because of the flooding. The
> floodwaters used to reach all the way to the primary school that is right across the road.
>
> I was a *campesino* and farmed corn and beans, took care of bulls and pigs. But this
> terrain is very low and cannot sustain the growth of farm animals. I had to go all the
> way to Capaculcho to earn 5 pesos a day. I only had school until the second standard.
> There was no school really at that time.

Like millions of his compatriots, Don Pablo was pushed to migrate to the United
States by harsh economic conditions in his home community. The themes he
points to—lack of infrastructure, lack of support for agriculture, and lack of access
to education—are ones that reverberate in the stories of his neighbors and of those
in other rural towns more than fifty years later. Due to the time period in which
Don Pablo migrated, he was able to make the journey with authorization from the
U.S. government. But U.S. immigration laws would change in the coming decades,
transforming many journeys like Don Pablo's into unauthorized ones.

Whether authorized or not, Don Pablo's journey and those of the other
migrants in this book are part of a larger story of racial capitalist relations between

27

the United States and Mexico driven by specific economic policies that act to benefit U.S. and Mexican elites and to extract resources, including human resources, from towns like Soyataco. Based in racialized characterizations of people like Don Pablo as "backward peasants" in need of modernization, these policies construct economic gaps in migrant communities that dislocate people from their home communities and displace them into industries where their labor benefits large corporate interests. The policies and practices that dislocated Don Pablo included divestment from agriculture and infrastructure spending, which had begun in the 1950s but accelerated in the 1980s, dislocating millions of Don Pablo's compatriots. At the time Don Pablo migrated, he was one of hundreds of thousands of Mexican farmworkers displaced into large commercial farms in the United States by the Bracero Accords. By the 1980s, women and men across Mexico were dislodged from their homes by neoliberal economic reforms prescribed by international banking institutions like the IMF and supported by the U.S. Treasury Department and the Mexican governing elite. These reforms—known as structural adjustment—involved fiscal austerity, privatization of state-owned industries, and market liberalization. Imposed on Mexican communities by the IMF and the U.S. and Mexican governments, structural adjustment would widen inequities in public support for agriculture, infrastructure, and education; flood the Mexican economy with foreign-owned manufacturing plants; and suppress wages across various labor markets. As the narratives in this chapter demonstrate, these policies and the continued adherence to neoliberalization in the decades that followed would propel people to leave an economically diverse set of home communities, cementing migration as part of the structure of racial capitalist relations between the United States and Mexico.

That migration is part of the structurally unequal economic relationship between the two countries has long been acknowledged by an interdisciplinary and international set of scholars examining Mexican migration.[1] The U.S.-based Chicano Studies scholars and historians Gilbert González and Raúl Fernandez trace the U.S.-Mexico relationship to the 1870s to formulate Mexican migration as "a transnational mode of economic colonialism" by the United States.[2] Examining more recent dynamics, the Mexican social scientists Raúl Delgado Wise and Humberto Márquez Covarrubius describe Mexico-U.S. migration since the 1980s as an "expression of the growing asymmetry that characterizes contemporary capitalism."[3] Similarly, the U.S.-based sociologist Tanya Golash-Boza theorizes that migration is part of a "neoliberal cycle of global capitalism" that both propels people to migrate and undergirds U.S. deportation policy.[4] Golash-Boza focuses her analysis on the deportation side of the neoliberal cycle, which, she demonstrates, maintains hierarchies of race.[5] This chapter merges these insights on race, colonialism, and capitalism by using the broader framework of racial capitalism. Through migrant community narratives, the chapter demonstrates that migrant dislocation is structurally bound up with the racial capitalist relationship between U.S. and Mexican elites, on the one hand, and more marginalized Mexicans who are racialized as inferior, on the other. Migrant community members do not use the terminology of racial capitalism explicitly, nor do they identify capitalism's incarnation as neoliberalism or U.S. colonial endeavors directly. Rather, they refer to the specific economic gaps that caused them to leave their home communities, gaps that can be traced to larger political economic structures built by international banks and the U.S. and Mexican elites to benefit one set of actors and dislocate others.

DISLOCATION IN ACTION

In the decades after Don Pablo migrated, waves of neoliberal reforms gutted economic structures, destroying livelihoods and transferring resources, including human resources, to large corporate interests in the "north" (northern Mexico, the United States, and Canada). These reforms reached into every community in Mexico whether rural or urban, Indigenous or non-Indigenous. The narratives in this book take place in four geographically, demographically, and economically distinct areas, yet the patterns they convey are remarkably similar (tables 1, 2). Soyataco, where Don Pablo is from, is in a tropical floodplain near the Gulf coast of Mexico. The other Tabascan town profiled is Chiltepec, a coastal village on the Gulf coast that was once supported by fishing. Across this northern part of Tabasco, the landscape is lush and green, with smooth paved roads. As one approaches the sea by road, the densely packed tropical forest is clouded with plumes of black smoke from the nearby oil refineries. Due west is the Mixteca region of Oaxaca, from which another set of interviewees hailed. Here the landscape is largely hilly and arid, with occasional specks of green interrupting what otherwise seems like earth hardened against life taking hold. Journeys by road are long here as they wind up and down hillsides and are pockmarked by frequent cracks and holes. Moving north, the varied communities of Tlaxcala include those that are urban, like San Francisco de Tetlanohcan (Tetlanohcan), which climbs a steep volcanic hill, and those that are rural, like Sanctorum, with its the wide, flat valleys. Both Tetlanohcan and Sanctorum are dotted with large nondescript buildings housing maquiladoras. And Tetlanohcan houses what seems like an overabundance of *abarrotes* (grocery stores). Finally, the nearby communities of Ozolco and San Pedro Cholula, Puebla, are small and large urban areas, respectively. Like Tetlanohcan, these *poblano* (of or from the state of Puebla) towns are nestled into Mexico's central volcanic mountain range. Roads in these parts of Tlaxcala and Puebla are well paved but slow as elevations rise. They are connected by highways that move from stunning mountain vistas to crowded intersections. As I would learn during my time in these communities, these landscapes were only partially natural. The black smoke looming over Chiltepec, the gray-brown earth of the Mixteca, and the ever-present haze wrapping the hillsides in Tlaxcala and Puebla were largely constructed.

Demographically, the three regions differ largely along the lines of indigeneity and diversity within Indigenous groups. Tabasco has a very small Indigenous population, with about 18 percent of the population identifying as Indigenous and

TABLE 1 Demographic, Economic, and Migration Rates in Communities

	Tabasco	Oaxaca	Tlaxcala	Puebla
Migration rate, 1980–89	Very low	Medium	Very low	Low
Migration rate, 1990–99	Very low	Medium	Medium	Medium
Migration rate, 2000–2009	Very low	High	Medium	Medium
Poverty rate, 1980–89	Low	High	Medium	High
Poverty rate, 1990–99	Low	High	Medium	High
Poverty rate, 2000–2009	Low	High	Medium	High
Leading economic activity	Mixed—agricultural/ small business	Agricultural	Mixed—industrial/ small business/ agriculture	Mixed—agricultural/ small business
Community organization present, 2012–17	None	FIOB founded 2004	CAFAMI founded 2007	CAFAMI expansion 2016
Number of 3x1 projects, 2013	0	35	7	20
Indigenous population, 1980–2017	1.7%	21.6%	3%	11.7%

SOURCES: Migration rates: Instituto Nacional de Estadística y Geografía (INEGI), "Tendencias y características de la migración mexicana a los Estados Unidos," 1990, 2000, 2010.

Poverty rates and leading economic activity: Consejo Nacional de Población, "Índice de marginación por entidad federativa y municipio," 1990, 2000, 2010.

Indigenous population: Instituto Nacional de Estadística y Geografía (INEGI), Tabulados básicos, 1990, 2000, 2010.

TABLE 2 Similarities in Reasons for Dislocation across Communities

	Tabasco	Oaxaca	Tlaxcala	Puebla
Poverty rate 2000–2009	Low	High	Medium	High
Leading economic activity	Mixed—agricultural/ small business	Agricultural	Mixed—industrial/ small business/ agriculture	Mixed—agricultural/ small business
Reason for dislocation #1	Lack of work (n = 18)	Lack of work (n = 13)	Lack of work (n = 14)	Lack of work (n = 9)
Reason for dislocation #2	Pay for education (n = 7)	Pay for education (n = 5)	Pay for education (n = 7)	Pay for education (n = 1)

Indigenous languages barely registering on the Mexican census.[6] This is in sharp contrast to the Mixteca region where 100 percent of interviewees identified as either Mixtec or Triqui in a state where the official Indigenous population is 35 percent.[7] Tlaxcala's Nahuatl-speaking Indigenous population is measured at 3 percent, but this hides a wide variation in communities.[8] For example, Sanctorum, Tlaxcala, has a Nahuatl population that is likely close to the state average. However, the other

Tlaxcaltec locality profiled in this book, Tetlanohcan, is 43 percent Nahuatl-speaking, and 100 percent of those interviewed in that municipality are Nahuatl Tlaxcaltecs.[9] In Puebla, the communities visited are also Nahuatl speaking, though they identified as Mexica, an importance difference with Tlaxcaltecs discussed further below. Officially Nahuatl speakers make up 11 percent of Puebla's inhabitants, but the number identifying as Indigenous is closer to 30 percent.[10] All of the interviewees in Ozolco identified as Nahuatl, as did the majority of those in Cholula.

Finally, the various towns had very different economic profiles as evidenced by their "marginalization" rates. "Marginalization" is a term used by the Mexican government to measure an aggregate set of economic indicators, including rates of educational attainment, illiteracy, and lack of access to basic necessities like running water, light, and flooring in housing.[11] Rates of marginalization range from "very high," indicating a widespread lack of these basic resources, to "very low," indicating the presence of most of these resources in a majority of households. Areas of very high marginalization are generally correlated areas with a significant population that speaks an Indigenous language, but within the communities profiled, this differed significantly among Indigenous groups. For example, the Mixtec and Triqui populations make up the vast majority of people living in the Mixteca region of Oaxaca, and the marginalization rates here are considered "very high."[12] This lack of basic necessities is visibly present in the villages profiled in this book. A number of houses had dirt floors and lacked indoor plumbing and electricity. In addition, many migrants reported having to leave school or being unable to pay for schooling for their children. This stands in contrast to Tlaxcala, which has a large Tlaxcaltec population but rates as having a medium level of marginalization.[13] Medium marginalization was evidenced by most households having indoor plumbing and finished floors but varying access to electricity and educational achievement. In an even more stark contrast, the municipality of Tetlanohcan, Tlaxcala, has a low marginalization rate despite its large Indigenous population.[14] This low marginalization rate was evident in the houses that mostly included finished floors, indoor plumbing, and electricity. In nearby Puebla, the relatively smaller Nahuatl community had a high rate of marginalization.[15] This was evident in the smaller dwellings some of which had dirt floors and no direct connection to running water. The smallest Indigenous population was in Tabasco, which, like Puebla, is considered to have a high level of marginalization.[16] Despite these differences, the top two reasons for migrating cited by all of the migrants discussed in this chapter were lack of work and cost of education (table 2).

The lack of work affects virtually all sectors of their local economies, from agriculture to manufacturing to services. The dearth of available jobs in agriculture and the instability of jobs in the manufacturing and service sectors were due to the mix of economic policies that made up the neoliberal incarnation of ongoing racial capitalist relations. Touted by international institutions like the IMF, the U.S. Treasury Department, and U.S.-educated Mexican elites as "efficient," neoliberalization was decidedly disdainful of small agricultural and industrial producers. Neoliberal policies imposed cuts to agricultural supports and social spending like education, encouraged foreign investment, and intentionally suppressed wages. As the remaining sections of this chapter outline, migrants' dislocation can be traced to these policies and in particular to three specific practices: divestment from small producing agriculture; investment in a low-wage, contingent manufacturing sector; and intentional wage suppression to offset inflation. The implementation of these economic reforms distributed resources to large multinational agricultural and manufacturing companies while choking off supports for small producers and businesses. The effects of these reforms were exacerbated by the intentional suppression of wages across all sectors of the economy, leaving little chance of making a sustainable living in large numbers of Mexican communities. These practices overlapped with a fourth vector of economic abandonment. When parents sought to educate their children, increasing their options to thrive, they were faced with cuts to education spending, which, like the policies disfavoring small business and wage earners, were prescribed by the IMF the U.S. Treasury Department and accepted by the Mexican elites governing the country. These policy changes continued to deepen over the decades, causing more and more people to experience the dislocation that Don Pablo experienced in the 1960s. In addition to Don Pablo's story, this chapter relates the stories of several migrants, family members, and community organizers from various parts of Mexico and demonstrates the ways in which successive incarnations of racial capitalist policies dislocated them from their home communities.

Divestment from Agricultural Supports

One of the most devastating reforms engaged in by the Mexican government during the 1980s was the reduction in supports to small agriculture. Racialized by Mexican elites as "backward peasants," small farmers saw supports for their produce diminish and wages for their labor suppressed. As a result, millions of Mexicans were dislocated from their home communities and displaced into large agribusinesses in northern Mexico and the United States. One of these small farmers was Don Margarito Santos (Don Santos). Don Santos spoke to me from the offices of FIOB in Santiago de Juxtlahuaca, Oaxaca. Juxtlahuaca, or "Jux" as it is called by county residents, is one of the county seats in the Mixteca, a region that encompasses the southwestern Mexican states of Oaxaca, Guerrero, and Puebla. The Mixteca is made up of 189 municipalities, ten of which are among the poorest in Mexico.[17] Several Indigenous groups live in the Mixteca region, including the Zapotecs, Mixtec, and Triqui. Don Santos and others interviewed in this region were all Mixtec or Triqui and spoke Spanish along with their mother language.

According to Don Santos, 50 percent of the people in his hometown of Laguna Guadalupe de Yucunicoco migrate to the United States "because there is no work": "The work there is you don't even make $100 [MXN] a day [the equivalent of

US$10] farming the milpa—corn, beans, and *chilacayote* [a kind of squash]. We do farm but only enough for us to eat. We invest more in the farm than we harvest." Don Santos could identify the exact years when the pueblo's out-migration rose. "There stopped being enough work in the pueblo in 1986–87, and that is when migration from the pueblo really began," he said. He migrated for the first time in 1987, because, he says, quite bluntly, "there was work there." He then added, "Not because they [U.S. growers] paid more but because there was work, period."

When Don Santos indicated that 1987 and 1988 were the years that migration "really began," he indirectly referenced the long history of out-migration that preceded the 1980s but accelerated in that decade. A leading scholar of the region, the anthropologist Michael Kearney, has noted, "The Mixteca has *never* seen any improvement in its economic infrastructure as a result of external investments—government or private."[18] One of the most crucial of these external investments was irrigation to help access nearby groundwater. However, instead of investing in irrigation that could allow small farmers in this area to flourish, the Mexican government engaged in massive public spending beginning in the 1960s to help irrigate and otherwise develop new large commercial farms in the border states of Baja California, Sinaloa, and Sonora.[19] Resources from Mexico were supplemented by a combination of U.S. businesses and food distributors that invested in the development of fruit and vegetable farms in northern Mexico to supply the U.S. market.[20] The decision to invest in the northern regions of Mexico was clearly beneficial to the United States as transportation costs across the Mexico-U.S. border were lowest. As a result, farms in these border states saw a huge increase in public investment for infrastructure, totaling nearly 50 percent of agricultural expenditures by the late 1970s.[21] As barriers to foreign investment were removed, U.S agribusinesses moved quickly to capture the Mexican food production and processing markets, owning about a third of such businesses by 1975.[22] These public and private investments of resources in large commercialized farms and food processing centers stand in stark contrast to the paucity of support for small farmers like Don Santos who, as he noted, "invested more in the farm than [they] harvest."

These conditions dislocated people who, following the path of financial resources, migrated seasonally to the industrial farms of Sinaloa and Sonora to work as wage laborers. Many of Don Santos's neighbors also migrated there. One of his Triqui neighbors, Doña Nancy, was only eight years old when she began working in Sinaloa's tomato fields. She migrated with her parents, part of a pattern of entire families recruited to work the northern fields. Large agribusinesses specifically recruited poor Indigenous families like Doña Nancy's based on racialized notions that they would not complain about the relatively low wages and harsh working conditions.[23]

The pattern of internal migration soon shifted to international migration in the 1980s, when, as Don Santos explained, "migration from the pueblo really began." This wave of migration was spurred by IMF- and U.S. Treasury–led interventions that changed the face of Mexican agriculture, social services, and business and wage structures. The interventions came as a response to a sharp decline in oil prices in 1982 that left Mexico in a financial crisis. Although the Mexican government initially resisted international assistance, the weight of the crisis eventually forced it to accept the conditional support of U.S. and international banking institutions.[24] The United States initiated a bailout by paying the Mexican government $2 billion to shore up the petroleum and agricultural industries.[25] In the next few months, a more permanent arrangement was reached with the IMF involving a number of loans and attached conditions.[26] Later in the decade, Mexico began to receive loans from the World Bank that were similarly conditioned on a set of economic reforms prescribed by that agency.[27]

Mexico agreed to these conditions in a series of Letters of Intent sent from the country's Finance Ministry to the head of the IMF.[28] Despite the appearance of involvement by the debtor country, the contents of such letters are highly controlled by the IMF's executive board, and certain terms must be addressed both in the letter and by the government in its policies.[29] Moreover, the IMF executive board is widely known to be controlled by the United States, particularly the Treasury Department, meaning that the conditions set are the imposition of U.S. Treasury policies on foreign governments in exchange for much-needed assistance.[30] Thus, Mexico's agreement to the conditions for the IMF loans was an agreement to continue to serve U.S. interests.

The conditions imposed by the U.S. and the IMF involved the three pillars of economic reform mentioned previously: fiscal austerity, privatization of state-owned industries, and market liberalization. These measures, known as structural adjustment, were predetermined conditions imposed on any country seeking loans from the IMF or the World Bank. Specific measures included sharp decreases in government supports for economic sectors such as agriculture (fiscal austerity measures), privatization of so-called inefficient public enterprises, the elimination of trade barriers, decreases in price supports, and the deregulation of industry (market liberalizations).[31] The IMF saw agricultural spending cuts as key to fulfilling the austerity goals it set out for the Mexican government as a condition of its loans.[32] The Mexican government duly responded, stating in its 1986 Letter of Intent that it would "eliminate . . . unjustified subsidies," reduce public expenditures, and reduce the number of public entities.[33] These promises translated into a reduced public role in provision of credit, commercialization of crops, price supports, and subsidies. As a result of these combined cuts, agricultural investment in small farms dropped by 85 percent between 1980 and 1989.[34] These deep cuts had a decidedly negative impact on southern states such as Oaxaca.[35] In addition to the fiscal austerity measures, market liberalizations that opened Mexican agriculture to foreign competition caused a sharp decline in crop prices, including the price of corn, which was cultivated ubiquitously in the Mixteca.[36] Price decreases, translated as wage or profit decreases for people like Don Santos, combined with bottomed-out public support to dislocate Don Santos and many others from their home communities.

The village of Sanctorum, two hundred miles due north of Laguna, is one of the few truly rural areas in the otherwise densely populated state of Tlaxcala. Even here, small assembly plants dotted the horizon before the landscape turned to flat farmland. Isaís is a farmworker who has made many trips to Canada under that country's farm labor program. He made his first trip in 2000 for a variety of reasons. He explained the reason that was chief among them: "My father and I were day laborers. But we only earned about 80 to 100 pesos a day. We could not get credit to buy our own land."

Isaís's inability to obtain credit resulted from another IMF-prescribed fiscal austerity measure that required reducing the availability of subsidized loans.[37] President Carlos Salinas de Gortari (1987–93) enthusiastically supported the measure and systematically downsized the national bank, National Bank for Rural Credit (BANRURAL), shifting existing BANRURAL loans to the private market.[38] As a result of these changes, government-subsidized loans to farmers fell sharply in the 1990s.[39] By 1992, private commercial lenders became the only option for small farmers seeking a loan to buy seed, fertilizer, or equipment. However, small farmers were not attractive borrowers in a commercial setting because of their low profit margins and relatively unpredictable crop yields.[40] The shift from public to private lending, according to one economist, was a "critical blow" to small farmers like Isaís, "whose relatively low profit margins and high-risk exposure make them unattractive credit risks for commercial banks."[41] Indeed, the privatization of credit has resulted in only 15 percent of Mexico's farmers having access to credit, of which the majority are large- and medium-scale farms.[42] Even if private lenders were willing to work with small farmers, it is unlikely that these farmers would have been able to afford the exorbitant interest rates private banks charged.[43] When Isaís said, "We could not get credit," he was expressing the frustration of 85 percent of Mexican farmers and likely a larger proportion of small farmers like himself.

The economic gaps experienced by small farmers were exacerbated by two overlapping events in 1994: a second economic crisis in Mexico and Mexico's entry into NAFTA with the United States and Canada. The economic crisis resulted in a massive devaluation of the peso and another round of loans from the United States and the IMF conditioned on further neoliberalization measures, including even deeper cuts to public spending and privatization of additional industries.[44] NAFTA, in turn, resulted in all three trading partners eliminating tariffs on imports and encouraging foreign investment. For Mexican farmers engaged in corn production like Don Santos and Isaís, this meant placing their unsubsidized products in competition with subsidized grain producers from the United States and Canada. The elimination of tariffs resulted in U.S. corn, in particular, flooding the Mexican market, reducing overall prices and driving many small farmers out of business.

The Mexican government attempted to address the worst of these consequences with a series of programs directed at extremely poor households.[45] Beginning with PROGRESA under President Ernesto Zedillo (1997–2002) and later named Oportunidades (2003–14), the programs transferred cash directly to households that met the criteria for extreme poverty if these households fulfilled certain education and health preconditions.[46] The approach was novel and held promise as it seemed to target the poor more directly and to give recipients control over expenditures.[47] However, most of the migrant families interviewed had not participated in either program. Isais and other migrants indicated that they had tried to participate but were told that they earned too much. In the Mixteca region of Oaxaca, mothers indicated that the program's requirement to attend health appointments were structurally impossible as a health care worker only visited the area once a week. Thus, it is not surprising that assessments of the effectiveness of direct cash transfers found that while it reduced levels of extreme poverty, it did not have a significant impact on overall poverty rates.[48] In fact, overall poverty rates were slightly higher in 2014 than they were in 1994, at the beginning of the crisis.[49]

It is also not surprising, then, that those who found themselves feeling the brunt of NAFTA's impacts on crop prices and competitiveness while also unable to qualify for social programs continued to find themselves dislocated from their lands in search of sustainable earnings. In fact, in many parts of Mexico, dislocation accelerated in the wake of NAFTA and further IMF interventions. In Oaxaca, out-migration increased 300 percent from the mid-1990s through 2005,[50] and in Tlaxcala, it increased more than 150 percent in the same period.[51]

The conditions that spurred Don Pablo's journey in the 1960s and Isais's first trip forty years later trace a long history of divestment from agricultural supports for small farmers raced as "backward" and therefore unworthy of public support. Their losses corresponded with gains for corporate agriculture in the form of public support and elimination of trade barriers. Multinational corporations such as Maseca, Bimbo, Cargill, Bachoco, PilgrimsPride, Tysson, Nestlé, Lala, Sigma, and Monsanto came into Mexico, gaining profits and market share while Don Santos and his compatriots were abandoned and left.[52] Ironically, many of these women and men who were dislocated by the distribution of resources ended up working in fields similar to their own in the United States or Canada. Thus, their labor was distributed in a way that benefited corporate agricultural interests over the communities from which they hailed.

Divestment from Manufacturing Support

A similar distribution of labor and wealth accumulation was constructed in the manufacturing industry. In the 1960s, at the same time that Mexico was diverting resources to U.S.-facing agricultural centers, the country also began to invest in maquiladoras. These manufacturing plants take components made largely in the United States, make them into finished products—from automobiles to

T-shirts—and then export them to the United States for sale by U.S. retailers. By 1967, there were fifty-seven maquiladoras located in the border cities of Tijuana, Nuevo Laredo, Ciudad Juárez, Mexicali, and Matamoros.[53] Eighty percent of these plants engaged in assembly or parts production for U.S. companies.[54] The industry expanded in the next decades, fueled by U.S. customs rules allowing for duty-free import of items manufactured abroad from U.S.-based raw materials and by decreased protections against foreign investment. One of the places that the industry expanded to in the 1980s was Tlaxcala.

Many maquila workers in Tlaxcala come from San Francisco de Tetlanohcan. Due to its location in the sierra, Tetlanohcan is hilly. The main plaza is located about halfway up the main hill. Farther up the hill is the Nahuatl barrio of Santa Cruz, which has some adobe homes as well as some more recently built two-story *migra casas* (migrant homes). "Nahuatl" refers to both an Indigenous ethnic group and the language they speak. It is the dominant Indigenous group in Central Mexico, where Tetlanohcan is located, and includes descendants of the Aztec Empire and their longtime adversaries in Tlaxcala, the Tlaxcaltecs.

At the base of the Santa Cruz barrio, I meet Irena, a Nahuatl woman whose husband has been in the United States for several years. Irena is one of thousands of women who at one time worked in one of many sewing factories that were part of the Malintzi Industrial Corridor near Tetlanohcan. Tlaxcaltecs like Irena were attracted to this work because it paid better than other work in the area. "The work is paid by the piece," Irena explains. However, like most maquilas, the Malintzi plants did not offer job stability. "They cannot give me more regular hours," said Irena of the shifts she was able to get. She goes on to tell me that between her hours at the sewing maquiladora and her husband's hours at a different maquiladora farther away, the couple wase making $1,700 MXN a week, decidedly less than the $5,000 MXN needed to meet basic necessities such as rent, food, utilities, clothing, and school expenses for their family of five. The depressed wages and unstable hours led Irena's husband, Efraím, to migrate in 1998 after they had their first child. While Efraím was in the United States, the maquiladora that Irena worked at closed, mirroring a nationwide contraction of that industry due to even more depressed wages in other parts of the world. When I met Irena in 2013, she was trying to sell her Nahuatl embroidery at local markets and fairs. However, what had once been a revered skill had fallen out of style in the era of fast fashion. Efraím had been back and forth to the United States since 1998 and had remained there since his most recent trip in 2007.

Irena's and Efraím's experiences reflect the displacement of Mexican-owned industry that concentrated on a Mexican market with U.S. owned maquiladoras that generated unstable, low-paying work and whose profits were realized by U.S. corporations. Until the 1980s, the Mexican government subsidized its domestic textile industry through supports for domestic enterprise and price supports in the domestic market.[55] These supports greatly assisted the textile industry in Tlaxcala, considered among the best clothing makers in the country. However, regulations put in place in 1972 to protect Mexican industry were reinterpreted during the Salinas administration to allow for complete foreign ownership of certain Mexican businesses and to increase the share of foreign investment allowed in others to greater than 49 percent.[56] Thus, a more diverse array of U.S. companies was now able to look to Mexican assembly plants as a way to reduce costs.

It was during this expansion in the 1980s that maquiladoras opened in large numbers in Tlaxcala. In particular, clothing retailers based in California saw a tradition of fine sewing and clothing production in Tlaxcala and decided to invest in maquiladoras there to assemble clothing bound for the United States.[57] These investments included maquiladoras in the Malintzi Industrial Corridor where Irena worked. During the time that Irena worked in these factories, the amount of products made in Mexico and bound for Los Angeles went from 10 percent (in 1992) to 60 percent (in 1997/98).[58] During this same time, the percentage of people from Tlaxcala displaced into the United States jumped by five times.[59]

By 1997, 80 percent of maquiladora owners were U.S. companies.[60] For these companies, the maquiladoras reduced overhead expenses and increased profit margins.[61] They also allowed for what the political economist Raúl Delgado Wise calls an "indirect exportation of labor or, alternatively, the disembodied exportation of the Mexican work force without requiring the workers to leave the country."[62] Maquiladoras are an isolated step in a larger supply chain that neither controls the products made nor benefits from profits earned. They buy raw materials from abroad, usually from the same companies that seek the final products. Maquiladora workers then assemble products such as automobiles or clothing for wages. Finally, the finished product is exported to be sold by the usually U.S.-based company that owns the assembly plant. This method of production allows companies to benefit from labor without having to import it, thus Delgado Wise's reference to an "indirect exportation of labor."

For workers like Irena and Efraím, wages in the maquiladoras was higher than what they could find elsewhere in Mexico. However, as Irena explained, the jobs were unstable. U.S.-based companies seeking to maximize profits found even lower waged labor in Central America and Asia. In addition, Tlaxcala's physical location far from the U.S. border did not offer as clear a geographic advantage as the plants located just south of the United States.[63] Moreover, due to pressure by U.S. companies looking to improve their profit margins and another economic crisis in 1994, the Mexican government froze wages during the last half of the 1990s.[64] As a result, worker's wages were reduced to subsistence levels.[65] This instability forced Efraím to begin migrating in 1998. Unsurprisingly, given the low wages and instability of the job market, Efraím's journey was part of a large uptick in Tlaxcalan out-migration in the 1990s. Thus, the indirect exportation of labor described by Delgado Wise eventually became a more direct pattern of unauthorized migration to the United States for many maquiladora workers.

While maquiladoras represent a significant part of the manufacturing sector, the most significant good extracted from Mexico (other than its people) is oil. On the Gulf Coast of Mexico, the sleepy seafront town of Chiltepec, Tabasco, is part of the municipality of Paraíso (Paradise). Paraíso is an ironic name for a town from which the black plumes of smoke can be seen at all angles. The smoke is a reminder of Tabasco's main industry. According to the Chiltepec's *delegado* (mayor), José Luis Sánchez Domínguez, oil was found on the Tabascan coast close to Chiltepec in 1979. After this, "the PEMEX [Petroleos Mexicanos, or Mexican Oil] boom started," said Sánchez Domínguez, "but skilled labor was imported from other states—Tamaulipas, Veracruz, and Campeche—to control the power of the oil workers' union." Moreover, profits from the oil were increasingly realized overseas. The once-nationalized oil industry, PEMEX, was opened to foreign investment in the 1980s and privatized in line with the IMF prescriptions of the era.[66] By 1997, U.S. and British investors such as Halliburton, Shell, Exxon, and BP owned large shares of PEMEX.[67]

Due to Tabasco's dependence on oil revenues for income, the state's governors, from Enrique González Perdrero (1982–87) to Andrés Rafael Granier Melo (2006–11), instituted regulations with the interests of these foreign investors in mind.[68] One such regulation from the 1980s was the prohibition on shrimping by farmers in the coastal town of Chiltepec because it would interfere with the oil drilling operations.[69] In addition to prohibiting local fishing, the state government stopped supporting the shrimp barge cooperatives financially, thus decimating the once-thriving shrimping industry in the town.[70] Thus, local employment and viability actually decreased after PEMEX arrived. Delegado Sánchez Domínguez decried these policy changes: "The situation of these workers [shrimp farmers] now is terrible. There is no retirement, no insurance, no unions who help them, and no benefits that come with the work. They simply work, earn money, and that is it."

This decreased level of employment in Chiltepec meant that people were ready to go to the United States when employers began recruiting in the area in 1989. One of these people was Serena, whom I met in the restaurant that she was trying to keep running on Chiltepec's small coastal boardwalk. Serena was a housewife when a cousin of her husband's mentioned that U.S. employers were specifically looking for women to train and work as *jaiberas*, or crab cleaners. Normally, Serena would not dream of migrating, especially on her own, but her husband had little work due to the evisceration of the local shrimping industry. However, she was convinced to migrate both because of economic need and because of the recruitment efforts of a U.S. seafood company. Like the California clothing retailers that located their maquiladora workers in areas historically known for sewing, the crab companies of the southeastern United States turned to areas like Chiltepec where traditional shrimping and crabbing were destroyed to fill their workforce. Serena became part of a massive movement of women from Chiltepec and other parts of Tabasco to the United States.

Intentional Suppression of Wages

When migrants like Serena, Don Santos, and Irena refer to the low wages for work in the fishing industry in Chiltepec, Tabasco, or the agricultural sector in Laguna Guadalupe de Yucunicoco, Oaxaca, or the maquiladoras outside San Francisco de Tetlanohcan, Tlaxcala, their diminished earnings can be mapped precisely onto the sectors of the economy that saw a loss of government support and intentional wage depression due to the demands of the IMF.

Lowering wages in all sectors of the economy was a key strategy advocated by the IMF and implemented by the Mexican government in the 1980s and 1990s. The IMF argued that compensation needed to be suppressed (alongside other measures) in order to keep inflation down and ensure that products were competitive for export.[71] The Mexican government wholeheartedly adopted this approach, even casting labor union demands for pay increases as "attacks on the country."[72] By 1983, the Mexican government had adopted the recommendations of the IMF to depress wages placing "a substantial share of the . . . burden" of reforms designed to reduce inflation on workers.[73] But IMF officials were not satisfied. In the same meeting minutes that delineated the policies that the Mexican government was willingly undertaking, IMF board members expressed concern at what they saw as the Mexican government's efforts to slow earnings losses in 1984.[74] These concerns translated into a promise the next year to peg any wage increases to productivity increases rather than a cost of living adjustment.[75]

The policy of intentional wage suppression in some sectors while also emphasizing world market competitiveness had mixed results.[76] Some industries became more successful, and some members of the middle class and elite were able to rise up the economic ranks.[77] For others, particularly in rural areas, real earnings plummeted during this period.[78] The economist Nora Lustig found that overall real wages dropped by a staggering 40 to 50 percent between 1983 and 1988.[79] In the maquiladora sector, compensation contracted less sharply, but there were still losses of 26 percent during these years.[80] For other manufacturing jobs, wages dropped by closer to 36 percent.[81] In agriculture, the patterns were slightly different because income is based on output. In the early years of structural adjustment, before cuts in subsidies and price supports took full hold, agricultural income rose slightly.[82] However, once these cuts went into full effect, agricultural output declined, and incomes were reduced by over 30 percent.[83]

Moreover, wage suppression continued to be a strategy well into the 1990s and 2000s, as Mexico sought to keep its place as a producer of exports to the United

States.[84] In particular, the Mexican government has kept payments to maquiladora workers low in order to ensure a continued comparative advantage for U.S. companies.[85] Overall, wages in Mexico plummeted after the peso crisis in 1994 and did not begin to recover until 2006. Irena and Efraím felt the effects of these cuts, and Efraím eventually migrated as a result. Even after 2006, the pace of wage recovery has been slow. As of 2014, real earnings (adjusted for inflation and cost of living) had increased slightly over their 1994 nadir and only barely surpassed wages from the pre–structural adjustment era.[86] The minimum wage, impacting many people like Irena and Efraim, actually dropped by almost 20% between 1994 and 2015 and unemployment increased during the same period.[87] Thus, Efraim has had to remain in the U.S. in order to help his family survive and to help his children invest in their futures.

Divestment from Education

Another key feature of IMF-prescribed fiscal austerity measures was cutting public spending on social programs. Between 1983 and 1988, spending on education and health care dropped precipitously, with cuts totaling 29.6 percent and 23.3 percent, respectively (figure 5).[88] This was despite ample empirical evidence at the time that suggested that education and health care spending was the key to increasing productivity.[89] In the education arena, this resulted in the reduction in payroll for teachers, reduced availability of materials, and school buildings falling into disrepair.[90] The reduction in education spending was accompanied by higher school dropout rates, particularly in rural areas, likely due to the need for young people to work and contribute to household income.[91]

Even when funding for education increased in the late 1980s and 1990s, it was still far below levels needed to ensure access to education for the population (figure 7).[92] Moreover, the IMF advocated for the decentralization of education from the federal government to the states.[93] This led to uneven development in which states with a higher income were able to spend more while education in states with lower incomes or with other priorities suffered. Decentralization had particularly negative impacts on southern rural states such as Tabasco and Oaxaca whose low revenues meant there was little to allocate to supplementing federal funding for education.[94]

It is no wonder then that paying school fees was the most common reason cited by U.S.-bound migrants from Soyataco and Chiltepec, Tabasco. Serena's main reason for migrating with authorization in 1997 was to pay for the education of her children. At the time, she had three children, ages twenty-one, nineteen, and twelve. And while she had an immediate need to pay for college fees for her eldest child, she continued to migrate for twelve years to pay for the other two children.

About an hour away from Chiltepec in Soyataco, Elias also found himself ensnared in the migration cycle because of the cuts to educational support. Elias

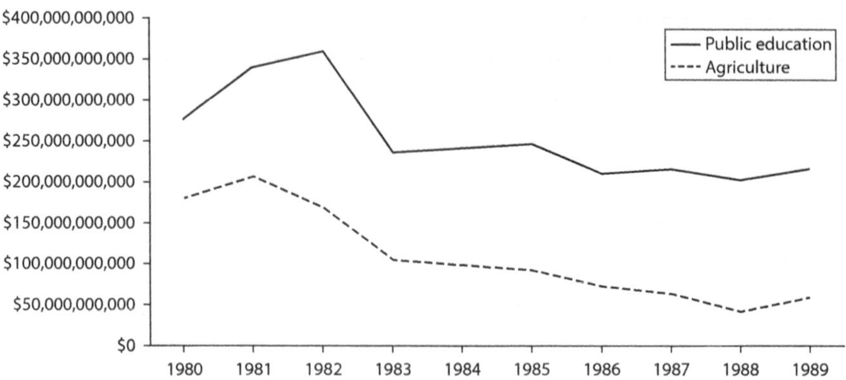

FIGURE 5. Mexico Public Spending, 1980–1989.

migrated without authorization in 1999, 2003, and 2006. In total, he spent nine years in the United States, returning for good in 2008. When asked why he left the first time, he said:

> Look, there is a great inequality between what one earns and the cost of the *canasta basica* [basic goods, necessities]. What one earns only gets you to *mediovivir* [his own phrase but translated as "half living"]. But as for why I left, point number one was to give an education to my children.

In 1999, Elias's kids were sixteen, fourteen, and twelve. Elias went on to explain that the lack of a high school in Soyataco meant that he had to pay for a taxi to take his oldest to and from the nearest school in Jalpa. The taxi cost $20 MXN a week, about 2 percent of his weekly income of around $1,000 MXN at the time. On top of that, the school fees were about $400 MXN a semester, a figure that was lower than the taxi fare but still substantial for a family that only earned about $4,000 MXN a month.

Elias made multiple trips to the United States to continue to pay for his children's education. Each time, he remained for several years and returned home to see his family for a brief few months. Once his children had all graduated from high school, Elias returned in 2008. He was very clear that he would not migrate again, having completed his goal. Since Elias's return, a high school has been built in Soyataco. However, it is a semiprivate high school requiring fairly high fees. Thus, it would be no surprise if educational costs continue to spur migration from Soyataco to the United States.

Five hundred miles to the southwest, in the Mixteca region of Oaxaca, educational access is even more scarce. Elfego and Ricardo describe the lack of educational facilities in two different Mixtecan villages over several decades. Though Elfego first migrated in 1985, before he had children, once the children were born, he was determined to educate them so that they could make a sustainable living in Mexico. By the mid-1990s, Elfego and his wife sought to send all four of their

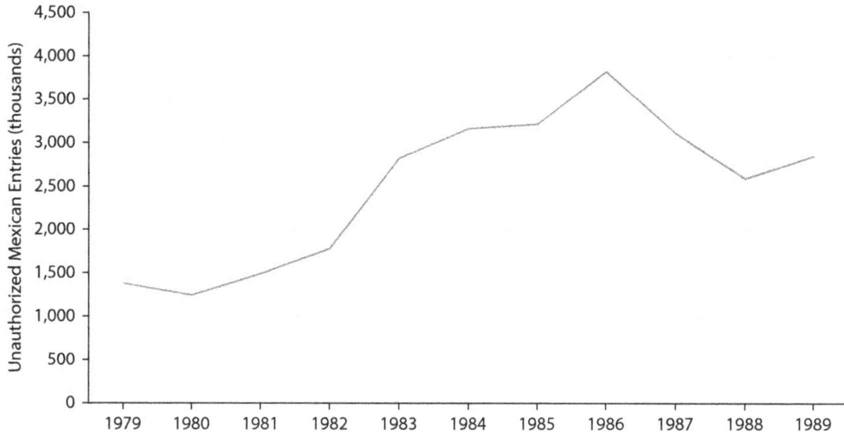

FIGURE 6. Unauthorized Mexico-U.S. Migration, 1979–1989.

children to school. According to Elfego, "They had to go to Tecomaxtlahuaca, and we had to pay for books, the subscription fee, for internet that they used at the school, etc. But with the money I made in the U.S., I was able to educate all four of my children through *secundaria*."

In Mexico, the basic educational system is divided into three parts: *primaria*, or elementary school (grades 1–6), *secundaria*, or middle school (grades 7–9), and *preparatoria*, or high school (grades 10–12). Finishing preparatoria is the equivalent of finishing high school in the United States. Thus, when Elfego says that he educated his children through secundaria, he was indicating that, even with migration, he could not afford to help them obtain a high school diploma. He explained, "They would have to go to Santo Domingo Tonalá [about two hours away] for preparatoria, and we just could not afford it." It was this lack of a local school that led his eldest son to migrate.

A similar pattern unfolded in Ricardo's family, who lived in the nearby town of Santa María Natividad. Ricardo and Luna, his wife, migrated in 2004. By then, he had experience traveling back and forth across the border. Ricardo first migrated in 1990, when he was just thirteen years old. "I went out of necessity," he said. "I was not in school. There was a primaria in our town but no others. And anyway, after that [primaria], in my time, kids went into the fields to help their parents. You had to look for work."

The need to leave school at a young age was fairly typical for children in extremely poor families like those in the Mixteca. Engaging the entire family in collective work has been part of the Mixtec economy for centuries.[95] But it was also due to a jarring lack of resources stemming from decades of economic abandonment in the region. As Ricardo said, "People live on their own power because the government does not make it to them. We invited the government to come, but they didn't visit us. There has never been a visitor from the government here."

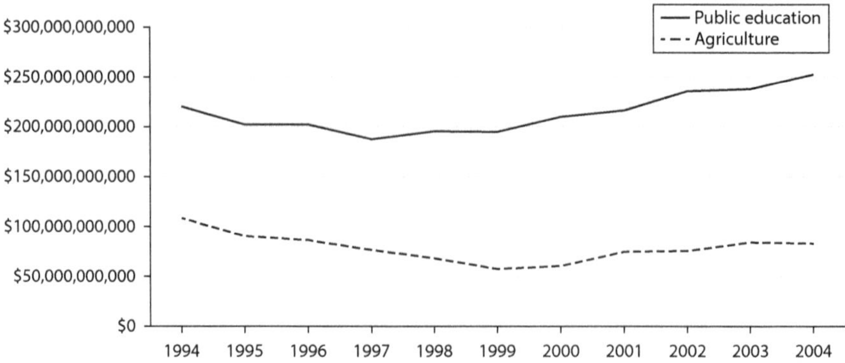

FIGURE 7. Mexico Public Spending, 1994–2004.

When Ricardo says that the "government does not make it to them," he is making a point about both historical context and present-day realities. As other observers of the Mixteca have noted, the Mexican government has never invested in infrastructure, development, or other projects there, including schools that are accessible and affordable to the local population.[96] A 2019 assessment of educational attainment found that rural southern states like Oaxaca continue to have a lower capacity to educate their residents and higher disparities in educational funding.[97] In fact, Ricardo goes further to indicate that the officials from the government have not even appeared in the Mixteca to see what living conditions were like and to understand the profound abandonment felt in this region.

Even in relatively richer states like Tlaxcala and Puebla, funding for education has concentrated on the development of private schools.[98] Thus, even in Tetlanohcan and Sanctorum, Tlaxcala, a significant number of families decided to have a member migrate to pay for the cost of education. Elísabet is the mother of six children in Tetlanohcan. She and her husband, Rodolfo are both Tlaxcaltec and speak Nahuatl and Spanish. When their eldest child, Manuela, was entering secundaria, the family decided that Rodolfo needed to move to the United States to earn money for her school fees. Rodolfo left in 1998 and spent twelve years in the United States without returning. However, when his mother became ill, Rodolfo had to return, which meant that some of Manuela's younger siblings could not complete their education. When I spoke with Rodolfo in 2013, he was trying to raise the money for a return trip to the United States. The construction work that he had done before 1998 had dried up, and work in the nearby maquiladoras was intermittent and did not pay enough. Rodolfo and Elísabet wanted to send their younger children to the newly opened bilingual school that would teach them Nahuatl. The school was opened after a long campaign by their community to recapture the Nahuatl language and Tlaxcatec traditions. However, having been developed in the time of neoliberalism, the new school

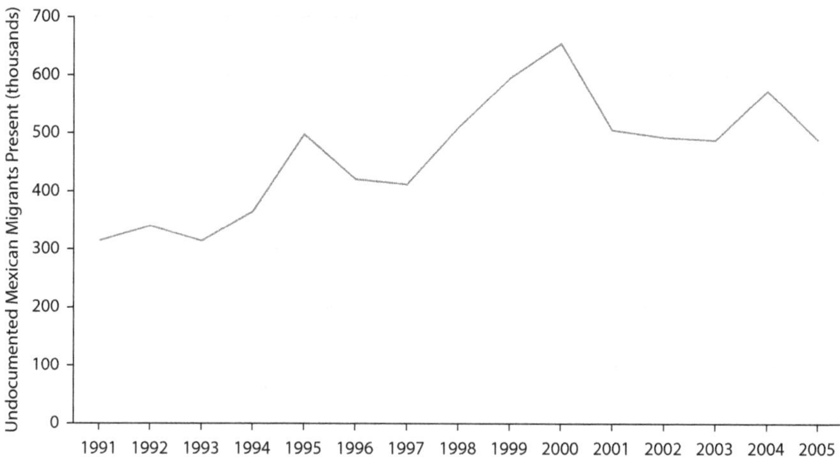

FIGURE 8. Mexico–U.S. Migration, 1991–2005.

was semiprivate, requiring tuition as well payments for books and uniforms. This placed the school out of reach for the family without Rodolfo's earnings from the United States.

The combined effects of cuts to education spending, suppression of wages across different economic sectors, and the distribution of resources to large corporate agricultural and manufacturing enterprises overlapped to construct a set of economic conditions that squeezed communities like Tetlanohcan, Soyataco, and Laguna Guadalupe de Yucunicoco. This newly constructed economic landscape, built on years of repression of Indigenous communities, exacerbated colonial practices with new forms of economic domination that left people like Rodolfo, Elfego, and Serena earning less but having to pay more for basic services whether they lived in urban, rural, or semiurban settings. Facing a constricted set of choices, more and more people entered the migration cycle in any way they could, whether or not their journey was legally authorized. As a comparison of figures 5 and 6 and 7 and 8 indicates, the dislocation caused by economic policies occurred on a large scale, impacting communities well beyond those profiled here, and persisted for decades.

A MIGRANT COMMUNITY PERSPECTIVE ON AUTHORIZED VERSUS UNAUTHORIZED MIGRATION

Rodolfo's inability to pay for his children's education led him, like so many others, to seek to enter the United States without authorization. Tellingly, the authorized journeys discussed in this book were made for the same reasons as the unauthorized ones. Isaís left Sanctorum, Tlaxcala, with authorization to help pay for his children's education around the same time that Rodolfo first left Tetlanohcan without authorization to pay for Manuela's secundaria. Similarly, in Tabasco, Serena left Chiltepec with authorization to help pay for her oldest to continue working toward his bachelor's degree around the same time that Elias left to help pay for his children to complete high school in Soyataco. In Oaxaca, Don Santos migrated both with and without authorization to help pay for his children's education while Elfego made numerous unauthorized journeys to educate his children. For all of these migrants, the need to fill gaps in public education funding overlapped with the inability to make a sustainable living due to cuts in agricultural, manufacturing, and banking supports.

Thus, from the migrant community perspective, the legality of a particular migrant's trip was subordinate to the forces dislocating them from their home communities. This was evident in the way migrants talked about their decisions to leave. When asked how they made their journeys, the vast majority of migrants simply said, "Me fui" (I went), and then mentioned the year they left or their destination. To discern whether the trips were made with or without authorization, more pointed questions were necessary. The responses to these questions were matter of fact, whether it was "Me fui contratado" (lit., "I went with a contract") or "Me fui mojado" (lit., "I went wet," referring to the historical method of crossing into the United States via the Río Bravo/Rio Grande).[99] But it was clear that all of the migrants were much more concerned about the conditions that were compelling their decision to leave. Rodolfo, Efraím, Isaís, Don Santos, Elfego, Elias, and Serena all spent much more time talking about the problems they faced paying for their children's education and the inability to make a sustainable living from agriculture (in the case of Isaís, Don Santos, and Elfego), manufacturing (in the case of Rodolfo and Efraím), or other industries. Thus, the migrant community perspective suggests that debates on immigration in the United States that focus on the distinction between authorized and unauthorized migration do not capture what migration actually is.

Legality did matter more for women, as many women indicated that they were not willing to risk the dangers of an unauthorized journey. For some, like Irena, this meant applying for permission to visit the United States and return. Irena was emphatic that she would not migrate without authorization even if it could help the family save more. "Migration [without authorization] is not for women," she said. "Some do it, but, no, it's too dangerous." For those who did make one unauthorized journey, subsequent journeys were ruled out. For example, Luna was clear that when she crossed the border in 2004, she went with other people "to feel protected." When we spoke in 2013, Luna said that she did think about returning to the United States, but then, she said, "I remember the journey," referring to its difficulty. And finally, Serena only considered migration as an option because she was able to obtain a visa for temporary work. Even when deciding not to make unauthorized journeys, women focused on the dangers they would encounter on the route to the U.S. border, not the risk of arrest or detention by U.S. border authorities. Like their male counterparts, they centered the needs of their families and community rather than the possibility that they were violating U.S. laws.

All of the migrants who reported making unauthorized entries acknowledged that their actions violated U.S. law. As Don Santos said, "One knows that a country has its laws." "But," he continued, "a person also has to do what he needs, what his family needs." In other words, Don Santos conveyed that his behavior was not subordinate to or less important than the law but that the law and his family's needs were on the same level. His response is consistent with other studies that have shown that decisions of unauthorized migrants to violate the law are made in part based on the perceived legitimacy of the law they are violating.[100] In Don Santos's case and in the case of many other migrants who entered the United States unlawfully, U.S. rules were considered legitimate but no more legitimate than the need to support their families.

Moreover, as the next chapter reveals, the dislocation of migrants like Don Santos benefited U.S. employers who sought unauthorized labor and public and private U.S. immigration enforcement interests that profit from the demonization of Mexican migrants. This follows a long historical pattern traced in the next chapter of importing Mexican labor into agriculture, mining, and other industries while simultaneously illegalizing their journeys. Some of this historical pattern has included authorizing Mexican labor, like the Bracero Program. However, much of this history has evinced a trend and even desire to employ those without authorization and simultaneously profit from immigration enforcement mechanisms. As the next chapter details, several sectors of the U.S. economy have a strong, ongoing preference for unauthorized labor while other sectors profit from trying to control that labor's movement. This has resulted in a pattern of permissions and prohibitions in U.S. implementation of immigration policies designed to maximize profits made from migrant workers while demonizing the people crossing into the United States. Thus the migrants are in some ways reflecting U.S. policies. They know that the migration is technically against the law but also that it is necessary—for them and for their destination country.

Displacement

We were treated like slaves. They saw us as beasts, nothing more.
—DON SANTOS

We're gonna let 'em in cause you need 'em.
—PRESIDENT DONALD J. TRUMP

When Luna left her village of Santa María Natividad in the Mixteca Baja region of Oaxaca, she was determined to cross into the United States with her husband, Ricardo. The couple was recently married and trying to make up for the lack of support for agriculture and schools in their town. Luna felt confident leaving the village. They had paid a coyote US$1,500 each to guide them safely across the border. That was the equivalent of about $15,000 MXN and represented more than a month's earnings for the young couple. They borrowed the sum from a local moneylender, hoping they could quickly repay the loan with their earnings in the United States.

Ricardo had previously crossed by himself in 1990. At that time, he just "swam across the Río Bravo," which stretches over 1,200 miles from Ciudad Juárez–El Paso to the Gulf of Mexico. Ricardo recalls that part of the journey being easy, saying, "No tuvo que cruzar la linea, me fui mojado" (I did not have to cross the border, I went "wet").

By 2004, when Luna and Ricardo made their journey together, crossing the Mexico-U.S. border had become more dangerous, and a coyote was essential. Luna recalls being in Tijuana "looking at the other side."

> I felt my nerves in my stomach. We were crossing with ten other people from different pueblos. The first two times we tried to cross, immigration arrested a lot of people. We had to run many times. We were turned back three times and only made it across on the fourth. Only four of us made it across. And that time, we only made it because it rained and the officers could not see us.

When Luna got to the U.S. side of the border, she was finally able to stop running. Only then did she notice that her knees were bloody from scraping against brush on the way. She described her journey: "We suffered a lot to cross that first time." Once in the United States, the couple was able to find work easily picking fruits and flowers in Washington State. They were not asked for documentation stating that they were authorized to work in the United States. Moreover, in the four years that Luna and Ricardo worked in different industries in the Northwest, they never encountered immigration enforcement officials. Luna said, "We were always looking out for the *migra* [Immigration Customs and Enforcement, or ICE], but I never saw them." The real problem, according to Luna, was the harsh working conditions and meager pay, which forced Luna and Ricardo to work several jobs at once and required them to leave certain positions to escape abusive treatment.

It was those conditions that finally convinced Luna to return to Mexico. She recalls living with a number of other people and having to take turns to cook and shower. Since returning to the Mixteca in 2008, Luna has thought about return-ing to the United States several times. However, she says, "I remember the jour-ney, and I decide to stay here," alluding to the high incidence of violence against migrants, particularly women. Ricardo returned home in 2012 and says that he no longer wishes to go back across the border. When we spoke in 2013, the couple had begun a small business selling ceremonial animals that was providing enough for a sustainable living. "We are fortunate that we do not have to return," Luna said in one of our last conversations.

IMMIGRATION ENFORCEMENT AS A TOOL OF RACIAL CAPITALIST RELATIONS

Luna's story takes place at a particular historical moment when both border and interior enforcement efforts were escalating. However, that escalation does not reflect a move toward stopping people like Luna and Ricardo. Rather, it reflects a new mechanism for wealth accumulation in the form of surveillance, tracking, and incarceration. By the time Luna made her journey, there were three modes of extraction from migrants who sought to enter the United States. The first, exem-plified by Luna's story, displaces labor into industries that have long demanded Mexican labor in particular. Policies facilitating this displacement are rooted in historical, overtly racist depictions of Mexicans as almost bestial and therefore particularly suited to agricultural and other grueling labor. A second, overlapping mode of extraction involves racialized depictions of Mexican migrants as bringing crime and stealing work,[1] which serves to fill public coffers and fuels private profit through various immigration enforcement policies and practices. These policies and practices include criminal penalties for unauthorized entry; enforcement infrastructures such as checkpoints, surveillance devices, air and land vehicles, physical barriers, and detention centers; and immigration enforcement person-nel, who make up the largest federal law enforcement workforce in the country. For migrants racialized as both perfect workers and carceral subjects, a third

TABLE 3 Similarities in Displacement to Industry across Communities

	Tabasco	Oaxaca	Tlaxcala	Puebla
Migration rate* 1980–89	Very low	Medium	Very low	Low
Migration rate 1990–99	Very low	Medium	Medium	Medium
Migration rate 2000–2009	Very low	High	Medium	Medium
Displacement industry #1	Agriculture/ food processing (n = 15)	Agriculture/ food processing (n = 11)	Service (n = 9)	Service (n = 9)
Displacement industry #2	Service (n = 7)	Building (n = 4)	Agriculture (n = 8)	Factories (n = 1)

* "Migration rate" is a measurement derived from Mexico's National Survey of Demographic Change (ENADID) in its quintennial report, "Tendencias y características de la migración mexicana a los Estados Unidos."

extractive mechanism requires them to pay coyotes to arrive at their destinations. Increasingly, this means that organized criminal enterprises have now joined the more formal U.S. private and public actors as sources of extraction.

This approach to analyzing immigration enforcement mechanisms integrates what other scholars have discussed as separate, historically idiosyncratic threads into one theory that encompasses the evolution of modes of extraction over time. For example, the Mexico-U.S. migration scholars Gilbert González and Timothy Dunn have demonstrated that immigration policies through the early to mid-twentieth century served the wealth accumulation goals of U.S.-based employers and other entities.[2] Moving forward in time, Tanya Golash-Boza, Harsha Walia, and Gargi Bhattacharyya have explained how twenty-first-century surges in immigration enforcement by the United States, Europe, and Australia are part of the racial capitalist relations between the state from which migrants originate and the state to which they tend to migrate.[3] As the stories in this chapter reveal, the mechanisms used to import labor and deter migration are part of a singular migration-as-extraction cycle.

To fully explicate the displacement phase of migration as extraction, this chapter begins with an analysis of policies that first actively and then passively recruited Mexican labor to perform agricultural and food processing work the United States. Through historical records and migrant narratives, it shows that these early recruitment efforts had long-lasting impacts across demographically and geographically diverse regions (table 3). Whether a person was from a state like Tabasco with its very low migration rate or from a state like Oaxaca with a high migration rate as of 2000, the labor markets that migrants were pulled into were (in order of frequency of response): the agricultural and food processing industries; the service industry (including hospitality, home services, and janitorial services); and construction and factory work. Agriculture/food processing and the service industry were the most prevalent locations of migrant labor displacement, reflecting patterns of recruitment dating to the early twentieth century.

These historical and contemporary migration patterns are analyzed against immigration enforcement policies that allow unauthorized labor to both enter and persist while simultaneously demonizing this entry and presence. Three enforcement policies—enforcement of employer sanctions, border enforcement, and interior immigration enforcement—are examined through the experiences of migrants to illustrate the selective enforcement of these policies in order to continue the free flow of desired labor while simultaneously profiting from the "homeland security state."

DISPLACEMENT OF MIGRANTS
AS EASILY EXPLOITED LABOR

Scholars from various disciplines have examined U.S. immigration enforcement efforts, particularly those targeted at Mexican migrants, as designed to help displace or transfer Mexican labor into specific, segregated industries in the United States.[4] Nowhere is this labor transfer more prevalent than in the agricultural and food processing industries. The stories of several migrants—including Don Pablo, who migrated as a bracero in the 1960s, Elfego, who migrated as an unauthorized agricultural worker in the 1980s, and Luna and Ricardo, who made the same journey as Elfego in the 2000s—illustrate the clear preference for these workers by U.S. and Mexican agribusinesses. Similarly, a large number of Mexicans, particularly Mexican women, have been recruited to work in food processing such as meatpacking and fish cleaning. The stories of women from Chiltepec and Soyataco, Tabasco, highlight one such migration pattern: from the Gulf coast of Mexico to the crab-cleaning plants of the Southeast. Whether authorized or not, these migrants discussed a litany of labor abuses and exploitative practices by employers: practices facilitated by the decided underenforcement of immigration laws prohibiting employers from hiring unauthorized workers while simultaneously targeting workers for immigration violations.

Displacement into Commercial Agriculture

Commercial agriculture, or agribusiness, in the United States has always relied on conscripted labor from other parts of the world. Modern commercial agriculture has its roots in the plantation system that relied on enslaved African labor to work lands expropriated from the Indigenous populations. Until the passage of the Thirteenth Amendment in 1865, the primary laborers in U.S. agribusiness were subject to chattel slavery. After the abolition of slavery, forced labor continued in sharecropping and other arrangements, but many descendants of enslaved Africans sought other work. Agribusiness had to seek out new types of laborers, leading to the importation of migrants from China, Japan, the Philippines, parts of Europe, and Mexico. By the late 1800s, however, racist ideologies in the United States led to the exclusion of Asian and Eastern European immigrants, and by the 1910s, these exclusions began to result in labor shortages on expanding commercial farms. The same racist ideology cast Mexican workers as ideal for the backbreaking agricultural work while also depicting them as "docile" workers who would not rebel against the dreadful conditions.[5]

There is little documentation of migrants' experiences in their own words from this era, but several songs included in Manuel Gamio's 1930 volume, *Mexican Immigration to the United States* recounted the recruitment of migrants in the 1920s. One such song was called "Los Betalberos" (The Beet Field Workers).[6]

LOS BETABELEROS	THE BEET FIELD WORKERS
Afio de mil nuevecientos veinte y tres	In the year 1923
en el actual	Of the present era
Fueron los betabeleros	The beet field workers went
A ese "michiga" a lorar.	To that "Michigan," to their grief,
Por que todos los señores	Because all the bosses
Empezaban a regañar	Began to scold,
Y don Santiago les responde:	And Don Santiago says to them:
Yo me quiero regresar	"I want to return
Por que no nos han cumplido	Because they haven't done for us
Lo que fueron a contar.	What they said they would;
Aquí vienen y les cuentan	Here they come and they tell you
Que se vayan para allí,	That you ought to go up there
Porque allá les tiene todo	Because there you will have everything
Que no van a batallar,	Without having to fight for it.
Pero son puras mentiras	But these are nothing but lies,
Los que vienen y les dicen.	And those who come and say those things are liars.[7]

The lyrics specifically refer to the "bosses" in the United States and to efforts to recruit workers for U.S. agribusiness: "Here they come and tell you / That you ought to go up there." But the song also describes the terrible working conditions that these recruited workers found in the United States. This is emblematic of the sugar beet industry, which is among the most deeply involved in the importation and exploitation of Mexican labor.

Sugar beet growers and refiners fought successfully to officially import Mexican labor in 1917, when World War I caused a severe labor shortage. The growers' advocacy was aimed at the U.S. Department of Labor (DOL), the agency charged with immigration management at the time. The agency responded to the growers' efforts by authorizing a waiver of the requisite head tax and other requirements to allow Mexican citizens to enter the United States to perform agricultural work. Thus began the first official collaboration between the U.S. government whose officials had to grant the entry waiver and U.S. agribusiness that sent labor recruiters to the border to fill their slots.[8] "Los Betalberos" refers to this agricultural waiver era. The waivers remained in effect until 1921, when the demand for labor created by World War I decreased. But access to Mexican workers continued after 1921 as growers from California and Texas pushed to continue to exempt Mexico from the national origins quotas passed by Congress that year and renewed in 1924.[9] Indeed, Mexican workers would not be subject to any numerical limitations on entry until many years later.

After this time, U.S. immigration policies continued to favor the entry of Mexican workers even as exclusionary measures against other ethnic groups were escalating. By the time Don Pablo, whose journey and work in the United States was highlighted in chapter 1, migrated as a bracero, the idea that Mexican labor was ideal for U.S. agriculture had become firmly entrenched.[10] The Bracero Program, under which Don Pablo migrated, set up an even more formal set of procedures for the importation of Mexican labor. Rather than a discretionary waiver for anyone who made it to the U.S. border, the Bracero Accords were a series of formal agreements with the Mexican government that allowed U.S. companies to recruit inside Mexico.[11] The first agreement was signed on August 4, 1942, and was formally called "Agreement of August 4, 1942 for the Temporary Migration of Mexican Agricultural Workers to the United States." Over the course of the next eight years, numerous other agreements were signed. In 1951, the contract labor system created by the Bracero Accords formally became part of U.S. law as Public Law 78 and remained in place until 1965. During those years, nearly five million Mexican men entered the United States to work as braceros in U.S. fields.[12]

In order to be eligible to enter the United States as a bracero, one had to be male and unmarried, have no children, and have agricultural work experience but own no land of one's own. In addition, applicants had to have a reference letter from their local authorities. This left out a good number of Mexican campesinos who needed work and excluded women completely. Moreover, not all U.S. states were able to participate in the program. Notably, Texas—where many agribusinesses were located and where Mexican labor had long been a feature of local agriculture—was barred from participating due to Mexico's concerns about that state's history of slavery and segregation. The combination of high dislocation rates in Mexico pushing migrants ineligible to enter as braceros and the demands of

Texan agribusinesses resulted in millions of unauthorized migrants entering the United States alongside legally authorized braceros.[13]

The U.S. government response to unauthorized migration at that time was to apprehend unauthorized migrants, "deport" them to Mexico, and immediately return them to the United States as regularized workers under the Bracero Accords.[14] Thus, the pattern of public-private collaboration to provide a ready workforce to U.S. commercial farms continued. For the workers, the program provided much-needed income. However, this was more than offset by the hazardous working conditions. They were so toxic that they drew the attention of civil rights and workers' rights movements.[15] Even DOL officials were concerned. Lee G. Williams, the officer in charge of the program in the 1960s, referred to the program as a system of "legalized slavery."[16] Under pressure from social movements and inside the DOL, the program ended in 1965.[17] Don Pablo does not remember the civil rights struggles, but he referred to the substandard conditions in his characteristic understated way. In explaining why he did not stay, despite his boss's efforts to retain him, he said, "The only thing over there is work and nothing else. One does not feel like one is in one's place." Perhaps the greatest evidence that working conditions were too arduous was the fact that, despite continuing economic difficulty and despite his U.S. employer's request that he return, Don Pablo did not return to the United States once the Bracero Program ended.

Perhaps Don Pablo was prescient as the end of the Bracero Program meant that most Mexican agricultural laborers in the United States became unauthorized. In 1965, the Immigration and Nationality Act was amended to place annual quotas on the number of people who could legally migrate from Mexico to the United States for the first time and partly as a result of fears of the population increase in Mexico.[18] Those quotas were further reduced in 1976, resulting in only 20,000 Mexicans being able to migrate as permanent residents in a year. The quotas combined with the termination of the Bracero Program converted the previously authorized stream of Mexican migrants into an unauthorized stream. Though the law technically provided agricultural employers with an alternative authorized means of employing foreign workers through the H-2 visa program, employers did not like the program because of its bureaucratic hurdles and requirements to pay for travel and lodging of H-2 workers. Unauthorized entries from Mexico ballooned from an estimated 87,000 in 1965 to almost 1.5 million in 1978.[19] This has led scholars to refer to the period between 1965 and 1985 as the "era of undocumented migration."[20] This did not mean that Mexican workers were excluded, however. U.S. laws during this time had attributes of what Gerald López calls "prohibitions and permissions,"[21] including laws that formally disallowed migration as well as laws that permitted unauthorized migrant life.

In 1986, U.S. law shifted to being both more formally permissive albeit time limited and formally prohibitive. The Immigration Reform and Control Act of 1986 (IRCA) included several provisions that gave unauthorized migrants a path to legalizing their status.[22] The first was not limited to farmworkers and allowed migrants who had resided continuously in the United States since 1981 to legalize their status. The other three provisions were specifically geared to agricultural workers. First, Congress enacted the Special Agricultural Workers program, which allowed those who had worked in agriculture for one year as of May 1986 to legalize their status to a permanent immigration status.[23] Second, Congress allowed for Replenishment Agricultural Workers to make up for any shortfalls in labor supply during the 1990s. And finally, IRCA split the H-2 visa into two categories: the H-2A for agricultural workers and the H-2B for all other temporary work.[24] The immediate legalization provisions (including both the general and farmworker provisions) were not limited to Mexican migrants, but the vast majority of people who benefited were of Mexican origin because the vast majority of people working in the United States without authorization at the time were from Mexico. Three million people applied for one of the many benefits, and 2.7 million were ultimately approved. Of those approved, 75 percent, or just over 2 million, were migrants from Mexico.[25] On the prohibitive side, Congress finally passed a law preventing the hiring of workers who lacked authorization. However, as detailed below, these prohibitions have rarely been enforced against employers in their nearly fifty-year history.

For those who did not benefit from the time-limited legalization program, the only option for lawful entry into the United States was an employer's willingness to sponsor them for an H-2A visa. The new H-2A visa had no cap on the number of temporary workers authorized to enter for work in agriculture.[26] Despite this unlimited pool of visas, fewer than ten thousand H-2A visas were issued each year before 1995,[27] and by 2015, they still accounted for only 5 percent of the agricultural workforce.[28] In contrast, over half of the U.S. agricultural labor force is undocumented, a majority from Mexico. Don Santos is one of many who migrated during this period. He was able to secure an H-2A visa for one year, in 1994, but explained, "I started going back without documents because the visa was expensive and the rent that the employer charged was very expensive. Also, we did not earn much." Don Santos also referred to the captured nature of H-2A visas. He had to work for the employer who sponsored him regardless of working conditions, whereas he was able to switch employers more easily when he was unauthorized. While Don Santos explains why a worker might decide it is better to work without authorization, it is also beneficial to employers to have a largely unauthorized workforce that can be disciplined more easily.[29] Moreover, having a visa did not protect workers like Don Santos from brutal working conditions. As he told me:

> We were treated like slaves. We began working before the sun rose, and you could not take a break. They managed us hard. You had to be fast. I was fast, but even I needed a break! If we tried to take a moment to rest from the sun, the exhaustion, we were yelled at, even hit. They saw us as beasts, nothing more.

These conditions were widespread enough that they led African American Representative Charles Rangel to comment in 2013 that the H-2A program was "the closest [thing] I've ever seen to slavery."[30]

Don Santos's and his neighbors' displacement into U.S. agriculture indicates the continuing reliance on racialized patterns of exploitation in place since the 1910 waiver programs. Three of every four agricultural workers in the United States are from Mexico, and the majority of those identify as Indigenous, showing a continued pattern of displacing Indigenous peasant farmers into U.S. agribusiness.[31] In the twenty-first century, public officials no longer have to explicitly racialize workers as "docile" or "bestial" to call for their entry for exploitation. As President Trump told a group of supporters in 2018, "For the farmers . . . it's going to get good. . . . We're going to have strong borders, but we have to have your workers come in. . . . We're going to let them in 'cause you need them. . . . We have to have them."[32]

"We're going to let them in 'cause you need them," echoes the policies since the early 1900s that bend immigration laws to the needs of large agricultural employers. Moreover, Trump's reference to having "strong borders" while simultaneously allowing "your workers [to] come in" hearkens back to depictions of Mexican workers as both a threat and a necessity in the 1920s and points to the continued use of immigration laws to control rather than prevent entry. Indeed, in the midst of the coronavirus pandemic, the Department of Homeland Security (DHS) declared that H-2A workers were essential and would therefore be exempt from the otherwise blanket rule barring temporary migration.[33] This "waiver" for agricultural work is starkly similar to the waiver programs over one hundred years earlier. Unlike the 1920s, the Mexico-U.S. border is now fortified, and Trump administration directives were to criminally prosecute 100 percent of those who sought to enter without inspection. This did interrupt the flow of undocumented workers, forcing employers to utilize the H-2A process. At the same time, DHS issued a rule change that effectively reduced the wages of these H-2A workers, already among the lowest paid in the United States.[34] The wage reductions for authorized workers brought their wages closer to those of unauthorized workers, essentially assimilating these two labor pools. And the pandemic choked off other labor markets, leaving workers with little choice but to toil under even harsher conditions. Thus, even as the border became less permeable for most migrants, the Trump administration ensured both the entry of necessary workers and an even more hospitable environment for exploitation in the agricultural industry, extending the century-long policy of importing colonized labor.

Displacement into Food Processing

Food processing is another industry dominated by foreign workers. One example is the crab-cleaning plants along the North Carolina and Virginia coasts. Initially concentrated in the Chesapeake Bay, blue crab farming and cleaning moved south to the North Carolina coast as waters became polluted and industrialization and gentrification pushed crab farms out of Maryland.[35] The work in these plants involves taking freshly caught and cooked blue crabs and painstakingly separating the meat from the shell. Pickers take up one after another crab and work a knife under and then around the rim of each carapace, lifting off the top and separating viscera and fat from meat with deft swipes of the knife. A number of women from Chiltepec and Soyataco, Tabasco, have been working in these crab-cleaning plants since 1989, when U.S.-based labor recruiters first began training and hiring Mexican women.

The first people recruited to work in these plants in the early twentieth century were African American women.[36] Recruitment was through an informal labor network and benefited from the proximity of the plants to coastal African American neighborhoods.[37] Payment was by the piece, necessitating speed to make a decent wage for a day's work. But speed led to injuries from the knives used to cut the flesh from bone. By the 1980s, the low pay and propensity for injury in these plants led many African American women to find other sources of income. The outflow of workers did not lead to improvements in labor conditions. Rather, much like their agricultural colleagues, the processing industry employers began to seek labor from outside the United States. Beginning in 1988, these plants began to formally recruit women from Mexico under the H-2B visa program.[38]

One of the earliest recruitment firms was Mariscos Bocas, an American firm that contracted with the crab-cleaning companies to find Mexican workers. Mariscos Bocas, known as "Bocas" in Mexico, recruited women primarily from Chiltepec beginning in 1989.[39] The company had a relationship with Chiltepec because one of its agents, known only as "Bobby," was married to a local woman. That first year, about twenty-five women migrated from Chiltepec to Elizabeth City, North Carolina.[40] This number increased each year. One of the women recruited and trained was Serena, a housewife and mother of three who was looking for ways to help pay for her children's education. She made her first trip on an H-2B visa in 1997, by which time there were nearly four hundred women moving from Chiltepec to Elizabeth City for the crab-cleaning season.[41]

The H-2B visa that facilitated the movement of Serena and other workers was split from the original H-2 visa that covered all so-called low wage work. The split occurred in 1986 as part of the Immigration Reform and Control Act. The H-2B's creation coincided with the period during which crab-cleaning and other food service industries were experiencing a loss of domestic workers. Unlike the H-2A, which concentrates on the recruitment of foreign agricultural workers, the H-2B allows employers to recruit workers in a broad range of nonagricultural settings. Also, in contrast to the H-2A, the H-2B has a cap of 66,000 visas per year.[42] Ironically, the total number of people entering on H-2Bs has actually exceeded the total number of H-2A entrants each year, despite the former being capped. Since 1993, the number of H-2Bs issued has risen annually from 9,691 to a peak of 129,000 in

2007.[43] The latter number reflects the George W. Bush administration's efforts to meet American business demand for H-2B workers by exempting returning workers from the 66,000 cap. Thus, since 2003, returning workers like Serena have been sought after as they do not count toward the total number of foreign workers that a company can hire. More recently, the Biden administration has increased the cap to almost double its statutory size, releasing an additional 64,716 H-2B visas for U.S. employers.[44] Thus, the U.S. government has continued to facilitate the transfer of workers into the U.S. economy through formal channels.

Migrating with authorization does not necessarily protect Mexican workers from abusive working conditions. They are systematically underpaid, work in dangerous conditions, and are subjected to sexual and racial harassment. So dismal are the wages and working conditions of H-2B workers that several studies have described the work as "the new American slavery," similar to descriptions of H-2A workers' conditions.[45] This gross underpayment ostensibly should be prohibited by the legal rules surrounding the visa application process. U.S. employers seeking to hire H-2B workers must first obtain a certificate from the DOL indicating that they have attempted to recruit persons already in the United States for the position and that they are offering to pay foreign-born workers wages that will not adversely affect the rate of pay for the position.[46] However, research has shown that the DOL regularly certifies employers at wage rates far lower than the average pay for the position and region.[47] And U.S. employers have continuously lobbied to allow these violations to continue unabated.[48] Between 2004 and 2014, wages in the crab and other fishing industries declined. Adding to the particular issues faced by jaiberas like Serena, the three states that use the largest number of H-2B workers in the crab industry—North Carolina, Virginia, and Maryland—also have among the lowest average wages in the country.[49]

Serena reported making up to $100 a day on a piece rate system that has existed since the early twentieth century. Thus, her average hourly earnings were dependent on her speed and accuracy in cutting the crab flesh from its shell. For Serena, the money was sufficient help support her children to complete their education. However, for many others, the wages are much more severely suppressed.[50] Serena's relative satisfaction with her wages did not extend to the working conditions at the plant in Elizabeth City, which she described as onerous: "We worked from four in the morning to four or five at night all the time we were depulping the crabs. It hurts your hands. The manager treated us very badly. He would insult us a lot. He used racism."

Though Serena did not want to expand on what she meant by "he used racism," she later recounted that the manager would use foul language in reference to Mexicans and women. Such abuses have been widely documented by transnational advocacy groups.[51] In addition to racist comments, women have reported widespread sexual harassment and abuse, as in many other industries.[52] These reported cases of abuse are likely wildly undercounted because women are afraid to speak out for fear of being blacklisted and therefore unable to return for work the following year. Serena did not report the abuses she experienced and witnessed, but others have been blacklisted after complaining about harassment or even violence.[53] Moreover, under the terms of her visa, Serena could not leave her employer in Elizabeth City. She was stuck working long hours and suffering racial and sexual harassment. Thus, the legal rules facilitate maximal extractive opportunities for employers of workers like Serena.

Exploitation Facilitated by Immigration Laws

U.S. immigration law ostensibly prohibits employers from hiring those who are not authorized by the U.S. government.[54] There is no concomitant prohibition against employees working without permission, though a person could become ineligible for certain immigration benefits if they work without authorization. The history of the employer sanction law, along with its current implementation, demonstrates that it is designed as "image craft,"[55] giving the appearance of deterring migration while actually seeking to control migrants and facilitate exploitation.

The U.S. Congress first considered a bill sanctioning employers who hired unauthorized workers in the 1950s. The bill was introduced in response to pressure from the Mexican government rather than any domestic efforts in the United States and was actively opposed by legislators in Texas, Mississippi, and Louisiana.[56] At that time, the United States and Mexico were renegotiating the Bracero Accords. The Mexican government was concerned that unauthorized migration out of Mexico was causing labor shortages for Mexican agribusiness. In order to try and continue the Bracero program, U.S. legislators agreed to try and help Mexican efforts to stem unauthorized migration. Lawmakers from Texas were the most vocal and effective opponents of the bill, understanding that it would have an outsized impact on agribusinesses in that state which were excluded from the Bracero Program and therefore employing tens of thousands of unauthorized Mexican workers.[57] Congressmen from Texas introduced an amendment to the Mexican government's supported bill called the "Texas Proviso." The Texas Proviso turned a law focused on employers into one focused on "harboring" and explicitly exempted employers from its reach. The amendment passed the Senate and the House and was signed into law in March 1952.[58] By taking employment out of the statute's reach, the new law served as carte blanche to employers seeking to hire unauthorized workers and "could not have been better suited to growers' needs."[59]

Lawmakers from large agribusiness states continued to successfully facilitate employer access to unauthorized workers over the next thirty years. In the 1960s and 1970s, these efforts were led by Senator James Eastland of Mississippi. A former cotton grower with strong segregationist roots and ties to agribusiness interests, Eastland chaired the Senate Judiciary Committee and its Subcommittee on

Immigration and Naturalization from 1965 to 1975. During that decade-long tenure, Eastland held exactly zero hearings of the immigration subcommittee, effectively blocking a vote on any sanctions bills in the Senate.[60] Eastland's departure from the Senate gave space for congressional hearings on the issue, but opposition to sanctioning employers continued to be strong.[61] Organizations representing agribusiness like the Farm Labor Alliance (FLA) formed specifically to oppose employer sanctions.[62] FLA members like Matthew Durando of California testified that employer sanctions would be harmful to their bottom lines as "probably in excess of 50 percent of [our] labor currently are illegal aliens."[63]

Eventually, employer sanctions did become part of the IRCA. However, over the course of the negotiations on the law, the FLA and its allies in Congress managed to water down employer sanctions and create a supplementary worker program to facilitate labor for southwestern growers. Criminal penalties were stripped from the sanctions structure, and employers were only required to voluntarily verify their employees' eligibility to work. In addition, a special guest worker program introduced by FLA allies Representatives Leon Panetta (D-CA) and Sid Morrison (D-WA) was passed giving the growers' lobby almost all of what it asked for.[64]

Given the ambivalence in Congress over employer sanctions, it is no surprise that there has been very little in the way of enforcement of these penalties in the years since its passage. Only one of the more than forty migrants interviewed reported having an employer ask for the required paperwork when they arrived to the jobsites, and none were required to leave due to lack of paperwork.[65] Instead, most migrants were hired easily. For example, Luna found work quickly after her harrowing journey in 2004. "We knew where to go even before we left the pueblo," Luna reported, referring to the migrant networks that stretched from the Mixteca through Sinaloa in northern Mexico and north along the Pacific coast to the Canadian border. "We used to work picking strawberries, cucumber, blueberries. This was in Seattle, Washington. Then we picked tulips for two to three hours a day to make some extra money." When asked about any encounters with immigration enforcement agents, Luna explained that they were a shadow rather than actual presence, "We were always looking out for the *migra*, but I never saw them."

The specter of immigration enforcement agents contributed to the harsh working conditions and low pay in the United States. "Life is very difficult there," Luna said. "We lived in a room with fifteen other people. It was so crowded. We had to stand in line to cook." Even when she found other work, she continued to encounter issues:

> I found work in a nursery that paid better. At first the boss was nice, but then we got another boss who was just looking for reasons to fire people. After I got fired from that job, I got another one, this time packing potatoes. But the supervisor, she would be looking closely to see if we even faltered a little.

Luna said that Ricardo and she withstood the uncertainty and low wages for six years, first to pay off their debt and then to save a little to start their own business. "Once we had enough to build the house and buy some goats, we came back."

Luna and Ricardo knew from the stories of other people who had successfully migrated to the United States from their region that they would find work. One of these people was Elfego, who had first migrated in 1985 and had spent the next thirty years moving back and forth from his home in San Martín Duraznos, Oaxaca, to various places along the west coast of the United States. Elfego's first trip took him to a ranch in Oceanside, California, where he picked tomatoes and strawberries, two crops most commonly worked by Mexican migrants. The work was "very tiring and badly paid," according to Elfego. But as this was his first trip to offset the lack of work in his home community, Elfego stayed on the ranch for three years. In subsequent trips, he was able to find work as a gardener, which he found "less backbreaking, but still not as well paid as I'd hoped." He asked this employer to sponsor him for a work visa, but the employer refused. Nonetheless, Elfego returned to this employer twice more, rationalizing that it was better than picking fruit in California. But then, in the early 2000s, Elfego learned of work in Washington State in carpentry. The hours and working conditions seemed better than the gardening job. Elfego made the longer journey to the Northwest and easily found work to sustain him and his family for the next several years. Throughout this time working in three different states and three different industries, Elfego never encountered interior immigration officials, but their presence weighed on him, as it did Luna. "One is always thinking that the *migra* can catch you," he explained. "But I had to keep going, to just keep working and counting the days before I could go home."

Even those who did not have extensive networks already in the United States were able to find work by journeying to locations where they knew others from their home villages had landed. Elias left his home in Soyataco, Tabasco, in 1999 without knowing anyone who was working in the United States. However, he knew that women from Soyataco and Chiltepec were being recruited to work in coastal towns in North Carolina and figured that he would find others from Tabasco in that area. His first journey brought him to Morehead City, about 150 miles south of where Serena and her coworkers were cleaning crabs. He was referred to work in a factory farm his first week in the small town. After working there for about three years, he moved on to cut lumber and then worked in a family-owned store. Elias recounted that he was "treated well" by the store owner, his last employer in the United States. This was in contrast to working on the farm and cutting lumber, which Elias described as "work meant for animals." He reported being able to move to a different employer easily. "I was never asked for papers," he said. Like Elfego and the other migrants interviewed, Elias was never approached by immigration officials during his nearly ten years in North Carolina.

The combined experiences of workers like Luna, Elias, and Elfego are reflected in the low number of employers facing sanctions. By 1990, only 8 percent of INS's enforcement efforts were dedicated to workplace raids.[66] Moreover, the number of fines issued against employers who hired unauthorized workers actually declined between 1991 to 2001, from a peak of a thousand employers fined in 1991 to a low of zero employers penalized in 2001.[67] This is the same period that saw a huge increase in unauthorized migration from Mexico, including first trips for many migrants like Elias.[68] And the share of unauthorized workers in agriculture exploded during this period, rising from 14 percent in 1989–91 to 55 percent in 1999–2001.[69] Thus, by the time migrants like Elias and Luna came to work in U.S. fields, almost all of their coworkers were unauthorized. The declining enforcement against employers at precisely the time when unauthorized migration was increasing demonstrates the law's continued facilitation of labor displacement despite its stated goal to the contrary. As one INS official said in 1999, "We don't want to have a negative impact on the production capabilities of these companies."[70]

In a sense, the migrants profiled in this book were lucky to never experience deportation as more than a shadow threat, operating as a backdrop to their working lives. For thousands of other migrant workers, deportation was a more material reality. From 2006 to 2008, the Bush administration carried out massive raids targeting migrant workers for deportation and criminal prosecution.[71] As a result, thousands were deported and hundreds were subject to criminal penalties for identity theft and other offenses. But employers continued to escape sanctions for employing these workers.[72] The administration of Barack Obama signaled a potential shift in policy in April 2009, instructing ICE agents to "prioritize the prosecution of the actual employers who knowingly hire unauthorized workers because such employers are not sufficiently punished or deterred by the arrest of their illegal workforce."[73] However, as in past eras, the practice was the opposite of prosecuting actual employers. Only a few hundred employers were fined through 2014, representing only 0.2 percent of employers nationwide.[74] Meanwhile, the Obama administration engaged in massive deportation of workers and other immigrants.

Even the Trump administration continued to facilitate the presence of desired migrant workers while ramping up raids and deportations. On the one hand, the Trump administration greatly expanded the scope of interior enforcement, making all unauthorized immigrants living in the United States priorities for removal.[75] Trump's director of ICE, Thomas Homan, stated in 2018 that his agency would quintuple workplace enforcement actions, but this time the U.S government was more explicit that it would be targeting workers and not their employers.[76] Moreover, Trump publicly reassured employers that they would continue to have access to migrant labor and continued his predecessors' pattern of largely ignoring widespread employer violations of the law. As the narratives in this chapter demonstrate, the lack of enforcement of this set of laws helped facilitate the displacement of unauthorized workers like Luna, Elias, and Elfego into industries where their vulnerable status was preferred for the ease with which these workers could be exploited. Combined with long-standing policies displacing Mexican migrants into particular kinds of work, the underenforcement of workplace sanctions facilitates extraction of migrants as labor.

IMMIGRATION ENFORCEMENT AS EXTRACTION: FROM EXPLICIT TO IMPLICIT PERMISSIVENESS

Extracting wealth from migrants extends beyond employers who extract from labor to public agencies and private companies who accumulate wealth from various forms of official immigration enforcement practices and extralegal endeavors that seek to profit from manufactured illegality. The remainder of this chapter focuses on extraction from Mexican migrants through three policies and practices: border enforcement, including the criminalization of unlawful entry; the resulting boom in coyotaje; and interior enforcement, including detention and deportation. Parallel to racialized efforts to facilitate the entry and ongoing presence of Mexican labor were efforts that raced Mexican (and other) migrants as threats to U.S. economic, personal, and national security to justify building massive public budgets and private contracts that accumulate wealth for public and private actors. This section traces the development of the latter form of racial capitalist accumulation and the resultant rise in the coyotaje industry.

Extraction Embedded in Border Control Policies and Criminalization of Unlawful Entry

In 1909, almost a century before Luna's journey across the Californias, there was no Border Patrol and no Department of Homeland Security. At this time, managing entry into the United States was explicitly tied to the demand for exploitable labor. As summarized by Frank Berkshire, a supervising inspector with the then Bureau of Immigration (BOI) under the DOL:

> We can exclude practically all of the Mexican aliens of the laboring class who apply for admission at this port as persons likely to become a public charge, for the reason that they are without funds, relatives or friends in the United States, and have no fixed destination; at the same time, we know that any able-bodied man who may be admitted can immediately secure transportation to a point where employment will be furnished him.[77]

Berkshire's sentiments were reflected in border control policies for nearly eighty years. The creation of the Border Patrol in 1924 provides one illuminating example. Separate from the BOI, which oversaw the lawful entry of foreign nationals at ports of entry, the Border Patrol was charged with apprehending those seeking to circumvent U.S. immigration laws by entering between ports of entry. According to government sources, the Border Patrol was created "to control illegal entry *from Mexico*."[78] The language here is important as it indicates the intent to target not Mexican migrants but Asian and European migrants who were taking advantage of the porous Mexico-U.S. border to circumvent U.S. immigration restrictions.[79] The new Border Patrol grew extremely slowly in its first decade. By 1925, the agency had hired 472 agents and two years later, 781.[80] These efforts did little to change the patterns of "border permeability" for Mexican migrants. As the historian Kelly Lytle Hernández documents, inspectors at the Mexico-U.S. border saw their role much like Inspector Berkshire did two decades before: not to "molest" Mexican migrants "except in the most extreme cases" because the laws "apply [chiefly] to European aliens."[81] Thus, the function of the Border Patrol was to manage entry into the United States, which largely meant facilitating the transfer of Mexican workers into industries that preferred their labor.

Parallel to the development and implementation of permissive border enforcement designed to extract from migrants as labor was the development of a carceral regime that extracted from migrants as arrestees and detainees. One of the key modes of carceral-based extraction was the criminalization of entry into the United States without authorization. The addition of these criminal penalties, beginning in 1929, was specifically designed to cast Mexican migrants as "illegal," despite their recruitment to the United States in the period immediately before the law's passage. Proposed by South Carolina's avowed segregationist senator, Coleman Livingston Blease, the law made surreptitious entry a federal misdemeanor and surreptitious reentry after a previous deportation a federal felony. Enforcement of the new crimes was directed specifically at Mexicans, and in the ensuing ten years, as many as 99 percent of those charged and convicted were Mexican migrants.[82] As Hernández has argued, this shift "had a massive social impact, rescripting the story of race in American by binding *Mexicanos* to the caste of illegals."[83] Equating Mexican migrants with a "caste of illegals" at the same time that they were cast as perfect workers served to both furnish employers with their desired labor and provide a mechanism for controlling that workforce.

The border's dual role as a door through which to usher in migrant workers and a site of criminal punishment has continued both rhetorically and materially to the present day. As narratives from migrants who entered without authorization demonstrate, border agents continue to facilitate the entry of a subset of Mexican migrants in the same way that Berkshire and his colleagues did in the 1910s. None of the migrants interviewed faced criminal penalties for entering without authorization. However, other sources have documented the continued targeting of Mexican migrants for criminal prosecution.[84]

For migrants like Elfego, the threat of border apprehension barely registered in the mid-1980s. As Elfego explained:

> Back then, it was easier. I did not have any money so I just crossed on my own. I left from Tijuana and started walking north. I was arrested once by immigration and returned, but I remembered the way and the second time I was able to make it across in about five or six days.

Elfego got information on how to "walk north" from cousins in Tijuana who had made the trip in prior years. Like Elfego, Don Manto also left the Mixteca Baja for work in the United States in 1985. "It only took an hour to cross the border," he said. In 1986, he moved his journey to the San Ysidro area of Baja California and California, slightly east of his first crossing. "It was easy," he said of the San Ysidro crossing, which he made to avoid a new U.S. Border Patrol checkpoint erected exactly where he had made his first journey.[85]

Some migrants were able to continue using the route directly from the city of Tijuana on the Mexican side to San Diego on the U.S. side. For example, Don Santos described his first migrant trip in 1987: "A friend of mine invited me, and I crossed the border with him. We did not use a coyote. My friend knew the way. We arrived in Tijuana. From there it took us a few hours to walk. We were both there for six months." Like Elfego and Don Manto, Don Santos migrated back and forth across the Mexico-U.S. border. His second journey was in 1988. "The second time," he said, "I crossed alone. I learned the route, and it took me one day walking, nothing more."

These first journeys of Elfego, Don Manto, and Don Santos occurred in the years following the first ever quotas on Mexican immigrants and a resulting surge in unauthorized entries. In 1965, the year the quotas were first enacted, experts estimate that about 87,000 entries from Mexico were unauthorized.[86] After quotas for lawful migration were reduced to only 20,000 per year, these same experts calculated that over one million Mexican migrants entered without authorization.[87] This surge continued after the neoliberal economic changes gutted the Mexican economy in the early 1980s. Elfego, Don Manto, and Don Santos were among the nearly three million Mexican migrants entering the United States without authorization each year from 1985 to 1989.[88] Like all three migrants from the Mixteca, about 86 percent of these millions of unauthorized migrants returned to their home communities within a year of arrival in the United States.[89] This circular pattern of migration was largely facilitated by a continued lack of any real border enforcement.

The porous border was about to become a more hardened line largely through the recasting of Mexican migrants as invaders who were causing unemployment. The language of "crisis" used by high-level immigration officials and President Gerald Ford worked to open up a new avenue of capital accumulation through border enforcement spending.[90] The rhetorical claim that unauthorized workers were responsible for unemployment was the rationale for the increases in Border Patrol funding provided by IRCA in 1986. Subsequent to IRCA's passage, depictions of Mexican migrants evolved again to associate them with drug trafficking, opening even more avenues for enforcement industry profit. This resulted in Operations Hold the Line, Gatekeeper, and Safeguard in the early 1990s and the passage of the Illegal Immigration Reform and Immigrant Responsibility Act (IIRIRA) in 1996, which targeted so-called criminal aliens. Migrants were again recast as national security threats after the September 11, 2001, attacks, resulting in even more resources and a reorganization of the agencies charged with immigration enforcement. The Immigration and Naturalization Service (INS) within the Department of Justice became the new Department of Homeland Security, which absorbed much of the former INS's role and split that agency's enforcement functions into two agencies: Customs and Border Protection (CBP) and Immigration Customs and Enforcement (ICE).

The evolution of migrant racialization resulted in an escalation of both public border enforcement expenditures and private profits from the industries of migration control. Public budgets for border enforcement ballooned from $665 million in 1986 to $17.7 billion in 2021.[91] Those budget increases include contracts with private companies like Boeing, Elbit, Lockheed Martin, and Raytheon, which totaled more than $3 billion by 2018.[92] These same companies help fund U.S. congressional campaigns for both parties.[93] As figures 9 and 10 illustrate, the resulting cycle has facilitated massive capital accumulation by both public and private actors undergirded by racialized depictions of migrants as a threat of one kind or another.

The journeys of a number of migrants demonstrate that despite the ever-increasing resources poured into the border enforcement measures, including criminal prosecution, many people continue to successfully enter without authorization. For example, Elias' trip in 1999 involved getting to a point in the southern Sonoran Desert by vehicle and walking across to Arizona. By this time, Operation Safeguard had expanded to all of Arizona, with Border Patrol agents stationed at regular intervals along the section of the border that Elias crossed.[94] However, Elias described the walk as "easy." He indicated that his group "made it across on the first try" without encountering any agents. Also, in 1999, Rodolfo made his first trip to the United States from Tetlanohcan, Tlaxcala, crossing from Tijuana by foot. In describing the journey, Rodolfo said, "It was extremely difficult. It took us twenty days to a month to cross." But even Rodolfo's group did not come across border agents, despite the beginnings of a border wall in Tijuana or the fortified presence of border agents under Operation Gatekeeper.

In addition to migrants who made their first trips, migrants like Elfego and Don Santos continued to make virtually "unmolested" subsequent trips to the

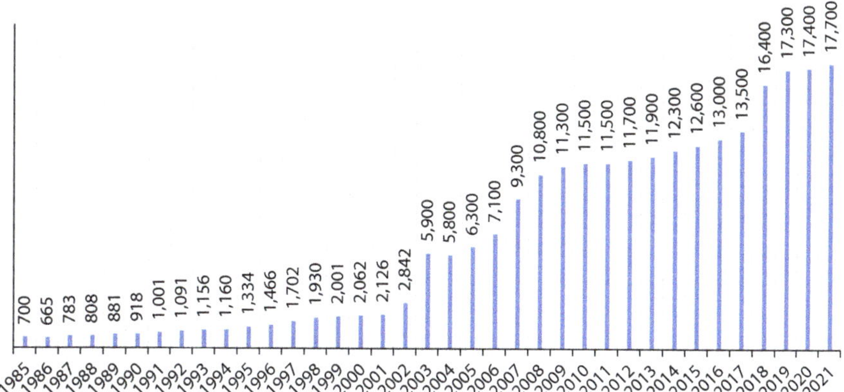

FIGURE 9. U.S. Border Enforcement Public Spending, 1985–2021.

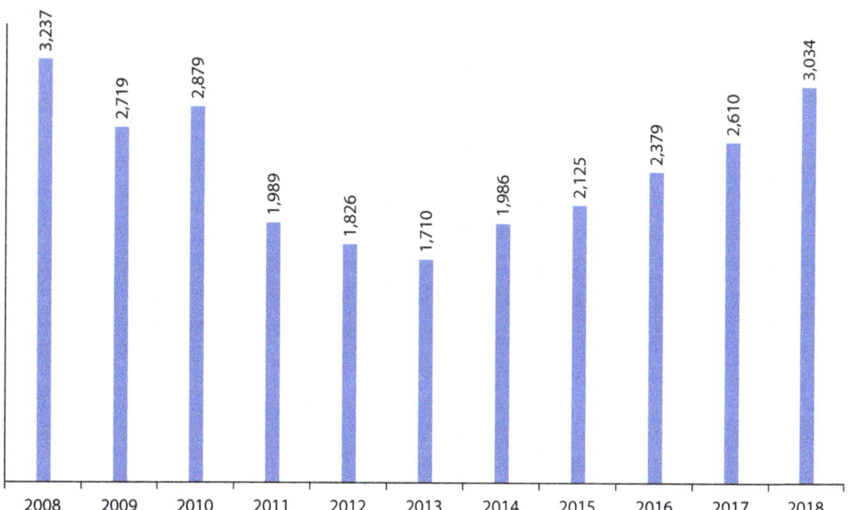

FIGURE 10. U.S. Border Enforcement Private Contracts, 2008–2018.

United States via Tijuana during the 1990s and 2000s. Don Santos did feel the policy shifts that brought about Operation Gatekeeper. "It was in 1994 when it started to get more difficult," he explained. That year, Don Santos convinced his employer to sponsor him for an H-2A visa. However, in 1995, Don Santos returned to the United States without authorization, this time paying coyotes to help him navigate the new border enforcement measures. His journey in 1995 was more difficult than his trips in the 1980s. He was arrested once and sent back across the border but was able to successfully enter the United States on his second try. Similarly, Elfego was arrested several times in his subsequent journeys to the United States. While he could not remember the exact years, Elfego made three trips to the United States between 1995 and 2009 and was able to successfully enter each time.

Elfego's experience reflects the continued permeability of the border even in the post-9/11 era. As Luna described, she and her husband, Ricardo, were able to eventually enter the United States in 2004 despite being arrested three times. As Luna explained, "The first two times we tried to cross, immigration arrested a lot of people. We had to run many times. We were turned back three times and only made it across on the fourth." A similar pattern emerged in Francisco Javier's retelling of his journey from San Pedro Cholula, Puebla, to Philadelphia in 2001. "We were arrested four to five times," Francisco Javier recalled. "And each time, we were returned immediately to the other side of the border. We finally crossed the fifth or sixth time."

Things had changed somewhat by November 2006, when Francisco Javier made his second journey. This time, according to Francisco Javier, "the *migra* took our fingerprints and told us that we would be punished if we tried again." The "punishment" in this case would be criminal prosecution for unlawful entry. In 2005, one year before Francisco Javier crossed, the U.S. government had launched Operation Streamline, requiring officials to prosecute 100 percent of people seeking to enter the United States for the crime of unlawful entry or reentry. The directive was limited to sectors in Texas, and Francisco Javier had crossed in Arizona. However, Operation Streamline was expanded to include Arizona and New Mexico by 2008. Thus, when Francisco Javier crossed via Arizona for a third time, in 2009, his prior arrest should have subjected him to prosecution for unlawful reentry. However, according to Francisco Javier, "I had the same experience as before. We were arrested, immigration took photos and took our fingerprints. I already had a record from when I tried to enter before, but they did not punish me." The Border Patrol officers who arrested Francisco Javier, much like their forebears in the early to mid-1900s, chose to allow Francisco Javier to try migrating again. And, like so many of his compatriots, he succeeded.

Despite evading incarceration himself, Francisco Javier's experiences at the southern border took place during a time of exponential growth in both the rhetorical criminalization of migrants and the actual imposition of criminal penalties. As a result of Operation Streamline, total convictions for unlawful entry across those sectors of the border went from 15,000 in 2004 to over 50,000 in 2008.[95] Prosecutions for unlawful entry continued to grow under the Obama administration, reaching a pre-Trump administration peak of over 65,000 in 2013.[96] Under President Trump, Operation Streamline was expanded to 100 percent of border sectors by April 2018.[97] As a result, prosecutions for unlawful entry and reentry would reach their modern zenith, with over 106,000 people prosecuted in 2019.[98] And despite the fact that unauthorized migration from Mexico was declining during this period, about 55 percent of prosecutions for unlawful entry and 75 percent of prosecutions for unlawful reentry were of Mexican nationals.[99] The cost of these new incarcerations generated nearly $1 billion in additional funding for U.S. prisons, including private prisons contracting with the U.S. government.[100] Thus, even as the United States continued to facilitate the entry of some Mexican migrants, it added a new source of capitalist accumulation through the expansion of the prison and related industries.[101]

Extraction through Coyotaje

The various permutations of extraction at the border resulted in a parallel development of extraction from migrants in the form of fees paid to coyotes to help circumvent ever evolving border enforcement mechanisms. The 1990s saw the U.S. government using new strategies that involved a much higher number of Border Patrol agents standing at short distances along common crossings like El Paso, Texas. These innovations had military-style names like Operation Hold the Line and Operation Gatekeeper. Studies on the effects of these operations showed that while the new lines of agents forced migrants to change their strategies for entering the United States, they did not deter most of them from making the journey.[102] This was certainly true for Elfego and Don Santos, both of whom had migrated several times before the Clinton-era operations and continued to migrate to the United States without authorization until the 2000s. It was also true for Elias, Rodolfo, Efraím, and Luna, all of whom made their first journeys in the years after Operation Hold the Line and Operation Gatekeeper. Although these migrants were not deterred, they had to make two key adjustments to avoid apprehension. First, they began to take more dangerous routes through remote and hostile terrain. Second, the dangers of the more hostile territory and the risk of getting lost led these migrants to pay coyotes to help them navigate these new routes.

For women, the new journeys came with a grave additional risk—that of sexual violence.[103] Researchers have calculated that up to 90 percent of women crossing the Mexico-U.S. border in the mid-2000s experienced some form of sexual assault.[104] Only one of the women interviewed spoke explicitly of witnessing gendered violence on her journey. The remainder of the women interviewed did not refer to sexual violence explicitly, but it was clearly in the background of a number of women's decisions on whether to make an unauthorized journey. Luna's first trip across the border included the harrowing chase that she described in 2004. She was clear that she went with other people "to feel protected." When we spoke in 2013, Luna had been back in Santa María Natividad for five years and was almost ten years removed from her arduous journey north. When asked if she would consider returning, she said that she did think about it, "but then, I remember the journey." "Remembering the journey" was as close as Luna came to recounting her possible experience of or witness to sexual violence. Others expressed fear at making even one journey. Efraím's wife, Irena, said, "Migration is not for women. Some do it, but, no, it's too dangerous." The fact that some women were deterred by the dangers of the new, longer journeys north demonstrates that the new border enforcement innovations "play[ed] out in gendered actions and interactions,"[105] increasing the risk of violence on journeys north.

Moreover, these innovations and the resultant risks deterred women who were perhaps among those less desirable as workers while continuing to facilitate the entry of needed labor.

For both men and women who did make the trip, coyotes were essential. Coyotes operate in a complex "bastard industry" of clandestine operations at the border.[106] Some coyotes are connected to criminal organizations like drug cartels or *bajadores* (thieves or bandits who rob migrants in the Sonoran Desert region).[107] Others are connected to their home communities or employers in the United States.[108] A few actually work alongside CBP agents, who are paid to allow migrants to pass through CBP checkpoints or walk unbothered through the remote areas between checkpoint stations.[109] But, whatever the mechanism by which coyotes operate, they wrest enormous amounts of money from migrants and their families.

The price that migrants paid for an unauthorized journey varied depending on what kind of coyote they hired and the methods the coyote used (figure 11). For example, Elias paid US$1,800 in 1999 to travel from Soyataco, Tabasco, to a point in the southern Sonoran Desert by vehicle and then walk through the desert to cross. He described the journey nonchalantly. "Although we had to walk a lot," Elias said, "it was easy. We made it across on the first try." Just a few months before, Don Rodolfo made his first trip to the United States from Tetlanohcan, Tlaxcala, with "friends" who were going. In sharp contrast to Elias, Don Rodolfo paid only US$300 to travel from Tetlanohcan to Tijuana by vehicle and cross into the United States on foot. The journeys that Don Rodolfo and Elias made within Mexico were roughly similar. Tetlanohcan is a little less than 1,800 miles from Tijuana, and Soyataco is a little more than 1,800 miles from the Sonora Desert. It is likely that the reason Don Rodolfo paid so little was that he was paying a more informal coyote who only worked with migrants he knew. Don Rodolfo and his friends quickly saw the drawback of using someone who did not have a vast network of connections. In describing the journey, Don Rodolfo said, "It was extremely difficult. It took us twenty days to a month to cross. We did not have any idea where we were going, but we ended up walking to Phoenix." People who wanted to find ways to avoid the desert and surreptitiously cross at checkpoints paid the highest fees. Among those surveyed, the highest amount paid was US$3,500 to hide in a car traveling through an official checkpoint.[110]

The amounts that migrants paid coyotes to try to ensure safe passage were exorbitant given that many of them earned less than US$400 per month. In order to pay these fees, migrants relied on loans from family members already in the United States, family members in Mexico, or informal moneylenders who sometimes charged double digit interest. At times, the cost of the journey was more than the price of the economic gap the migrant was seeking to fill. For example, Elias took out loans from a local *prestamista* (loan shark) totaling US$6,800 for his

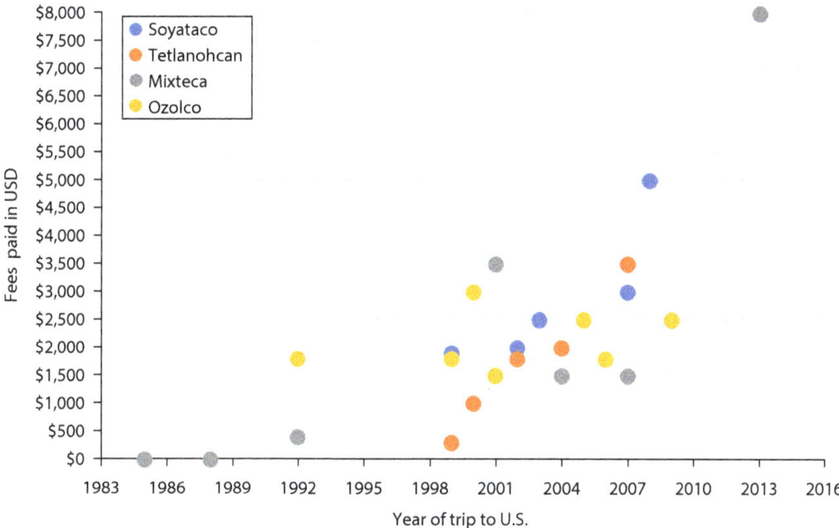

FIGURE 11. Fees Paid to Coyotes.

three trips to the United States. He made these trips primarily to pay school fees and the cost of transporting his children to school, items that would have cost him about US$4,200 over the course of his children's educational careers. However, the only other method for paying school fees was to seek a loan for that expense directly. Personal loans are not available in Mexico, so Elias would have had to borrow money from the same prestamista he used to pay for his trips to the United States. Interest rates on these loans are high, 20 percent in some cases. Thus, one needs almost twice the original loan amount to repay the lender. In the absence of sufficient earning potential in Mexico, Elias had no way to pay the $4,200 he needed for his children's education. The only way to make the finances work was to earn in U.S. dollars.

As expenditures on border enforcement strategies rose in the 2000s, so too did the cost to migrants of their journeys north. For example, Elias paid US$2,500 for his second trip in 2003, an almost 50 percent increase over what he paid in 1999. As in his previous journey, Elias managed to cross the border without being detected by U.S. border agents. In contrast, Luna and Ricardo paid significantly less in the same period. Their journey cost them US$1,500 each. However, their journey was also marked by more interaction with U.S. authorities. Eventually, the couple was able to cross but not with the same ease that Elias crossed with his more expensive guide.

Still others remained in the United States for longer periods to pay off their debts to the coyotes and to avoid having to pay a second time. Indeed, in Tetlanohcan, all but one migrant interviewed were still in the United States, sometimes several decades after leaving. For example, Efraím made his most recent trip to the United States in 2007 and has remained there since. Efraím had paid US\$3,500 in 2007 to cross, and it took him three years to pay off the debt. Similarly, on his last trip in 2009, Francisco Javier paid US\$2,500. This was a 28 percent increase from the price he paid to cross the border just three years earlier. And prices rose rapidly after Francisco Javier returned.

By 2013, fees had risen so high as to create a barrier to crossing into the United States. That year, Efraím said that the main reason he could not return to Tetlanohcan to visit his family was "the cost, the expense. It is like \$80,000 [MXN] (the equivalent of US\$8,000) to cross now. I don't have that, and I cannot ask for that much." Luna and Ricardo quoted the same sum if they were to try to get to the United States in 2013. "The line is very difficult now," Ricardo explained. Though he himself was not interested in crossing again regardless of the cost, Ricardo thought that many of his neighbors in the Mixteca would have trouble repaying the loans they would need to take out to pay the high fees. Figure 11 shows how these costs changed over time based on community of origin.

The amounts that migrants paid rose at the same time that U.S. enforcement methods picked up. However, they also reflect the changing nature of coyotaje. In some parts of the border region, coyotes became increasingly involved with international criminal organizations that dealt not only in the smuggling of people, but also drugs (to the United States) and weapons (into Mexico).[111] These efforts raised the cost of unauthorized migration exponentially.[112] Thus, extraction from migration benefited organized crime as much as it did U.S. employers and U.S. business and government interests involved in border enforcement.

Extraction Embedded in Interior Enforcement

Once in the United States, Mexican migrants found they were haunted by the specter of detention and deportation. These interior enforcement mechanisms, like border enforcement, were designed to facilitate access to and control migrant workers. Just as the dual system of permitting entry while simultaneously criminalizing it developed at the border, massive raids in the 1930s saw the repatriation of 500,000 Mexican workers who had entered to work on farms, to build railroads and to mine copper.[113] The repatriation efforts were couched as necessary to expel "illegal invaders."[114] These "invaders were described as having "nothing higher than animal function" and acting, ironically, "to the ultimate ruin of American agriculture . . . and to the detriment of . . . political and racial characteristics of the native American people of these regions."[115] In the 1950s, former army commander turned INS commissioner, Joseph Swing, repeated the "invasion" metaphor to justify a multiyear, derisively named Operation Wetback that would expel six million Mexican migrants.[116]

These operations correlated with economic downturns in the United States, including the Great Depression of the 1930s and recessions of the 1950s and 1960s.[117] Like the justifications for border protection, they characterized Mexican migrants as stealing work. However, the stated justifications masked justifications to hold on to the Mexican workforce, particularly in agriculture. Even as Commissioner Swing was carrying out the largest mass raid in history, he was guaranteeing employers that he would find replacements of any unauthorized workers who were removed with authorized ones.[118] These guarantees were acted on, as most of the six million migrants expelled from the interior were "dried out" at the border and returned as braceros.[119] Thus the massive raids, justified through racialized characterizations of Mexican workers as stealing jobs, operated less to expel Mexican migrants than to exert dominance over this workforce, particularly during times of economic downturns.

Both the racialization of Mexican migrants and the mechanisms of interior enforcement evolved over the next decades but continued to garner more resources for immigration control. In the 1980s, associations of Mexican and other migrants with crime brought new interior enforcement resources to the public and private sectors, matching similar spending increases and its justifications at the border. Interior enforcement began to include detention, a tactic that mirrored the rise of mass incarceration in the criminal legal system a decade earlier.[120] In the post-9/11 era, migrants became associated with threats to national security, and interior enforcement was expanded through the reorganization of the former INS into the Department of Homeland Security and the creation of ICE as an agency solely dedicated to interior immigration enforcement. These evolving associations of Mexican and other migrants with crime and national security concerns alongside ongoing association with the loss of U.S. jobs have coincided with massive increases in resources for interior enforcement. As shown in figure 12, successive legislation from 1985 to 2021 has increased interior enforcement spending on arrest, detention, and deportation by 2,700 percent, from $300 million to $8.3 billion. The largest single-year increases came in 1997, 2003, 2009, and 2018. As was the case with the large-scale removal operations in the 1930s and 1950s, these larger jumps in funding coincide with economic recessions in the United States, evincing the need to manage the supply of workers and to maintain their subordination. Like border enforcement measures, interior immigration enforcement does not just fatten public coffers. It also funnels funds to private contractors, like CoreCIVIC, Inc., and GEO Group, Inc., that garner over $1 billion in profits from operating private immigration prisons (figure 13).[121]

Luna and other migrants profiled here escaped direct experience with interior enforcement, but the specter of detention or deportation loomed large in their consciousness. As Luna indicated, "We were always looking out for the *migra*." This "looking out" prevented Luna and many others from complaining about substandard working conditions, low pay, and even employers' abuse. One of those other migrants was Elfego, who labored in strenuous and exhausting conditions without complaint because, he said, "one is always thinking that the *migra* can catch you." Even those who migrated with authorization felt the weight of possible deportation. Serena, who migrated with a visa, did not report the racist insults and

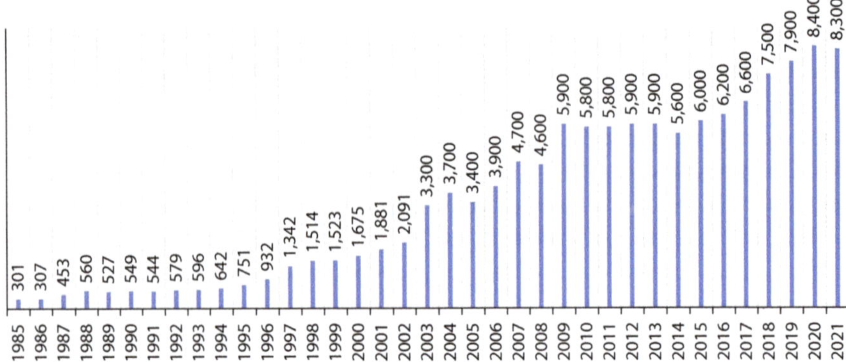

FIGURE 12. U.S. Interior Enforcement Spending, 1985–2021.

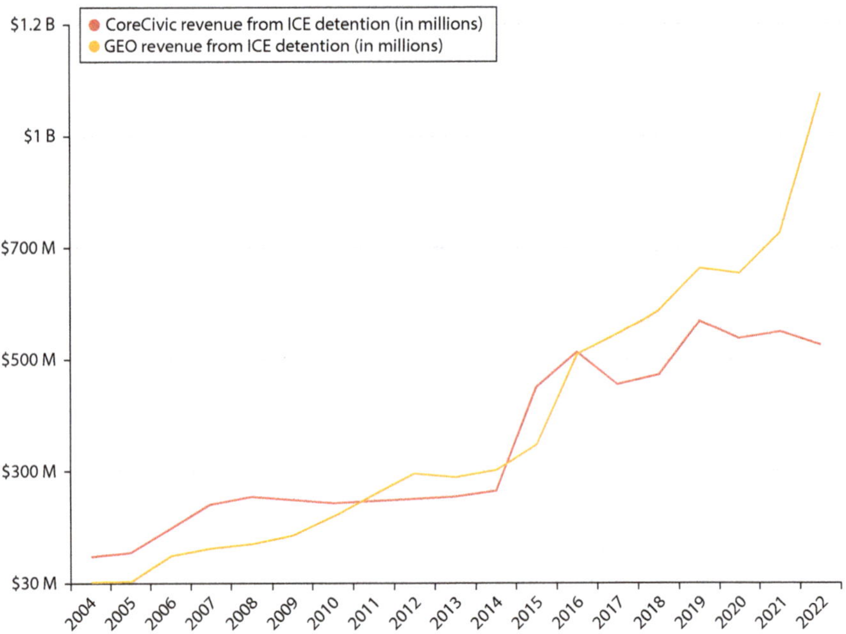

FIGURE 13. U.S. Interior Enforcement Private Contracts. Credit: ACLU. Reprinted with permission from American Civil Liberties Union.

grueling working conditions she experienced in part to avoid being blacklisted but also to avoid being fired and therefore subject to deportation. Thus, the massive spending and profits from interior detention and deportation operated to maintain the segregation of migrant workers in industries that preferred their labor—unauthorized or not—and exacerbate the harsh conditions migrants worked in while in the United States.

JOURNEY HOME

The other side of migrants' journeys to the United States were their journeys home. The vast majority of migrants interviewed had either already returned to Mexico or were contemplating return. Unlike many of their compatriots, the southward journeys of these migrants were voluntary, reflecting a broader pattern of largely voluntary return migration to Mexico in the late 2000s. Migrants regularly reported "voluntarily returning" to Mexico because their ability to perform the work available to them was exhausted. Elfego, for example, though he was only forty, said, "I returned because of my age and the work there [in the United States] was too difficult." Still other migrants returned because they became ill or injured at work and could not obtain health care. Don Santos returned for good in 2008 because he broke his back laying electrical wire in Tennessee and could not obtain necessary treatment there. Doña Mathilde, one of Elfego's and Don Santos's neighbors, had to return after only one year in the United States because she learned she had a heart condition.

Returned migrants were then confronted by the limits their contributions could make to the overall economic health of their home communities. Elfego had to return to preserve his physical health despite not being able to complete payments for his son's high school degree. This led his son to migrate. Don Santos noted the irony of being injured laying electric lines in the United States when his own pueblo lacked electricity and a proper school building as late as 2013. Even those who returned after completing their goals for their families saw the limits of their contributions. Elias returned after completing the payment of his children's school fees in 2008. "I always knew I would come back, and when the time came, I did," he declared. But many others from his town continued to migrate to pay those same school fees. Luna and Ricardo also returned to Mexico in 2008 after saving enough to start their own business. But their business could not lift up their entire community. These migrants' journeys north had enriched U.S. employers, government contractors, and coyotes much more than they enriched their home communities. This was not for lack of trying on the part of migrants. But the systems that migrants were operating in sought to entrench the gaps left by neoliberal disinvestment and the subsequent need for successive groups of people to move— the next phase of migration as extraction.

Entrenchment

The family also migrates and is completely transformed.
—MANUELA

Twenty-nine-year-old Manuela is the director of the Centro de Atención de Famil-ias Migrantes e Indigenas (CAFAMI; Indigenous Migrant Family Care Center) in San Francisco de Tetlanohcan, Tlaxcala.[1] Manuela was born and raised in Tetla-nohcan. Her father migrated to the United States without authorization when she was fourteen years old.[2] As the oldest of six children, she saw firsthand how migra-tion affected her family. "It was really hard emotionally for my mother. She had to play two roles, the role of mother and father. And it was also hard for my siblings. They needed both parents, you see," she explained. Manuela went on to say that her younger siblings were able to finish high school because of remittances that her father sent from his work in the United States. When asked what it was like for her, she said, "Well, for me, I suppose it was different. I was older when he [my father] left. And I was able to go to university. But yes, it was also hard." "Also hard" was about as much as Manuela was willing to say about the impact of her father's migration on her. She was much more comfortable describing how hard migration was for her siblings and for other people in her community: "When I was young, I saw people just destroyed emotionally. It was really hard to see. And it continues, you know? Migration is not just about the migrant . . . the family also migrates and is completely transformed."

Manuela's current thinking about migration as transformative for families resulted from her participation in activities that would lead to the formation of CAFAMI. In 2001, a group of anthropology students from the Instituto de Inves-tigaciones (Research Institute) in the neighboring state of Puebla conducted a one-year project in Tetlanohcan. The project sought to build relationships with youth through activities like photography and video. Manuela explained why she joined: "I liked what they were saying, that they wanted to help us build capacity and communicate how we were seeing things in our community." Soon it became clear that the main issue facing most of the youth was that one or both parents had migrated. Manuela and her fellow students chose to use their new videography skills to document life in Tetlanohcan for their parents in the United States. They interviewed their grandparents and others who were helping care for them. "We wanted to show them what life was like at home," Manuela said, "to help them connect to us but also for us to feel connected to them." Through this project, Manuela learned of the many difficulties other youth in her community were facing as a result of migration. She also saw how to open a space for dialogue and healing the wounds of family separation.

Manuela took a pause from the project to attend university but returned to her hometown in 2007, determined to build the same kind of community that she had been part of for women like her mother. Though migration from Mexico generally includes a significant number of women, migration from Tetlanohcan was male dominated. Tetlanohcan follows a pattern in many Mexican communities in which staying behind is feminized.[3] Many of the women Manuela worked with described themselves as *amas de la casa*, or housewives. Most of their husbands had migrated to the United States in the 1990s and had not returned. In more recent years, these women saw a second generation of migrants in their children. This new generation included many more women, but the family members they left behind tended to be their mothers and younger female siblings. This meant CAFAMI's membership remained almost exclusively female.

Over several months, many of these women spoke of their own multifaceted experiences of the migration of their family members. Those experiences and the experiences of their compatriots in other communities were encapsulated by Manuela when she said, "The family also migrates . . . and is completely transformed." Manuela's words describe the intersectional impacts of migration on both the emotional and economic levels, robbing migrant communities of their closest familial relationships and their ability to thrive economically. "The family also migrates" means that family members experience the same extractive forces that dislocate their loved ones and displace them into exploitative labor markets or as a justification for border fortification. For family members of unauthorized migrants in particular, dislocation and displacement are experienced as family separation prolonged by the illegalization of migration. Thus, spouses, parents, and children and a variety of other kinship ties are transformed into transnational relationships that are stretched and strained.

Dislocation and displacement are also entrenched through development policies that hold transnational families responsible for improving the very conditions that dislocate migrants and displace them into exploitative and/or carceral settings. Development policies touted by international banking institutions and the U.S. and Mexican governments seek to make migrant remittances central to economic betterment. Racialized as backward or economically unviable while in Mexico, migrants are characterized as "heroes" once in the United States because of the large sums they send to their families. The reliance on remittances sent by these "heroes" to improve living conditions reinforces the state's abandonment of its responsibility to provide for basic human needs and shifts such responsibility from the state to the very individuals feeling the brunt of divestment. Migrant community narratives expose the pernicious side of the hero metaphor and the myth that reliance on migrant remittances can lead to development. While remittances did improve access to certain basic human needs—clothing, food, housing, and education—they did not reverse the extractive forces of decades of economic abandonment. Though Manuela was not being strictly literal when she said "the family also migrates," the children of migrants often had to migrate because their parents' remittances could not fill the gaps left by neoliberal divestment. Thus, migrant families are "transformed" into successive generations responsible for undoing the harms of state divestment and reliance on migration.

Most studies examine one of these two intertwined dynamics—either exploring the impact of migration on familial relationships or its economic consequences[4]—but rarely talk about how the two intersect. One exception is Leisy Abrego, whose work on transnational Salvadoran families sheds light on the mixed economic and emotional impact of migration on parents who journey to the United States and their children in El Salvador.[5] Abrego writes that for migrants, "remittances are more than mere economic markers; they represent a sense of obligation between family members and often the expression of deep emotional bonds between relatives across borders."[6] This chapter examines the corresponding experiences of family members who receive remittances in both economic and emotional terms. It also broadens the analysis of migration's interwoven economic and emotional impacts beyond individual families to the community level. As the Mexican authors Rodolfo García Zamora and Juan Manuel Padilla have illustrated in their work on Zacatecan migrant communities, migration leads to depopulation, which has an impact on both family structures and economic opportunities.[7] This chapter builds on these insights in the context of diverse communities in Oaxaca, Puebla, Tabasco, and Tlaxcala where out-migration rates are more mixed but where migration's impacts on family relationships and community-wide economic health are similarly adverse. As the narratives here demonstrate, the impacts of migration mirror the dislocation and displacement of migrants with a third phase of the migration-as-extraction cycle—one that entrenches economic underdevelopment and family separation for those left behind.

To delineate the ways in which migration as extraction is entrenched in migrant communities, I first trace the emotional impacts of migration on family members of migrants and then move to the intersecting economic impacts on these same families. The stories of various actors in migrant communities—including family members, returned migrants, and community leaders—reveal the overwhelming emotional loss suffered by migrant families and the limited economic gains that entrench patterns of migration. It also compares the limited benefit of remittances to migrant communities with the clear benefits to the Mexican treasury and private financial interests in Mexico and the U.S. Just as unauthorized Mexican labor migration benefited U.S. industries, including the immigration enforcement industry, remittances benefited private and public elites in Mexico and the United States far more uniformly than it advanced the economic health of migrant communities.

MIGRATION AS EMOTIONAL EXTRACTION

Like Manuela, many migrant family members addressed how they "migrated" through the loss of their loved one, changes in parenting and other caregiving structures, and changes in their view of themselves. One of the people who was most outspoken about the sense of emotional loss that accompanied migration was Gabriela, a young member of CAFAMI whose father and older siblings had all migrated to the United States. During a CAFAMI meeting in her aunt's house, Gabriela said, "When I think of migration, I think of family disintegration. It is a wound that a mother cannot overcome." Like Manuela, she saw the pain that migration caused her own mother. And Gabriela felt the pain of family separation both for herself and for others in her community.

> For us, as young people it [migration] is a disaster. I see lots of young people who are addicted to drugs because they do not have parents here. Even the priests at our church are talking about it. About how our feelings can no longer be left to the side when talking about migration.

The "disaster" that Gabriela spoke of was unfortunately evidenced throughout Tetlanohcan. As Gabriela mentioned, one aspect of this was a high rate of drug addiction among young people. Tlaxcaltec youth (defined here as between the ages of twelve and seventeen) report using drugs such as alcohol, tobacco, marijuana, and inhalants at nearly twice the rate of the national average.[8] Though statewide statistics do not provide reasons for this, CAFAMI organizers were very clear that most youth are using drugs to help manage the separation from their parents.

Drug use was one of the more dire consequences of migration. But other, seemingly mundane consequences had a serious impact on migrant families. Irena, whose husband, Efraím, had been migrating to the United States since 1998, spoke about the impact of Efraím's absence on herself and her children: "While he was gone, it was very hard for me. I am not from Tetlanohcan. I did not know anyone and was always just in the house." When her children began attending school, it was even harder for her. "I am like a single parent," she said. "But the children don't listen to me like they would their father. Sometimes, I just have to let them do what they want." One of the hardest things for her was the uncertainty: "Efraím will stay in the U.S. a little longer so we can build a business, but we don't know how much longer. And that, yes, it hurts me."

The disastrous effects that Gabriela discussed and Irena's extended single parenthood are directly related to the U.S. policies that have made earlier patterns of circular migration from Mexico all but extinct. Migrants like Gabriela's family members and Irena's husband must remain in the United States for extended periods because they cannot afford the cost or the physical risk of crossing the border multiple times. The migrants' entrenched displacement into U.S. industries has a mirror effect in Mexico, where illegalized migration entrenches family separation and is social consequences. Moreover, these emotional losses are not made up for by economic gains. Gabriela attends school thanks to remittances from her older siblings. And Efraím has been able to support his children's education and build a house with remittances from his salary in the United States. However, these limited economic benefits do not erase the pain expressed by Gabriela and Irena. Another CAFAMI member put it succinctly: "Migration built the house I live in, but on balance, [migration] was not beneficial because it does not help me to have a house and not have my family together."

The pain of family separation also extends to parents who remain behind while their children migrate. This was the case for Celia, whose two sons had followed in their father's footsteps and migrated to the United States. When we spoke, Celia had not seen her sons for over ten years. "To me," Celia said, "it is the saddest thing. It is like little knives in my chest all the time. And I worry. It is so hard not to see my sons, to not know how they are doing." Celia's children were the second generation of her family to migrate. Her husband had been able to send enough remittances to support their children through high school. However, their diplomas did not allow them to obtain stable jobs. Stuck in Tlaxcala's volatile and underpaid maquiladora industry, Celia's sons decided to make the journey together to the United States. Celia's family, like many families throughout Mexico, was experiencing the multigenerational nature of the migration cycle.

ECONOMIC EXTRACTION

The inability of families like Celia's to stop the migration cycle is rooted in economic development policies that do not aim to reverse the policies of dislocation outlined in chapter 1 but rather seek to entrench those policies and displace responsibility for development onto migrants. By "development," I mean the ability of communities to meet basic human needs such as nutrition, education, health care, and housing and to have a social safety net.[9] International financial organizations, the Mexican and U.S. governments, and some migration scholars have long posited that remittances sent by migrants could be used to improve access to these basic human needs in migrant sending communities.[10] Stephen Castles and Raúl Delgado Wise have dubbed this malapportionment of responsibility the "remittances to development agenda" because of the extent to which it "places the role of remittances at the forefront in . . . development."[11] In the context of ongoing neoliberal economic restructuring, the remittances-to-development agenda emerges as a means to entrench state divestment from migrant communities, privatizing and outsourcing development to the very people dislocated by such divestment.

Mexico in particular has developed policies like 3x1 that require investments from migrants in order to obtain state resources for development projects. This excludes most migrant communities, including the majority of communities profiled here. Thus, in practical terms its impacts are extremely limited. But even in the communities where 3x1 projects have been successful, the theoretical basis of the program is circular: it relies on migration to solve the economic problems that caused migration. Moreover, it offloads the state's obligation to provide for its citizens' basic human needs onto migrants, counting on "some of the most exploited workers in the world [to] make up for the failure of mainstream development policies."[12] Thus, 3x1 and other remittance-to-development programs are not designed to counteract neoliberal economic abandonment. Rather, they are new forms of neoliberalism that act to extend and concretize the cycles of dislocation and displacement as they cause communities to become reliant on remittance transfers from abroad rather than facilitate the development of local sustainable sources of income. The remittances-to-development agenda serves to entrench migration as a solution to the economic gaps left by neoliberal development.

Migrant community narratives expose the extent to which the remittances-to-development agenda is a myth. As Irena and Celia describe, remittances help families meet basic necessities, build better homes, and educate their children, but they do not sustainably increase access to food, shelter, and education for the community as a whole. Rather, the remittance-led development model results in further dependence on migration and remittances, entrenching the economic gaps that dislocate people from their home communities and displace them into exploitative industries in the United States.

The Myth of the Remittances-to-Development Agenda

Some 228 miles south of Tetlanohcan, Don Margarito Santos, one of the *autoridades* (public officials) for Laguna Guadalupe de Yucunicoco (Laguna), summarized the impact of migration on communities as a whole. In talking with me about conditions in Laguna, Don Santos lamented: "People think that migration is a benefit, but we don't have anything in my pueblo. If we can get good work [in the United States], we can build a house for ourselves, buy clothes, a car. But it does nothing for the whole pueblo."

One of the other key resources "the whole pueblo" needed was water for the small farmers, which would require an irrigation line. Once an area that could thrive on rain-fed agriculture, the Mixteca region where Laguna is located had seen climate change–induced reductions in annual rainfall from the 1980s on. The lack of irrigation in this region is tied to resource distribution policies beginning in the 1960s that favored government support for large commercial farms close the U.S. border and actively disinvested from small farms like those in the Mixteca. These policies destroyed the livelihoods of almost all small farmers, forcing them north to find work. Don Santos and many others had migrated from Laguna precisely because of this lack of irrigation and cuts to agricultural supports from the 1980s. To try to help other community members stay in Mexico, Don Santos and other migrants had raised about $150,000 MXN on top of the moneys they sent to their families to participate in 3x1. The basic structure of 3x1 is to match private funds collected by migrants from a particular community with equivalent levels of public funding from the three government, federal, state and municipal levels with jurisdiction over that community. The community's governing municipality collects funds from federal and state agencies and then disburses these "three" parts to match the migrants' funds. To be eligible, migrants have to form a hometown association in the United States that collects funds exclusively for use in the 3x1 program. Don Santos was a member of a hometown association and raised money for the association over and above the amounts he sent to his family members.

Because Don Santos was part of an Indigenous community that had set up an *autoridad* (collective governing council) under the *usos y constumbres* (ways and customs) form of government,[13] the funds for the 3x1 program should have been disbursed through the budget line item Ramo 33.[14] But as Don Santos explained, "The resources do not get to us. We were supposed to get $325,000 MXN in 2012, but we were left with only $120,000 MXN." In this case, Don Santos was describing the unwillingness of the state government of Oaxaca to release funds to the municipality of Santiago de Juxtlahuaca, which in turn could disburse funds under Ramo 33. The efforts of Don Santos and his fellow community members finally forced some resources to be released in 2017, which allowed the pueblo to build an irrigation system. However, even those funds were not fully distributed.

> This year [2017], we were able to get resources for infrastructure projects, but the money did not cover all the expenses of the project. We got $57,000 to $67,000 MXN under Ramo 33. But it did not cover all the cement that we needed. We got water to come to the lower half of the village, but those that live up the hill don't have water. They have to draw water from the well below and walk up with it.

At least part of the reason for the delays was the political disagreement between the autoridad that Don Santos and others were part of and municipal government, which was led by the Partido Revolucionario Institucional (PRI; Institutional Revolutionary Party). The PRI in Mexico has a long history of selectively distributing funds only to those who supported them in prior elections,[15] and Don Santos and others supported the opposition party. Thus, a combination of patronage politics and what seemed to be bureaucratic inefficiency was impeding rather than supporting the project that so many migrants had contributed to. The result was that nearly ten years after migrants raised funds, half of the community in Laguna was still left without the necessary resources to make their land usable.

Similar patterns played out across the Mixteca region of Oaxaca. In the village of Santa María Natividad, years of work by autoridades in Mexico and the community members in the United States resulted in the approval of a 3x1 project in 2009 to build a drainage and sewer system. The hometown association had raised $250,000 MXN, and the project was decided on by a process involving the autoridades in the village and migrants living in the United States. Like the irrigation project in Laguna, it took years for the federal, state, and local governments to disburse their share of the funding. And as in Laguna, the residents of Santa María Natividad had supported the candidate opposing the then-mayor of their governing municipality, Ixtapantepec Nieves. By March 2013, when I visited Santa María, the autoridades held a day-long meeting to discuss how to obtain the funds that remained undisbursed. Their discussions included potential political as well as legal interventions. Their efforts worked to some extent as they were able to receive some funds. However, by 2017, it had become clear that there were insufficient funds to complete the project. Pipes had been laid, but they had not yet built the water treatment system for sewage. This led one of the organizers working with the autoridades in Santa María to lament, "All that work will amount to nothing if we can't finish the project." In effect, the enormous financial contribution made by migrants themselves was in danger of being wasted due to bureaucratic maneuvering.

While the communities in the Mixteca were able to participate in 3x1, the vast majority of communities in Mexico cannot. As Manuela's father, Rodolfo, indicated, "We had a hard time trying to use 3x1 [in Tetlanohcan] because the minimum contribution from us is $100,000 MXN, and many people do not have that kind of money. You also need a club in the U.S. with a permanent person to help organize the funds." Empirical data show that Rodolfo and his neighbors' inability to participate in 3x1 was not unique. Only one percent of remittances sent by migrants is matched through 3x1.[16] In 2013, about 584 municipalities participated in 3x1,[17] whereas 1,123 municipalities showed at least a medium level of out-migration during the same period.[18] Tlaxcala, the state that Rodolfo was from, had a few 3x1 projects listed. However, Tabasco, the state where many of the migrants interviewed were from, did not have a single project.

To put into perspective the level of state involvement in development projects, Rodolfo García Zamora points out that in 2006, the Mexican government spent $15 million pesos (the equivalent of about US$1.3 million) on 3x1 *for the entire year*, while Mexican migrants were remitting $62 million pesos

TABLE 4 Similarities in Use of Remittances across Communities

	Tabasco	Oaxaca	Tlaxcala	Puebla
Community organization present 2012–17	None	FIOB founded 2004	CAFAMI founded 2007	CAFAMI expansion 2016
No. of 3x1 projects in state in 2013	0	35	7	20
Uses of remittances #1	Basic necessities (n = 21)	Basic necessities (n = 10)	Basic necessities (n = 14)	Basic necessities (n = 6)
Uses of remittances #2	Education (n = 7)	Education/build a house/buy land (n = 5 for each)	Education (n = 7)	Build house (n = 4)

(or US$6 million) *a day*.[19] Consequently, the entire amount spent by the Mexican government equaled not even 10 percent of what its citizens from abroad contributed to Mexican households. As the stories from the Mixteca region show, the low levels of support provided by 3x1 and the political corruption that exists in many municipalities have led projects to stagnate. Meanwhile, the gaps left by neoliberal underdevelopment—gaps like lack of irrigation or basic sewer drainage—remain intact and even entrenched.

Dependency on Migration

The failure of remittance-to-development programs like 3x1 to reverse structural economic gaps parallels the more widespread inability of remittances from individual migrants to lead to economic development for communities as a whole. Where access to 3x1 was limited, all of the migrants and migrant families profiled participated in individual remittance transfers. The amount of money that migrants remit each year is quite significant, whether viewed at the individual, familial, community, or even countrywide level. Individual migrants like Rodolfo and Irena's husband, Efraím, reported sending close to half their earnings to their families in Mexico. Their narratives are consistent with studies showing that undocumented migrants sent 49 percent of their earnings and documented migrants sent 44 percent of their earnings to family members.[20] Rodolfo's and Efraím's family members—Manuela and Irena, respectively—reported being able to meet some basic human needs like food, shelter, clothing, and access to education with these remittances (table 4). At the community level, individual remittance transfers are even higher. For example, the communities of Soyataco and Chiltepec, Tabasco, received as much as US$10 million a year from 2013 to 2018.[21] And at the national level, remittances provide a significant infusion of income for the Mexican economy overall. In 2018, Mexico received US$33.4 billion in remittances from its citizens abroad, making remittances one of the largest contributors to Mexico's gross domestic

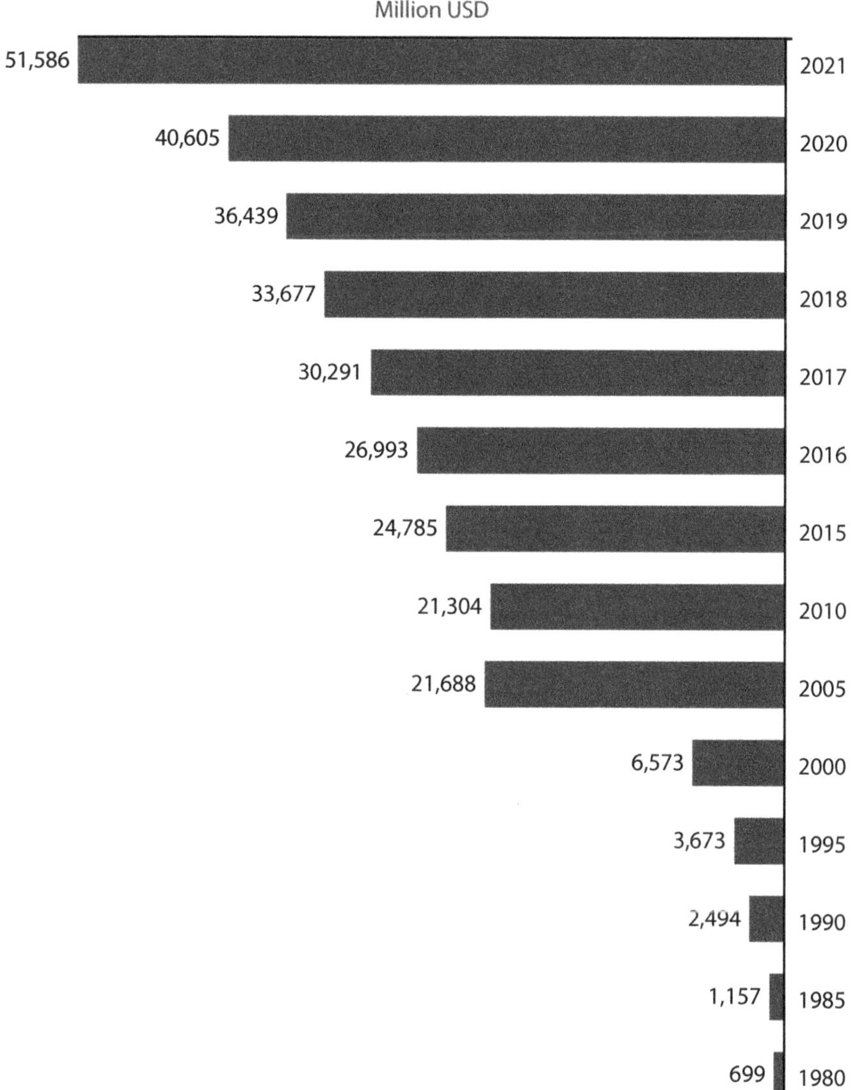

FIGURE 14. Remittances Sent from the United States to Mexico, 1980–2021.

product (GDP) (figure 14).[22] Despite these very large distributions of funds from relatively low-income individuals, it is clear from the collective experiences of people in migrant communities that these funds were insufficient to build up the industries destroyed by neoliberal economic restructuring. In particular, remittance investments in agriculture or land, in small businesses, or in education made important improvements for individuals or families but were unable to reverse state divestment from agriculture, manufacturing, and education (see chap. 1). They left intact the dependence on migration.

Abandonment of Small-Producing Agriculture

One of the most important uses of individual remittances, from the migrants' perspective, has been the acquisition of land. Land has historically and contemporaneously been viewed as a source of financial security and freedom in rural Mexico. Indigenous communities have struggled to maintain control of land since the sixteenth century. In the more recent past, after decades of land confiscation and consolidation under Porfirio Díaz (1876–80, 1884–1911), the Mexican Revolution broke out in large part to wrest control of land from large plantation owners. As a result of the Revolution, the Mexican Constitution contains Article 27, a unique provision that in its original form declared that all land belonged to all people in Mexico and gave the government power to seize large landholdings for the purpose of redistributing it to agrarian communities as *ejidos* (collectively owned parcels of land with usufruct rights).[23] The same provision restricted the amount of land that could be owned by foreigners.[24] In the twenty-first century, access to land continues to have deep meaning for many small farmers, hearkening back to the revolutionary struggle engaged in by many of their ancestors. However, the ejido system established by Article 27 only redistributed a small fraction of the arable land and that small fraction has been subdivided into ever smaller parcels for successive generations. To realize their dreams of landownership, then, small farmers take work in northern Mexico or the United States to earn enough money to buy additional tracts that they aspire to make profitable. These aspirations have been stymied by the interests of Mexican and U.S. elites who successfully cast these small farmers as less economically viable and therefore less worthy of support than their large, corporate counterparts.[25] These characterizations resulted in far more support for large, irrigated, export-facing commercial farms than the small producers who became migrant farmworkers. Thus the promise of Article 27 has been undermined by a continued effort to enrich large corporate interests at the expense of small farmers.

One of these small farmers was Don Remedio, who took work as a contract farm laborer in the United States to realize his dream of owning his own land. With his earnings in the United States, Don Remedio was able to buy a one-hectare parcel after he returned from his first trip in 1980. For the first few years, Don Remedio was able to make enough profit from this small parcel to pay his family's expenses. However, those earnings dropped dramatically after the neoliberal reforms of 1982–88 gutted agricultural supports for small farmers. Don Remedio explained:

> I used to farm cacao and coconut. The government co-op used to buy from us for about $2.50 MXN a kilo. We used to harvest so much that we would get about $3,000 MXN biweekly but no more. The government stopped supporting us. The co-op closed about twenty years ago [approximately 1993]. We were losing huge amounts of money, like $7 million MXN.

When Don Remedio said "the government stopped supporting us," he was referring to the decreases and eventual termination of price supports for small producers like himself. These supports, along with other agricultural subsidies for small farmers, were cut sharply—by 85 percent—between 1980 and 1989.[26] At the same time, large commercial farms continued to enjoy stable or even increasing levels of public support, effectively distributing resources away from small producers like Don Remedio to large corporate farms like Anderson Clayton. The impact of these changes on small farmers in the South and Southeast in particular was devastating. The price of the cacao that Don Remedio grew on most of his land dropped a colossal 70 percent between 1984 and 1992.[27]

Exacerbating the manufactured drop in prices for locally produced goods was the elimination of existing public support for stabilizing agricultural earnings. In saying that the government co-op was "no more," Don Remedio was referring to the elimination of the cooperative store run under the now-defunct Mexican agency, Compañia National de Subsitencias Populares (CONASUPO; National Company of Popular Subsistence).[28] CONASUPO's main role prior to 1986 was to provide fairly intense support to agriculture in the form of import tariffs and quotas, price supports for producers of stable crops, and subsidies for agricultural inputs like fertilizer and machinery.[29] It also guaranteed a market for farmers and a minimum price in those markets.[30] However, the IMF saw cutting CONASUPO's budget as key to fulfill the austerity goals it set out for the Mexican government as a condition of its loans.[31] By 1991, CONASUPO had severely reduced its supports for all crops other than corn and beans, and by 1999, the agency was terminated altogether.[32] Don Remedio, like millions of other small producers, were caught in a vicious cycle labeled economically unviable for failing to thrive in these austere conditions while funding continued to flow to large corporate agribusiness.

The inability of small farmers like Don Remedio to make their lands profitable was exacerbated by NAFTA in 1994. Because of NAFTA, small grain farmers in Mexico (e.g., corn, wheat, and sorghum producers) would soon face competition from highly subsidized and mechanized U.S. imports. Due to widespread public pressure, the Mexican government introduced a program they said would counteract NAFTA's most disastrous impacts. The Programa de Apoyos Directos al Campo (PROCAMPO; Program for Direct Support to the Countryside) would subsidize farmers at a level amount per hectare, ostensibly targeting supports to the smaller producers. However, access to the program was limited in ways that actually excluded small producers like Don Remedio. The payment by hectare model extended and exacerbated Mexican policies benefiting large agribusinesses. Don Remedio's one hectare would only have drawn about US$68 a year,[33] less than one-tenth of what he had invested from his own earnings in the United States a decade earlier. Meanwhile, many large corporate farms could stand to obtain upwards of US$10,000 a year.

Political corruption added to the inability of returned migrants to make use of PROCAMPO, even when they had more land. Don Remedio's neighbor, Don Pablo, had secured eight hectares with his earnings from the United States in the 1960s. But making the land profitable was challenging because, as he said, "[the government] do[es] not want to risk giving you money because there is no irrigation so you are at the mercy of the rains," and "there are no banks that give agricultural credit. There is not that custom." These structural barriers, faced equally by farmers in the Mixteca, made sustaining a living from the land difficult for Don Pablo. After many years, Don Pablo was one of a few small farmers to gain access to PROCAMPO but never saw the funds he was promised, much like the communities in the Mixteca never saw their 3x1 funds materialize. Don Pablo detailed his experience with PROCAMPO as we toured his landholdings.

> About six years ago [approximately 2006], [the] government . . . took us to a meeting and said that they were going to give us $10,000 MXN annually. They gave us a card that we could use to go to the bank and get the money that they deposited. But after the first time, they never deposited money again. The money just stays between themselves. There is little help for the farmland. They say that they are spending millions but it does not arrive.

The theme of money not arriving unfortunately resounds through all of the areas profiled in this book. In Tlaxcala, Don Isaís experienced impediments similar to those of Don Pablo and the returned migrants in the Mixteca. Don Isaís said that when he attempted to apply for PROCAMPO, "They told me no, they will not help me because I went abroad." Clearly, prior experience as a migrant is not a disqualification as Don Pablo was able to participate in the program as a returned bracero. Both Don Pablo's experience of being promised money that never arrived and Don Isaís's experience of being blocked from applying altogether highlight the myriad ways in which the implementation of these policies is corrupted. These political manipulations, combined with the paucity of funds available for distribution to small farms, means that very few returned migrants can make agriculture profitable even with investment from abroad.

Where migrants like Don Remedio, Don Pablo, Don Isaís, and those in the Mixteca continued to face roadblocks to materializing sustained benefits from their remittance-based investments in agriculture, large corporate farms enjoy the majority of government support. More than half of all agricultural supports still flow to large commercial farms in northern Mexico, despite the fact that the majority of producers in Mexico are small. This skewed distribution of resources is rooted in paternalistic characterizations of larger corporate enterprises as "economically viable" and small producers like Don Remedio as requiring "a social welfare approach."[34] The resulting flow of resources entrenches patterns of divestment from migrant communities that dislocate and displace people

into the extremely exploitative agricultural labor markets in northern Mexico
and the United States.

Abandonment of Locally Based Manufacturing

The remittances-to-development agenda extends beyond agriculture to maintain
that remittance-based investments in small businesses should be able to produce
sufficient income to replace migration as a source of sustenance and economic betterment.[35] However, as with remittance-based investments in agriculture, migrants
faced unfair competition from larger businesses, impeding the returns they could
garner from their investment. In Tetlanohcan, Tlaxcala, for example, migrant families like Irena and Efraím's were unable to overcome the "maquiladorization" of
their community with local businesses. Parallel to its investments in large commercial farms, the Mexican government has invested since the late 1980s in expanding
the maquiladora sector in Tlaxcala. In particular, large U.S.-based clothing retailers
located assembly plants in Tlaxcala, displacing the local artisanal embroiderers into
contingent, low-paid work. Irena was one of thousands of women displaced from
local production into the maquiladoras with unsafe conditions and unstable hours.
Efraím also worked in the sector, but the couple found that they could not meet
their expenses with the unsteady and low-wage work. The displacement of local
industry and investment in corporate retailers eventually displaced Efraím into the
United States, separating the family for a lengthy period. When Irena and I spoke,
Efraím was trying to remit enough to cover both the family's expenses and a business selling shoes and embroidered blouses. The money that Efraím sent allowed
Irena to purchase materials and a storefront with the goal of showcasing her goods.
However, the remittances are not sufficient to allow Irena to stop working full-time
in the maquiladora. "I hardly do any business," Irena lamented. "[So] we are dependent on remittances." Thus, despite Irena and Efraím's sacrifices, their ability to turn
their investment into a sustainable income was elusive.

A similar pattern emerged in Chiltepec, Tabasco, where multinational oil companies had pushed small shrimpers out of business starting in the 1980s. One of
the most well-resourced returned migrants to Chiltepec was Serena, who had
worked in the United States as a jaibera for over a decade. Serena tried to use some
of her earnings to open a business. "With the money that I made in the last years
[in the United States], I bought a restaurant on the malecón of Chiltepec called
El Costeño," she said. Serena's investment was significant, using almost half of the
US$20,000 that she had saved from her work in the United States. But she also
invested wisely. As she explained, "I bought [the restaurant] from my mother-in-
law, so I did not have to pay a lot." Serena and I were speaking in the restaurant for
the better part of a day, but there were no customers in El Costeño or other nearby
restaurants that had been opened by returned jaiberas. After talking several times
similarly uninterrupted by customers, Serena conceded, "The restaurant does not
make much money."

The lack of customers on Chiltepec's malecón stemmed from the same maldistribution of resources as that found in the agricultural and manufacturing sectors. Just as the Mexican state provided disproportionately higher support for corporate agribusinesses and maquiladoras, public support and infrastructure were distributed away from small local businesses like Serena's toward multinational oil companies. As outlined in chapter 1, foreign corporations like Exxon and British Petroleum benefited from the privatization of Mexican oil refining and regulations prohibiting shrimp farming. These policies devastated Chiltepec's historic fishing and shrimping industries and spurred massive out-migration. Migrants like Serena who tried to invest in the local economy were thwarted by ongoing support for those same multinationals that spurred the building of U.S.-based hotel and restaurant chains in nearby El Bellote. These chains bustled with activity while Serena's and the other jaiberas' restaurants remained empty. A fitting metaphor for the distributive inequities was the road to Chiltepec. A two-lane, paved highway from Tabasco's capital ends in El Bellote, a physical marker of the support for that enclave and the economic abandonment of towns like Chiltepec on the other side of the highway. Serena and other returned migrants were trying to push for the highway's expansion so that travelers could patronize their local businesses, but as of 2013, they had not been able to secure meetings with any state or federal officials. Just as with agriculture, the distribution of state support away from small enterprise created a structural barrier to the success of remittance investments like Serena's.

Even businesses that had more success for their immediate owners had limited impacts on the surrounding community. When Don Santos said, "People think migration is a benefit, . . . but it does nothing for the whole pueblo," he was explicitly referring to his pueblo, Laguna. But his words encompass the experience of many of the communities in the Mixteca. In nearby Santa María Natividad, for example, Luna and Ricardo had returned to their hometown with several thousand dollars that they were able to save from their time in the United States. Ricardo was now an autoridad, one of the governors of the town, and I spoke with Luna and him during the autoridades meeting at which they discussed the 3x1 drainage pipes project. Luna and Ricardo had a business raising and selling goats. "There is a market for these goats," Luna explained. "We sell them for festivals and celebrations. We used to sell to a wholesaler in Huajuapan [the closest town], but he paid cheap so now we sell them directly to people because they know us." Indeed, as we spoke, one of their goats was cooking as part of the formalities for the autoridades meeting. According to Luna, large goats like the one being cooked for the meeting we were attending sold for $1,800 MXN or about US$175. Luna and Ricardo and Ricardo's cousin Juan raise and sell about three hundred goats a year, netting the business associates about US$45,000 annually. From this, they have to maintain their own families, pay for festivals as autoridades, and help support other family members who have not migrated. The total sum Luna and Ricardo earn in a year is lavish for Santa María Natividad. Yet their earnings do not necessarily have what economists call "multiplier effects" that benefit the community as a whole.[36] Luna and Ricardo's business did allow them to earn a sustainable income for themselves but not enough to employ or create adjacent sources of income for neighbors. As long as large-scale support was limited to multinational corporations, migrant investments in smaller enterprise would continue to spur more migration but would not be able to offset the divestment from migrant communities.

The Education Gap

Migrant investments in land and small businesses cannot overcome one of the most widespread gaps left by neoliberal restructuring and still experienced by migrant communities despite decades of out-migration and remittance investments: the lack of funding for education. Nearly all of the migrants interviewed indicated that at least part of their earnings went toward paying for educational expenses for their children. This was equally the case for migrants who journeyed north in the 1960s as it was for those whose journeys occurred over forty years later. Education is underfunded in rural areas of Mexico, and people must pay fees. As I learned from Don Santos, even in 2017, after large sums of migrant remittances had been invested in community projects in Laguna, "there are a lot of necessities in the community." He went on to specify, "The school needs work, we need electricity. The school we have is only a *primaria*, and it is not comfortable because there are no windows. We don't have a *secundaria* or *preparatoria* in the town. The kids who can go to Santa María, which is about 35 to 40 minutes [away]." Don Santos's description of his particular locality reflects larger patterns of divestment from education in rural states like Oaxaca that mirror other patterns of resource maldistribution favoring industry in the north of the country.[37] These patterns pushed successive generations of parents to migrate from all of the areas profiled. And it also pushed some of the children whose education was funded by remittances to migrate themselves.

A significant gap left by educational divestment, as outlined by Don Santos, is the lack of support for building schools in rural areas. As a result, parents in places like Laguna are required to pay to transport their children to schools in far-off villages or city centers. These additional expenses, not faced by parents in larger urban settings, exacerbate educational inequality in rural areas. Don Santos's nearby neighbor, Elfego, related that the lack of schools in San Martín Duraznos pushed him and now his two oldest children to migrate. Elfego began migrating in 1985 before he had children. However, he continued to migrate for much longer than he had planned to try to help his children receive more education than he had. When we spoke, Elfego beamed as he told me, "With the money I made in the U.S. I was able to educate all four of my children through *secundaria*." Because of the slowdown in investments in education, there was no secundaria in San Martín Duraznos. He had to send his children 30 kilometers (about 18.5 miles) to Santiago de Juxtlahuaca. Elfego and his wife decided to have their children commute rather than stay in town because the journey was about an hour each way. But this added to the expenses for the school. "We had to pay for the travel to Jux, and we had to pay for books, the subscription fee (tuition), pay for internet that they used at the school and other things." With all of these expenses, Elfego was not able to pay for his children's education beyond secundaria. "The oldest started to attend Santa Domingo Tonalá [about two hours away on the road to Huajuapan] for *preparatoria*, but we just could not afford it." As a result, Elfego's oldest two children journeyed to the United States to work, entrenching migration as a survival strategy for Elfego's family.

The experience of Elfgeo's immediate family mirrors the reliance on migration at a community-wide level in all of the regions profiled. A closer look at migrant narratives from Soyataco shows how migrant investments in education have devolved from supporting children to complete higher education to requiring support for children to enter and complete high school. Those like Don Pablo and Don Remedio who migrated from the 1960s to the late 1980s were able to facilitate significant social mobility for their children through a bachelor's degree. Even then, some of these children migrated due to suppressed wages. But as adherence to neoliberal economic policies became entrenched, migrants who sought to replicate these returns in the 1990s and 2000s were thwarted by deepened cuts to education spending. In these later years, people were pushed to migrate to pay for basic pre-college educational fees.

In the 1960s, Don Pablo had used his earnings from the Bracero Program to "achieve sending my eight children to school. . . . They all finished their studies, and we are at peace, thank God." But this "peace" was not achieved immediately. Don Pablo described how one of his children had to migrate despite becoming a doctor. "He actually went to the U.S. illegally because he could not find work here. But he did not like it there, did not like having to look for work every few weeks, so he came back. He works in Nacajuaca now but has a very low salary."

Almost twenty years later, as the IMF-led economic transformation was under way in Mexico, Don Remedio was remitting money from his trips to the United States and Canada. He told me about one of his key achievements from these trips: "I educated all nine of my children. They are all professionals now." Like Don Pablo's family, Don Remedio's family experienced a significant step up the economic ladder thanks to the investment of remittance dollars. However, by the early 1990s, the Mexican government decentralized school funding and governance, resulting in a sharp decrease in education funding in rural areas like Soyataco. Primary and secondary schools began charging tuition to support their budgets. The enormous sums remitted by Don Pablo and Don Remedio could not counteract these ongoing cuts to education. Their neighbor, Elias, migrated in 1999 precisely to pay for the additional costs of high school brought about by neoliberal disinvestment. Elias explained:

I never intended to go to the United States. If the basic education was more affordable or I was able to earn enough to pay the fees, I never would have gone. I agree that
parents should pay something for an education. People should contribute. But right
now, the fees are ridiculous.

The "ridiculous" fees that Elias had to pay were new in Soyataco and forced many
more people to migrate. Though Elias eventually succeeded in supporting his children to complete high school, he could only do so by migrating to the United
States, and his separation from his family lasted much longer than Don Pablo's or
Don Remedio's. Thus, while Elias's family certainly benefited from migration economically, they endured an emotional cost. And like Don Pablo's and Don Remedio's private investments in their family, Elias's investments did not improve access
to education in Soyataco as a whole.

A similar pattern emerged in Sanctorum, Tlaxcala, another rural community
that was abandoned by Mexican policy makers in the drive toward neoliberalization and the remittance-to-development agenda. As in the rural communities of
Oaxaca and Tabasco, schools in Sanctorum began to charge fees when their public
funding was reduced in the 1990s. Isaís, a migrant from Sanctorum, explained,
"Before you did not have to pay for these schools. But now you do. Now you have
to pay for fees, uniforms, books, internet. And sometimes they collect money
for other things for the teachers." These fees could total as much as $2,500 MXN
(US$250 USD) a year for primaria, $3,000 MXN a year for secundaria, and $5,000
MXN a year for preparatoria. For small farmers like Isaís, this represented close
to 30 percent of their income. Since 2000, Isaís had been migrating to Canada
as a contract laborer to pay for his children's education. Seventeen years later,
he was still working so that his children could complete college degrees. As Isaís
explained, his continued migration was necessary in an economy that had simultaneously decreased support for basic education and increased the credentials
necessary to obtain almost any kind of work. "It is different today, the type of life,"
Isaís indicated. "You need a college degree now for any work. If you have a college
degree, you can get paid."

Isaís's neighbor Julio exemplified the need for ever higher educational levels for
a wider range of jobs. Julio was the child of U.S. returned migrants. He had grown
up in Sanctorum and was able to complete high school thanks to his parents' contributions to his educational fees. However, he was not able to turn that diploma
into a sustainable job in Sanctorum. Julio described applying for jobs in offices and
even at restaurants and being turned down for a lack of credentials. The one job
that Julio could get was work in a maquiladora, but Julio said that the pay was low
for what they wanted and more importantly, "the work was too temporary." As a
result, even after the investment that Julio's parents made in his education, he had
to migrate to the United States to "get ahead."

About 22 miles from Sanctorum, in the more urban center of Tetlanohcan,
Rodolfo was reflecting on his ability to help Manuela and her younger siblings

attend school. However, Rodolfo also saw the larger economic picture, beyond his family and even beyond his community in Tetlanohcan. "Migration benefited my family," he said. "I sent money to maintain my children. But I think that the remittances helped the government more than my own family. It helps the government to say all this money is coming into the country." Rodolfo was describing the importance of remittances as a source of foreign exchange for countries like Mexico. The availability of foreign exchange in developing countries is seen as a sign of the country's overall economic health and leads to better credit ratings and the ability to attract foreign investment and loans.[38] By 2006, the nearly US$26 billion sent in remittances had joined oil exports, foreign direct investment, and the maquiladora sector as the leading sources of foreign exchange for the Mexican government.[39] And by 2019, remittances had reached US$36 billion, surpassing oil exports to become the leading source of foreign exchange.[40] As longtime scholars of the Mexican economy have observed, "For Mexico's macroeconomy, remittances are the most dynamic source of foreign exchange and the mainstay of the balance of trade."[41] "Migrants' hard currency," argue others, "helps reposition the country in the global financial world, subsidizes the import of goods and services to modernize national industries, and maintains the consumption of foreign goods."[42] Remittances from migrants like Rodolfo, Elias, and Elfego are the vehicle by which the Mexican government has managed to leverage additional foreign debt and maintain a good credit rating. And while the foreign investment this attracts could theoretically assist in improving overall economic conditions, it actually operates to redirect resources from small local enterprises like those of Serena, Irena, and others and toward multinational corporations.[43]

In addition to shoring up the Mexican treasury, the billions of dollars remitted by migrants help families subsist and partially cover the social costs and minimal infrastructure previously supported by public investment.[44] As exemplified by the stories in this chapter, remittances helped cover the costs of basic necessities for families like Irena and Efraím's, helped pay for educational expenses for the children of Elias, Elfego, and others, and helped all of these families build better homes. Thus, remittances enrich the Mexican state in two key ways—by allowing it to continue to show the world an economically stable face and by allowing it to argue to its own citizens that it is pursuing economic development for their benefit without taking responsibility for that development.

Migrant remittances also contribute to the profits of U.S.-based institutions involved in the transfer of funds from migrants to their families. By 1996, Western Union and MoneyGram controlled the transfer of 97 percent of moneys remitted from the United States.[45] These two companies abused their market share and extracted from migrants through transaction fees, temporarily investing migrant's hard-earned funds before transferring them and artificially establishing exchange rates disfavoring the dollars migrants were seeking to transmit.[46] Though these practices were eventually curtailed, they laid the groundwork for what would become a "remittance transfer industry," involving a number of U.S.-based corporations in the delivery of funds from migrants to their families abroad.[47] In the 2000s, the bilateral Partnership for Prosperity encouraged migrants to use formal banking institutions, transferring much of the profit made by money exchanges to multinational banks. Companies like J. P. Morgan Securities and Merrill Lynch and Company made hundreds of millions of dollars by securitizing the expected amount of remittances that would enter the formal banking system as a result of the Partnership for Prosperity.[48] The remittance transfer industry became so profitable that a wide range of corporations, from AT&T to CitiBank to WalMart, became involved.[49] These companies joined their counterparts that extracted from migrant labor or migrant incarceration with extraction from migrants' efforts to support their families.

Migrants like Rodolfo and migrant family members like Manuela see the benefits that inured to U.S. corporations and Mexican governmental interests while their communities suffered. They recognize the effects of the remittance-to-development agenda as foisting migrants into the role of heroes that can develop the nation while the state continues to forgo its obligations and successive generations are dislocated and displaced. They experience the pain of family separation, even family disintegration, as migration became entrenched as the model for economic development. And migrant communities are responding to the abandonment of their communities with organized demands and programs to wrest resources from the state, create local alternatives to migration, and build bridges to reconnect families. These efforts are highlighted in the next chapter, showing that migrants are not passive participants in the migration-as-extraction cycle but rather actively seeking to disrupt that cycle and replace it with greater self-determination and greater economic and emotional stability.

4

———

Resistance

We need the government to see us and invest in us.
—SERENA

Doña Mathilde was sitting with her sister and father outside their joint family house in Santa María Asunción, Oaxaca. The house was on a hillside and had a sweeping view of the steep valley below, including the family's farming plots and the road we had traveled to arrive at their house. The road was uncharacteristically well-paved, making the journey from the county seat in Santiago de Juxtlahuaca ("Jux") relatively quick. Doña Mathilde's greeting conveyed warmth. "Ven, ven, sientate" (Come, come, sit), she gestured to me. After recounting her one and only journey to the United States in 1990, Doña Mathilde began to tell me about why and how she joined the FIOB: "There was a staff member who came and interviewed us, had meetings, and engaged in trainings about the rights of women. I started to change my way of thinking with the organization. And the pueblo changed too. Now there are women at the assemblies."

The changes that Doña Mathilde made as a result of the FIOB meetings and trainings were profound. She contrasted her experiences when she first returned from the United States more than twenty years earlier: "At that time, I was stupid. I did not even leave the house. Women at the time had to be in the house all the time. You could run to give food to your husband, but you had to come right back to the house. Women used to be hit. I was not, thankfully, but I know a lot of women who were."

Though Doña Mathilde did not report suffering physical violence, she said she was subject to the control of her movements that characterizes many women's lives. Doña Mathilde says she only began to recognize how this manner of living was oppressive when she began working with FIOB. Once this process of realization began, Doña Mathilde's thinking and actions evolved rapidly. From not leaving the house, Doña Mathilde had become a local community leader, participating in both economic projects and political decision making. She was involved in a wide range of income-generating projects, including a mole paste–making project with other women, a cloth-making venture with other women and an organic farming project that included men and women. She also indicated that she and the other women had a savings club which they used like a bank to help each other in times of need. In addition to these projects, Doña Mathilde had begun to participate in the autoridad assemblies in Santa Maria Asunción. It was through these meetings that she reached the conclusion that "the pueblo changed too." In describing the current work of the autoridad assembly, she characterized it as falling on the more democratic side of the spectrum, allowing for women to express their opinion alongside men. "We are discussing now how we are going to ask for more work in the town so that people do not have to go to the U.S.," she said.

Two hundred twenty-five miles due north of Doña Mathilde's family farm in Santa María Asunción stood a small, freshly painted house at the top of a hill in San Francisco de Tetlanohcan, Tlaxcala. Tetlanohcan is one of several towns in Central Mexico with a majority Nahuatl population, and this house stood at the edge of a densely populated barrio. The house is the central meeting place for CAFAMI. Inside the house, several members of CAFAMI were talking about an upcoming market where they would be selling their line of herbal beauty products. After the meeting, I walked home with Celia, one of CAFAMI's earliest members. She told me that she had joined with her sister. They had both heard about a group of college students who were working with migrant families. "I heard that a group had been able to visit their families on the other side, and I wanted that opportunity too." Celia was talking about a group organized by CAFAMI that had brought a culturally unique performance to the United States in 2007, including a play produced according to the methods of Theater of the Oppressed.[1] These workshops wrought a "script" from the words and movements participants used to describe their experiences.

When it came time for Celia to participate in the theater workshops, however, she found it challenging. "It was hard at first," Celia said, "Normally, we do not talk about these things. But I took strength from the others, especially my sister. I did not know that we had the same experiences. Now I feel that I can speak about things." The "things" that Celia found hard to talk about were her experiences with migration and domestic abuse. Her realization that her sister had the "same experiences" was echoed by many women who participated in the theater workshops. Celia went on to be part of the second group to visit the United States, bringing a production about the pain of family separation in migrant communities like San Francisco de Tetlanohcan. But her "speaking up" was not limited to speaking of her experiences. She also participated in efforts to lobby the state and federal governments for more resources for the Nahuatl communities of Central Mexico. She described one of the most recent efforts over dinner in her house.

We have a workshop to generate demands for a senator in Mexico City. We are going to demand more work, and to allow people over the age of forty to work in the plants here in Mexico. We also need a health center where the doctors come in the morning and afternoon. Right now, there are only fifteen appointments each day, and then you have to wait to the next day.

In stark contrast to the dusty hills where I met Doña Mathilde and Celia, Serena spoke to me from her restaurant on the malecón in Chiltepec, Tabasco. Over 400 miles southeast of Tetlanohcan and over 500 miles northeast of Jux, Chiltepec was surrounded by a riot of tropical green on one side and the sea on the other, a view that was pockmarked by the black-gray plumes of smoke from the nearby oil refinery. Serena had migrated to the United States many times on a visa for temporary unskilled workers known as the H-2B.[2] She worked as a jaibera and was one of many women from Chiltepec and nearby Soyataco to do so. These journeys to the United States changed her view of herself, her domestic relationships, and her desire to advocate for more resources to reach her town of Chiltepec. She described the process that unfolded over the many years that she journeyed to the United States: "There they see your work. Even after my children finished school, I went back for another three years. A person gets used to working and having their own money." "There" referred to the United States. In saying that her work was seen abroad, she was also referring to the unseen work she had been doing for years as a housewife. And by "getting used to . . . having [her] own money," Serena drew a distinction from her experience before migrating when her husband was the person in charge of the household finances despite the fact that Serena worked part time outside the house at a nearby school. When Serena returned, she looked for ways to remain financially independent from her husband. She started her own business, the seafood restaurant where we first met. Her decision did not come without conflict with her husband, who expected her to return to a full-time role as a housewife. However, Serena prevailed, involving her mother-in-law in what Deborah Boehm would describe as a "series of negotiations through which women are exercising increased power in some circumstances but also facing the reassertion of male dominance."[3] Unlike Doña Mathilde and Celia, Serena did not have an organization to plug into when she stopped migrating. However, Serena's experience running the restaurant also shaped her interest in organizing other women to seek resources from the state. "We need the government to see us and invest in us," she said.

Women's Transformations and Community Resistance

Doña Mathilde, Celia, and Serena experienced massive shifts in their self-perception as a result of their experiences with migration, either as a migrant themselves or as someone whose family member had journeyed to or settled in the United States. These shifts in self-perception led all three women to renegotiate their positions within their families and communities and to create and join efforts to establish economic self-sufficiency and repair the emotional loss of family separation. These shifts, moreover, carry into their families and towns as a whole, galvanizing entire communities to confront the various threads of migration as extraction with efforts to make migration a choice. Their efforts are beginning to reverse the harms of divestment, displacement, and entrenchment embedded in the extractive process of migration through demands for state resources, creation of sustainable local sources of income, and transformation of emotional loss into new forms of connection. This chapter therefore begins with a deeper description of the ways in which women's experiences and initiatives inform the organizing strategies of FIOB and CAFAMI and inform demands coming out of less formally organized migrant communities like Chiltepec.

In the Mixteca, the experiences of women like Doña Mathilde were consciously channeled by FIOB organizers, increasing women's participation in existing *asambleas* (assemblies or meetings) but also informing the development of existing and new projects that sought to wrest resources from the state and create alternative sources of income. FIOB District Coordinator Rosa Mendez put Doña Mathilde's story in a larger context.

> They began to understand their own experiences of exclusion within male-dominated *autoridad* assemblies despite being the majority of people present. We also organized consciousness-raising workshops that started with what the women wanted to talk about. And, for many women, it was their own experience of migration that brought them to FIOB.

The efforts that Rosa described began in the late 1990s when women's participation in the governance of Indigenous municipalities was abysmally low despite comprising the vast majority of people attending the decision-making asambleas.[4] The efforts began to build steam by 2004, as Centolia Maldonado Vásquez and Patricia Artía Rodriguez, two scholars and FIOB members, observed:

> The women of the FIOB have made significant gains in finding ways to improve their well-being and to advance their social economic and political rights. After a long journey, the women have begun to create and enter spaces where they can exchange experiences, speak their minds and gradually build leadership.[5]

These "significant gains" continued to build over the years. When I last spoke with Rosa in 2017, she described the change in women's roles throughout the region.

> In Santa María Asunción [where Doña Mathilde lives], there has been an increase in participation from women who were migrants. Some of them went to the U.S. Upon their return, they have started a project in organic vegetables. They also have projects to make mole, and *totopos* [tortilla chips] from the organic corn they grow. In San Miguel Tlacotepec,[6] the women rose up, and now there are 80 percent women in the [autoridad] assembly. In Benito Juárez [Yucunicoco], women began to vote in their local assemblies after FIOB did a consciousness-raising workshop with them.

Thus, the interrelated process of women's changing self-perception and FIOB's organizing efforts have moved women toward equally interwoven expressions of self-determination, both political and economic. For another returned migrant, Doña Nancy, the decision to join FIOB was mostly about "having her own money." Doña Nancy was Triqui, and her family had migrated to Santiago de Juxtlahuaca from their home community in Putla, Oaxaca, because of violent political conflict there. Like many others, she experienced multiple dislocations, moving with her family to northern Mexico to pick tomatoes as a child and finally moving to the United States with her husband in 2002. Doña Nancy had not liked her experience in the United States, indicating like many others, "It is not the same being in your country as in another country that is not yours." And being in the United States meant that Doña Nancy had to work in arduous conditions. Despite these hardships, the ability to earn her own income afforded Doña Nancy a level of independence that she did not want to give up when she returned to Jux. She told me about the decision to join FIOB at her stand in the main plaza of Jux where she sold embroidered blouses and purses.

> I joined FIOB three years ago [2010]. I joined because I had been accustomed to having my own money when I was in the United States. I did not want to depend on a man. My husband started to work when we came back, but I did not. So I liked to have my stand in the main plaza where I can sell my things. I also work with FIOB to make blouses and purses to sell abroad.

In not wanting to "depend on a man," Doña Nancy was expressing the same desire for self-sufficiency described by Doña Mathilde and Serena. The economic activity led to leadership development. The other women in the collective clearly regarded Doña Nancy's experience as valuable as they elected her president of the collective for the purposes of filing legal paperwork. Doña Nancy's and Doña Mathilde's leadership in various aspects of FIOB's work mirrors the leadership of women in transnational Mixtec movements to improve local living conditions in Mexico and the United States.[7] As Abigail Andrews has documented, women in various parts of the Mixteca who have very different organizing goals are moved to leadership by their experiences of and reactions to migration, which have in turn resulted in critical shifts in their self-perception and the way they interact in their homes and communities.[8] These women's participation in political processes means that the demands that organizations like FIOB make are being informed by a more inclusive contingent of the community.

CAFAMI presents an even more clear-cut example of the power of women's organizing. Whereas FIOB initially focused on male-centered organizing and has come to include women over the years, CAFAMI originated and continues to be an organization dominated by women. These are the women who have been left behind as fathers, husbands, older brothers, and, increasingly, older sisters migrate to the United States. CAFAMI opened up a physical space for these women to gather and discuss issues of importance to them. As expressed by Celia, this resulted in women beginning to express themselves more openly. Like Celia, Doña Silvestre participated in the Theater of the Oppressed workshops that invited women to share their experiences and build a "script" for a play from those experiences. Doña Silvestre shared how the theater workshop energized her to speak up. "At first, it was difficult for me to speak up in public," she said. "But then it was easy because it was just telling our experiences. I feel very good having been part of these works. Now I speak up more."

Through the theater workshops, Celia, Doña Silvestre, and the other women expressed their dialectical experiences of loss and freedom from abuse that accompanied the migration of their husbands and sons (and fathers in the case of other members). These were then translated into a series of performances that covered themes of domestic abuse and the loss of family members to migration, showing the prevalence of pain from both family violence and family separation. The second play was named *La Casa Rosa* (The Pink House) in reference to one of the migra casas that had been built by a migrant in the United States but was sitting empty waiting for their return. Each of the women performed her stories of loss inside this empty house, a powerful metaphor for the abandoning experience of migration. Even more profoundly, the women of CAFAMI produced the play as a way of reversing that experience of loss and reconnecting with loved ones in the United States. As Celia indicated, "Seeing my children again was the most important . . . part of being in the play." Thus, women's willingness to access profound sources of pain transformed into an ability to mobilize a creative and powerful mode of repair for those wounds and a restoration of community connections torn apart by migration.

These investments in building community also resulted in organizing to wrest resources from the state and create new sources of economic stability. Irena connected the emotional need that brought her into the group with the demands and projects she participated in. "I joined CAFAMI two years ago," said Irena. "I liked the atmosphere. I could find people to talk to about raising my children without their father, my worries for my husband [in the United States]." Irena soon found herself engaged in much more than communing with other women about her experiences. She became involved in a theater project with Celia and Doña Silvestre, a documentary about life in Tetlanohcan, with similar goals of reconnecting migrant families, and an income-generating alternative medicines project, which sought to both reestablish local sources of income and supplement the often-insufficient remittances from family members abroad. The opening of a space for women to share experiences has resulted in tangible efforts to repair the emotional damage wreaked by migration and invest in new ways of relating to family members and new sources of economic stability.

In Tabasco, there is yet a third dynamic at work, this one among largely female migrant community members who have returned but who have not as yet formally begun to organize collectively. As outlined in previous chapters, the communities I visited in Tabasco did not have the same strong Indigenous identities I witnessed in Tlaxcala and Oaxaca. This may be part of the reason that collective organizing was not as present in this region. Another factor may be the difference in access to lawful migration methods. Women from Tabasco generally migrated to the United States with visas, whereas men from the area tended to migrate without authorization. The community may not have the same set of collective experiences from which to draw cohesive organizing strategies. However, the lack of formal organizing did not stop individual returned migrants from expressing many of the same demands as FIOB and CAFAMI members. When Serena commented that the government needed to "see" people like her, she was expressing the invisibility she felt that was brought on by the profound abandonment of migrant communities like Chiltepec. This abandonment was particularly stark in a place like Chiltepec, which was less than three miles from a bustling hotel and restaurant plaza serving the oil industry. Since the 1970s, when oil extraction began, the local fishing industries that once sustained Chiltepec have been dismantled, and almost every working-age adult has migrated to the United States. Thus, when Serena indicated that the government needed to "invest in us," she was expressing a desire for a return of resources directed at oil production and benefiting largely foreign corporations.

The stories of Doña Nancy, Doña Mathilde, Serena, Celia, and Doña Silvestre point to profound shifts in gender perceptions and norms as a response to the extractive process of migration. Each of these women confronted migration in different ways, but all took steps toward self-determination. In most cases, these women did not act alone. Particularly in FIOB, women and men worked together to push for change, but even in Tetlanohcan, where CAFAMI is exclusively female, and in Chiltepec, where the experience of migrant women dominated, women's experiences were creating change for everyone in the community. Their efforts both initiated and supported campaigns to redistribute state resources, create local and sustainable sources of employment and income, and repair the emotional damage wrought by migration.

The remainder of this chapter details specific ways in which these highly varied migrant communities are resisting migration as extraction. Though none of the communities used the term "extraction" or specifically saw "migration as extraction," their efforts are clearly aimed at reversing the three phases of migration as extraction that dislocate their communities, displace them into exploitative and/ or carceral spaces, separate families, and entrench migration as the purported solution for economic development. Despite the differences in identity and level of formal organizing, the chapter illustrates that these communities have built similar analytic frameworks and projects that seek to (1) wrest resources from the state, as a reinvestment of resources dislocated to support large corporate entities; (2) create local sustainable sources of employment and income that counteract the

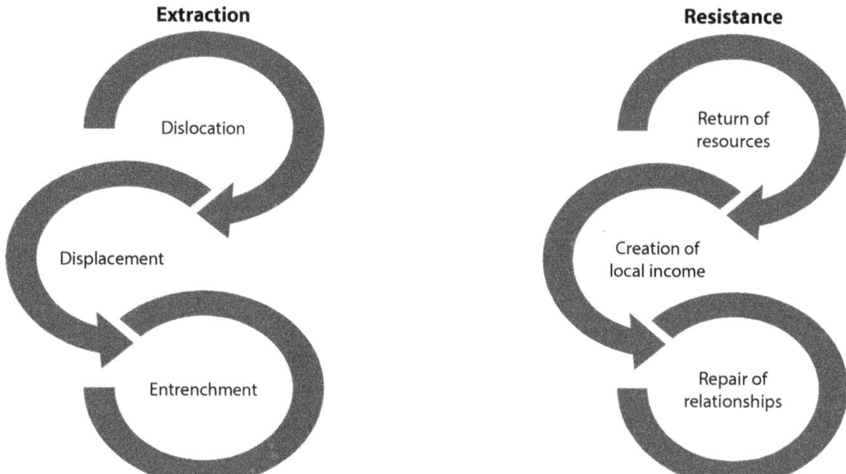

FIGURE 15. Extraction and Resistance in Migrant Communities.

displacement of community members abroad; and (3) repair familial bonds torn by migration (figure 15).

RESISTING EXTRACTION WITH THE RIGHT TO STAY HOME

Of the communities I visited, the most long-standing and analytically developed response to what I call migration as extraction was FIOB's campaign for *el derecho de no migrar*, or the right not to migrate. In claiming a right *not* to migrate, FIOB was drawing attention to the various intersecting policies and practices that compel people to move. FIOB cofounder, Gaspar Rivera Salgado, has defined the right not to migrate as expressing the need to recognize economic rights like "the right to go to school, the right to make a living from farming, or the right to health care and decent housing."[9] Underlying this assertion of rights is a call for sufficient resources directed at things like education, agricultural supports, health care, and housing, alongside other economic projects like job creation. Moreover, as Rivera Salgado has also indicated, the right not to migrate expresses a demand for autonomy, meaning that "people in communities of origin, therefore, not banks and corporations, should control the economic development choices that . . . make it possible for people to stay."[10] Thus, the right not to migrate encompasses demands for self-determination over economic and political decisions and campaigns asserting that autonomy to reclaim resources appropriated by economic and political elites.

The right not to migrate is fundamentally different from the right to free movement, rooted in liberal political theory.[11] However, it is not the opposite of the right to migrate, nor does it contradict arguments in favor of free movement. Arguments for the right to move freely challenge border controls and deportation powers as inconsistent with the commitment in liberal polities to individual rights.[12] Where the right to migrate challenges a nation-state's power to exclude, the right not to migrate excavates further, surfacing and challenging an economic and political ordering that compels migration for accumulation of profit and then spreads this wealth accumulation to include control of migration. Thus, the right not to migrate is not so much about regulating migration in ways that are consistent with an existing regime of political rights but rather requires a fundamental rethinking of what migration is and what rights are. Migration, in the context of the right not to migrate, is a part of racial capitalist relations that redistribute wealth and a labor in ways that benefit economic elites. Thus, when Gaspar Salgado argues that there is a *right* to go to school, a *right* to make a living from farming, and a *right* to health care and decent housing, he is arguing for a fundamental rethinking of rights as economic, cultural, and social. Framing education, earning a living, and health care and housing as rights, moreover, challenges the normalization of state policies divesting from these institutions in the name of modernization and structural adjustment. Under the right not to migrate framework, investments in these institutions are required, and it is the state's responsibility, rather than migrants' responsibility, to invest.

Even as the right not to migrate seeks to make it possible for more people to thrive in their home communities, it is not an argument for no migration. Rather, it is an argument that migration should be a choice. This fundamentally challenges the ability of corporations, and the governments supporting them, to determine who is allowed to migrate and where with a framework in which migrant communities, critically in this case, Indigenous migrant communities, have more control. Thus, the right not to migrate is both a set of material demands and a political project seeking to realize these material demands through reclaiming the right of Indigenous migrant communities to self-determination, including migration if that migration is by choice.

The struggle for political control and demands for economic investment that make up the right to migrate movement are rooted in a long history of decolonial struggles in the Mixteca. Mixtec communities have been resisting colonization since the sixteenth century. Twentieth-century resistance has seen the formation of organizations like the Unión Nacional de Organizaciones Regionales Campesinas Autónomas (UNORCA; National Union of Autonomous Regional Peasant Organizations),[13] which, since the 1970s, have fought (at times in literal violent conflict with state leaders) to demand better agricultural working conditions, control of the use of land, and control of local political decision making free from the intrusion of political parties.[14] Part of what emerged from these various movements was the call for a return to a system of governing indigenous municipalities known as usos y costumbres. This is a form of self-governance for Indigenous communities who had been excluded from the formal Mexican state. It provides an official entity through which to demand resources and to demand autonomous decision making over the use of land and other resources.

Oaxacan communities had been fighting for this form of self-governance for decades. In 1994, the Ejército Zapatista de Liberación Nacional (EZLN; Zapatista National Liberation Army) in Chiapas gained international attention. The short-lived armed rebellion was followed by years of negotiations with the Mexican government, which produced a mixed set of recognitions of Indigenous rights to self-governance.[15] In Oaxaca, where many indigenous groups supported the EZLN, the armed rebellion and the negotiations that followed paved the way for an amendment to the Oaxacan constitution making the usos y costumbres system of self-governance official state law in 1995.[16] Two years after that constitutional reform, 418 of Oaxaca's 570 municipalities had chosen to adopt usos y costumbres as their electoral system. Many of those, including Laguna and Santa María Natividad, are located in the Mixteca.

Under usos y costumbres, the municipality would be able to run their own local elections independent of the political party system, making decisions through participatory democracy, and monitoring compliance through a parallel (and often informal) system of law enforcement and community justice.[17] Elections are run by a general council made up of elders from the community who have success-fully served in a submunicipal level of governance, an autoridad. Autoridades are groups of individuals from the same village within a municipality.

It is in this context of increased localized political power that the precursor to FIOB was formed in 1991. The Binational Mixtec-Zapotec Front was initially orga-nized in the United States by migrants from these two Indigenous communities who sought to improve working conditions for people displaced and transferred into agricultural positions in that country. The movement soon expanded through circular migration and cross-border communication to take on the forces of dis-placement more directly, in a process that Andrews calls "remitting resistance."[18] As the group expanded to include members from Indigenous groups other than the Mixtec and Zapotec, it became known as FIOB. In this earlier formation, FIOB sought to promote effective community development projects in the Mixteca that would allow people to remain in their communities and with their families.[19] Thus, even before the right not to migrate was named, FIOB resisted dislocation of its community members. As the group evolved, it "developed a framework for see-ing the connection between the displacement of people in their countries of ori-gin and exploitation and repression of those communities in the countries where they go to work."[20] This framework informed the connections made in this book between the dislocation and displacement phases of migration as extraction.

By 2013, when I visited, the framework connecting dislocation and displace-ment had matured to also include a critique of so-called development policies that worked to entrench migration as a survival strategy. FIOB's work had expanded to encompass a wider range of strategies including gaining access to information, campaigns to demand more state resources, and the creation of *autoempleo* (community-created jobs). Their analytic framework was mirrored in calls by CAFAMI to make migration a choice, invest in local sources of income, and to repair the economic and emotional damage wrought by migration as well as the calls by migrants like Serena for the government to "see" communities like hers. These calls translated into three concrete strategies for reversing the extractive dynamics of migration: 1) wrest resources from the state, as a reinvestment of resources dislocated to support large corporate entities; 2) create local sustainable sources of employment and income that counteract the displacement of community members abroad; and 3) repair familial bonds torn by migration.

Wresting Resources from the State

Tucked into the foothills known as the Sierra de Oaxaca, Jux houses the Oaxacan office of FIOB. It was here that I met Don Margarito Santos, one of the autoridades of Laguna. Don Santos was at the office to meet with Bernardo Ramirez Bautista, state coordinator of FIOB, to discuss plans to ramp up efforts to obtain resources from the state and municipal governments. Laguna had been allocated funds under Ramo 33, a funding line for Indigenous communities. However, the funds were not forthcoming. "We have to protest to get them to pay," explained Don Santos. He went on to describe protests in 2012 and the state's reaction: "We went to the municipal presidency last year, but the government sprayed us with gas instead of doing anything. They did not do anything. We also went all the way to Oaxaca [the state capital] last year, but they did not do anything either."

Despite the violent reaction of municipal officials and the indifference of state officials, Don Santos and others from FIOB persisted in pressuring the state and local government until they were able to get some funds disbursed in 2017. As outlined in chapter 3, this resulted in the partial construction of irrigation pipes channeling water from a valley into the mountainside where most farming was done. The efforts to obtain state funds is one of many ways that FIOB organizes to build migrant community power and reverse the extractive forces of migration.

Reinvestment of state resources is a key demand of FIOB, CAFAMI, and individual returned migrants in Tabasco. As Don Santos of Laguna outlined, resources that have been allocated for the community's benefit do not always make it to the intended beneficiaries. Bernardo indicated that an investigation by FIOB members, including Don Santos, had uncovered that between a quarter and a third of the resources that had been allocated to Jux under Ramo 33 never arrived. This information led to the protests that Don Santos described to obtain sorely needed revenues.

Moreover, each pueblo participating in FIOB is spurred on by the knowledge that other involved communities have prevailed in getting the full resources they are owed. For example, in Santa María Asunción, access to information has resulted in real infrastructure improvements. Don Manuel, who is Doña Mathilde's husband and one of the autoridades in that pueblo, reported, "We learned more about what we were promised. And we went to the municipal heads and the state officials and we talked to them, we protested. Now the government gives us more support under Ramo 33. For the last six years, they have done more. They paved the road that passes through the town, for example." Paving a road may seem like a small victory, but in a region like the Mixteca, this is an enormous improvement. Most roads are either dirt or were paved so long ago that they are badly damaged and difficult to pass. Journeys of 30 to 40 kilometers (16 to 26 miles) take hours, and some routes are circuitous. This makes it particularly difficult for farmers and other makers to bring their products to markets in larger towns and cities. The new roads in Santa María Asunción paved the way for these makers to improve their earnings.

The fight to reinvest in communities includes a participatory democratic process about what projects to pursue, in contrast to the top-down decision making involved in government-run projects like 3x1. For example, Don Santos recounted the process used in Laguna.

> First, we hold an assembly to ask the people what they are going to do this year. We take proposals from the community and then ask the people to decide. It is done through community discussions. Sometimes this takes a few days. The community gathers, discusses, and comes to a decision, "This is what we want to do this year." Then we [the autoridades] go to the municipal presidency to ask for the project. We do the application. It used to be hard to fill out, but now we have a form created for us [by FIOB staff], and we just have to fill in blanks with the name of the municipality, the name of the authority, the community, the work, and the quantity of materials requested.

As Don Santos described, sometimes the democratic process is slow. But the process for completion of projects can be even more drawn out, requiring the constant vigilance of community members. In the case of Laguna, the irrigation project voted on in 2012 was still not completed as of this writing. A similar dynamic played out in nearby Santa María Natividad. In March 2013, I attended a meeting of the town's autoridad at which officials discussed progress on a project begun with the help of FIOB. The project had been approved by the community's asamblea, similar to the one described by Don Santos in Laguna, and entailed building a sewage and drainage system. Funds for the project came from the Mexican government's 3x1 program, which required a financial commitment of $250,000 from community members and matched those funds with equal amounts from the municipal, state, and federal governments. All of these steps had been completed over years of close collaboration between the autoridad and FIOB organizers to ensure democratic participation in the selection of a project and to ensure that the promised funding from the public entities materialized.

Funding for the 3x1 project had been approved in 2009, and work had begun shortly after, thanks to constant pressure by the autoridad and FIOB. By 2013, one of the autoridades at the meetings I attended indicated that the pipes had been laid but they had not yet built the water treatment system. Most of the conversation during the half-day meeting (translated from mixteco baja to Spanish by an FIOB organizer, Cipriano) was about how to complete the water treatment system. It seemed that the municipal government, charged with disbursing funds, had finally done so and that work was progressing slowly but steadily.

After the meeting, everyone gathered for a meal of earthen roasted goat, a specialty made possible by Ricardo and Luna. Both Luna and Ricardo were happy about the work being completed in the village, but Ricardo emphasized that the investment from the government had come only after a lot of pressure from the people. Ricardo's comments speak to the ways in which Indigenous communities continue to lack political power despite the gains in autonomous governance since the 1990s. Government officials do not feel the need to visit Santa María Natividad because they do not feel accountable to people in this area. Don Santos similarly spoke of the lack of attention of government officials when they failed to disburse funds allocated under Ramo 33. This results in the need to constantly pressure state officials through protests and other means. FIOB regularly used protests as part of a larger strategy. On February 18, 2013, there was a peaceful march in Oaxaca to get resources for projects that were promised in 2011. Five years later, in 2018, FIOB was again having to threaten to protest in order to get work completed that had been promised in 2017. As Don Santos points out, the protests alone are often not enough to get the work done. But they are an important part of the overall strategy of political and economic power building, which includes learning what resources were allocated, meeting with government officials, and street protests.

Demanding resources from the state is also an imperative in Tlaxcala. Though basic infrastructure is better here than in Oaxaca, decades of divestment have left gaps in education and health care funding. Similarly, the development of the maquiladora industry with its insecure and dangerous work has resulted in the lack of sustainable employment opportunities in the area. As in Oaxaca, divestment has displaced thousands of people from the community. It was this dislocation that led to the formation of CAFAMI in 2007 to serve as a space for those left behind by migration. Like FIOB, CAFAMI's organizing vision has evolved based on the demands of the migrant communities in Tlaxcala and the collaborations they have with migrant communities in other parts of Mexico. And like FIOB, CAFAMI fundamentally seeks to reverse the migration as extraction cycle by fighting for sufficient investment in local communities that would allow people to remain in Mexico. As Itzel Polo, one of the organization's supporters remarked: "We can create an economy from the local, from the communities, and not from the perspective of [globalizing] forces like large corporations. The phrase we organize around based on the community perspective is 'migration should be an option, not a necessity.' "

CAFAMI members have sought to "create an economy from the local" and make migration a choice in a number of ways. For example, CAFAMI has participated in a number of protests in Mexico City seeking better employment creation and other investments from the state. As described by Celia, one of these was a workshop to generate demands for a senator in Mexico City. CAFAMI's advocacy has long sought to have the Mexican government reinvest in migrant communities. This includes fighting for greater resources for job creation, education, and health care to allow more people to remain in Mexico. In more recent years, CAFAMI has also joined with other organizations to make life for returned migrants easier. However, they face indifferent bureaucrats and lawmakers.

Gabriela was only fourteen years old when she had her first taste of the difficulties of this advocacy work. "We have been demanding a lot," she said of her work with CAFAMI. "We visited Congress after the trip to the U.S. We demanded a law to help create jobs, make it possible for people to continue working after forty, but the government does not care." She got the impression that the senators representing Tetlanohcan did not care because they only met with them for a few minutes and then only praised the all-woman delegation's migrant relatives. "They don't take responsibility. They could do a lot of things but they don't do it," she lamented.

Both Celia and Gabriela emphasized demands for more work and opportunities for employment. These demands carry deep and substantial meaning in a place like Tetlanohcan where available work has become more and more fleeting as neoliberal reforms dug deeper into the community. The once-stable agricultural and wage labor work evaporated as structural adjustment policies removed supports for agriculture and suppressed wages. Available work became even less stable as trade protections crumbled and U.S.-owned maquiladoras moved in with their contingent positions, low wages, and high lay-off rates. The rampant age discrimination that Celia described was a sign of the search for "perfect workers" inside Mexico in much the same way U.S. employers sought "perfect" Mexican workers across the border. Older workers were considered too feeble or slow to carry out the punishing demands of work in the maquiladoras. And the focus on maquiladora development meant the absence of investment in other industries that could create more stable jobs and whose profits could remain in the community rather than benefit large corporate interests in the United States.

Even in Tabasco, where there are no formal organizations like CAFAMI and FIOB, returned migrants understand that the key to a sustainable future for their communities is to redirect state resources. For example, Serena's experience with migration showed her that self-sufficiency was possible. Unlike most of the migrants I interviewed, Serena had been migrating to the United States on a visa and was therefore able to have a bit more control over when she stopped working.

She had used her remittances to buy a small restaurant offering a number of local seafood specialties. However, disinvestment and pollution in Chiltepec brought on by the incursions of the petroleum industry meant she lacked the customer base needed to make her business profitable. When we spoke, Serena identified the issue as rooted in a lack of resources from the state. "We need the government to see us and invest in us," she said, referring to the lack of infrastructure that would allow people to access Chiltepec. A two-lane, well-paved highway ended in Paraíso, only a few miles from Chiltepec but boasting an oil refinery and a U.S.-based hotel chain. Thus, Serena's call for the government to "see" her was a call for more government investment, echoing the demands of more mature organized groups like FIOB and CAFAMI.

Creating Alternatives and Filling Gaps

At the same time that communities fought for more state investment in job creation, they also took it upon themselves to create local sources of income to counteract the need to migrate and satisfy the economic gaps that remittance income could not quite fill. A key feature of these income-generating programs was their noncapitalist nature. Rather than reinforce the structures that captured surplus value from workers in agriculture, manufacturing, or other industries, migrant communities created cooperative structures in which those performing the work were in charge of the means of production (whether that was producing food, herbal medicines, or leather bags) and in which all members shared in the profits of the venture. Though they operated in the larger context of capitalism, and more specifically, neoliberal capitalism, the projects are examples of attempts to carve out niches of more egalitarian and democratic relationships than those present in the larger economic system. FIOB's Rosa Mendez described two employment creation programs in the Mixteca. One project sought to help farmers grow organic products. Rosa indicated that this project was funded by the Ford Foundation, whose materials describe the project's goals thus: "Help small farmers in Mexico increase crop production and access U.S. and Mexican markets; and demonstrate more productive use of remittances in poor rural communities where migration is common."[21] The foundation's description of project goals is consistent with historical neoliberal understandings of the need to "modernize" Indigenous communities so that they can be more productive and better participants in capitalist markets.[22] The last goal, "productive use of remittances," is a direct reference to the remittance-to- development mantra touted by international banks and the Mexican government that seeks to absolve the state of its obligation to support its citizens and instead saddle migrants with the responsibility.[23]

In practice, FIOB members operationalized these projects in ways that created worker-owned cooperatives in which profits were distributed equally among members. Thus, while the project operated within the confines of existing markets that may themselves have been exploitative, the project itself was arranged to distribute resources in a more egalitarian and democratic manner. Elfego, who had returned to San Martín Duraznos in 2009, said he had the idea with his friends to cultivate organic mushrooms, or setas, which were becoming a delicacy in the more touristy parts of the state. "We started to organize ourselves to go on a better path [than migration], and from there we were introduced to FIOB," he said. In 2011, with FIOB's support, he was able to obtain a starter kit for the setas and training on how to plant, care for, and harvest the fungi. During our conversation in 2013, he walked me through his son's half-finished house, which was serving as storage for his first harvest. "These have come out well," he beamed. "The plan is to talk to restaurants in Oaxaca about buying these and maybe get a contract." Elfego was well aware that one way to realize the employment-creating potential of setas was to tap into the global market that visited Oaxaca. But Elfego was also thinking about local sustainability. Mushrooms were a relatively sustainable product in the soil-eroded Mixteca as they do not require planting directly in the earth. Moreover, they can withstand the eight-hour bouncing, winding ride from San Martín to the capital, making them well suited to the underdeveloped infrastructure. And Elfego and his friends would share equally in the profits from selling to upscale Oaxacan businesses.

In addition to mushrooms, Elfego and his companions had planted basil, pomegranate, and Mexican limes. In describing these efforts, Elfego discussed the potential for simultaneously expanding community involvement and increasing income. "We need a big greenhouse so that more people can come and work on the organic products project," he said. "It would create more employment if we had a greenhouse and could grow more things. We could also do more business because we would have more to sell." But he also saw challenges in getting people to join the project. "The seeds we get from Mexico City do not always produce," he said. Those seeds were provided by the Ford Foundation's Mexico City office, according to Rosa. Elfego went on to explain, "We lose a lot of crops. For that reason, many of the other farmers do not want to bother with organic. They want to continue doing things their way." Continuing to do things "their way" involved the use of fertilizers and pesticides, which became common in the Mixteca in the 1980s as rainfall began to decline. Continuing to use these products, despite knowing that they might harm the soil in the long run, spoke to the precarious economic health of these farmers and their families. A bad crop could be devastating in an environment void of economic security nets. Despite these issues, the project persisted, and Elfego continues to try to convince his neighbors to return to organic methods.

Similarly, Doña Mathilde worked on a number of different projects to create employment and supplement remittance income. Some of the projects are with other women from Santa María Asunción, and others are projects that she is doing alone. One of the group projects was to cultivate organic produce, similar to the one Elfego was involved with in his community. Looking out over her family's property, Doña Mathilde described the variety of products her group was able to cultivate, "We are planting tomatoes, tomatillo, lettuce, cilantro, radish, chard, broccoli." Despite the fact that it was Doña Mathilde's family that owned the land, "everyone shares in the income." In another of her groups, Doña Mathilde told me, "we are making *mantel* [cloth used for women's blouses] to sell during our fiestas, especially August 15 [the feast of the assumption of the Virgin Mary, for whom the town is named]. We make about $10,000 MXN during the fiestas." These proceeds are distributed among the group. That amount can stretch to cover about two months of expenses in this region. In some of her ventures, the spirit of collective work and profit sharing was not as successful. In a third project, Doña Mathilde explained:

> There used to be a group of five of us who made and sold mole paste, but two died and another one left the organization with $9,000 MXN of our money. The investment for the paste is pretty big—$5,000 to 10,000 MXN—so we need to be able to make a profit. I decided to continue without the group to see how it goes. Now I sell in the market in Juxtlahuaca by order.

Even with these risks, Doña Mathilde's involvement in various employment creation projects was not unique in Santa María Asunción. She indicated that 134 people from her village (with a population of 1,600) were engaged in different ventures, mostly through FIOB but also some independent projects. She proudly stated, "My entire family is involved, including my ninety-year-old father." Doña Mathilde connected her family's efforts to larger efforts to create more locally sustainable sources of income for the entire community. She said, for the upcoming municipal-wide asemblea, "we are discussing now how we are going to ask for more work in the town so that people do not have to go to the U.S." The "ask" was a demand for state investment in employment creation in order to reverse the migration as extraction cycle.

In addition to agricultural projects, FIOB organized its members, particularly women, to try to leverage Indigenous artistry as a source of income. One such project was to train existing artisans how to make blouses and bags that could be sold in the United States and Canada. Rosa described the overall project: "Oxfam Mexico funded us to help the artisans make designs and stitching of a quality that would be bought for export. Oxfam is helping by giving tips based on work they did with a group in Zacatecas. They also have bought some of the material for the women to use in the project and have other resources." Among the other resources were industrial sewing machines, which were being set up during my first week in Jux. Another resource was a trainer from the nearby state of Puebla who came to help the women learn about how to make sure that their purses and bags would be appreciated on the international market. The profit-sharing structure of this project, like that of agricultural projects, was democratic. The women would share equally in the profits made by their collective sale of the bags. However, in this situation, the women did not have as much control of which products to make or how to make them. Rosa spoke to the challenge that posed for attracting women to the project and keeping their interest.

> Most of the women already make crafts but in their own form. These do not sell that well, and so they are learning how to make their work more marketable. One of the key things the women are learning is how to measure with a measuring tape so that products turn out the same size every time. . . . There were twenty-two women involved in the project at first, but that decreased to twelve and now to six. It is difficult when they have so many other things going on. It is also personality dependent. Some do not like to change their design. Others like learning new things.

In describing the need to change these women's artistry from "their own form" to something "more marketable," Rosa was articulating the shifts needed to participate in the globalized capitalist market. The resistance of some who "do not like to change their design" shows that these singularly profit-seeking shifts were not overwhelmingly welcome and that the participants sought to maintain their designs as an artistic expression. Moreover, the lack of control over the designs meant that the women themselves did not feel as enthusiastic as Elfego and Doña Mathilde did about their endeavors. "I'd like the women to take charge of the project themselves and not depend on FIOB so much," said Rosa. However, in the months that I visited the sewing site, one of the other FIOB staff members, Isabel, was initiating sewing sessions and regularly checking in on the women to see how they were doing. Though it was not clear exactly why women did not take ownership in the way that Elfego and Doña Mathilde did, it may be that they felt less included in the decisions about what kinds of products to make and how they should be made. It may also have to with the fact that the women on this project were Triqui, a different Indigenous group than the Mixtecs that formed the majority of Jux's population and FIOB's staff.

One of the women involved in the sewing cooperative was Doña Elena, a Triqui woman who moved to Juxtlahuaca from San Juan Copala with her mother and older brother. We spoke in her stall in the main plaza of Jux where she sold Triqui blouses, purses, and bags of her own design. "Originally, I got to know FIOB because they helped the plaza venders when the municipal president tried to make us leave the plaza." Once she joined, she learned about the project that Rosa described and decided to join because of the possibility of selling her products to a wider market. However, Doña Elena soon faced challenges trying to adapt her craft for an international market. "We had a workshop with the store owner from Puebla where she showed us how to cut the leather and make patterns so we could sell them to fancier places," she explained.

> I liked learning the new techniques, but they are very difficult. The cuts and weaving have to be exact. With our traditional products, we just make the things in square forms, sew them up, and there it is. Because it is difficult, we are losing women

> from the group. There were twelve, and now there are only six. I don't know if I can continue with the project. My back may not be able to handle the work. Also, I don't know if this woman [the trainer] knows what she is doing. I took her advice on one of my bags, and it turned out so badly.

Doña Elena was not alone in expressing frustration with the project. Doña Nancy, who is also Triqui and also moved to Juxtlahuaca at a young age, said, "The work is difficult. The blouses are especially difficult. The work is very fine, and I am not sure my back can stand the work." Like Doña Elena, Doña Nancy learned about FIOB from others in the plaza and joined in 2010. Though she was not enthusiastic about the work, she was interested in the cooperative aspect and the possibility of creating income streams for herself and other Triqui women. "FIOB is helping us become a legal cooperative," she indicated. The application had already been submitted, with Nancy listed as president of the cooperative.

Two hundred twenty-five miles due north of Juxtlahuaca, in San Francisco de Tetlanohcan, a different organization was helping a different Indigenous group create income to help fill economic gaps left by structural adjustment. Here the women of CAFAMI initiated a business venture on their own, without assistance from or decision making by outside funders. Like the project in Juxtlahuaca, CAFAMI's business venture drew on Indigenous knowledge and practice. CAFAMI's cooperative cultivated medicinal plants to create a variety of health and beauty products for sale. In this alternative medicines project, the collective made products that addressed a variety of issues, from body aches and infections to acne and dandruff. The knowledge of plant-based medicines itself was cultivated by CAFAMI's programming. Early in its history, migrant families sought to reclaim their language and hired a teacher to give classes in the Nahuatl language and other aspects of Nahuatl culture. One of those cultural lessons was about traditional plant-based medicines. Thus, the confluence of affirming Indigenous culture, building connections between women, and seeking local sources of income merged to create the alternative medicines project.

One of the unofficial leaders of the group was Doña Luisa, who did not have any migrants in her family but joined CAFAMI because she "liked the atmosphere." Doña Luisa's family was one of the few large landholders in Tetlanohcan, and she provided some of that land to CAFAMI for growing medicinal plants. She had some knowledge of these crops from her family but also learned a lot in the workshops at CAFAMI. She was the first to experiment with using the products when she traveled with CAFAMI to the United States in 2008. Doña Luisa took part in the organization's production of a "carnival" showcasing regional dances, foods, and herbal medicines. While she was in the United States, she "administered a lot of this traditional medicine to people from the community." The ailments she treated ranged from dandruff to back pain.

Helping her community members in the United States made Doña Luisa and others think about investing more in the knowledge and cultivation of medicinal plants for profit. Like the structures created by FIOB members, the women in the alternative medicines project are worker-owners. They do all the work to cultivate the plants and formulate the various products and share in the profits equally. The challenge that they face is that state structures continue to favor large corporations over smaller enterprise and favor goods from transnational U.S.-based corporations over locally produced goods, making profitability a distant goal. As Doña Luisa theorized:

> There needs to be support for the creation of natural products. They sell all the American brands here, but these natural products, Indigenous products are better. Instead of products from the U.S. coming here, we should be able to find a market for our products in the U.S. Then maybe the children, they would not have to go there.

The difficulty of getting support for a local, Indigenous product mirrors the larger economic shifts in Mexico that continued colonial forms of extraction. Since the 1960s, resources have been allocated to large-scale agriculture and industry, while supports for local farming and manufacturers evaporated. This has famously resulted in the replacement of diverse varieties of locally produced Mexican corn with an influx of government-supported, commercially farmed monoculture corn from the United States. It has also resulted in the replacement of local manufacturing and enterprise. A key example is the textile industry in Tlaxcala, which has been replaced by maquiladoras where textiles are assembled rather than made for U.S.-owned retailers. This same pattern affects the ability of the alternative medicines group to obtain the support they need to launch a full-scale business, much less one that can market its products outside their local economy.

Organizers with CAFAMI have taken note of these limitations. In 2013, Norma Mendieta spoke of CAFAMI's efforts to connect with pro bono counsel to obtain business licenses and apply for funding for the project. By then, the product line had a name, Herbalini, and included six women. However, the licensing process wore on for several years. By 2017, Doña Luisa and the other women were less hopeful, almost resigned to distributing the herbal medicines locally and to their family members in the United States as a service rather than a business. But the continuation of this project, despite these setbacks, demonstrates the resilience of CAFAMI members in general. Doña Luisa and others expressed their frustrations at a fair in the capital, Tlaxcala, where they were able to inform a number of people about their product line and make a few sales. And one of the members, Leticia, expressed hope. "Many people stop and ask questions, but not a lot of people are buying yet," she said. Leticia believed that with increased awareness of the health risks of factory-manufactured products and the health benefits of herbal remedies like the ones produced by Herbalini, they would attract more paying customers.

Whether or not the efforts were financially successful, the creation of locally based income streams represented an important step within migrant communities to disrupt their own or their family members' displacement into extractive industries that generally created income for others. By coalescing around the development of products drawn from Indigenous knowledge—like the mole pastes that Doña Mathilde and her colleagues made, the blouses and purses made by Doña Nancy and others, or the herbal products of Herbalini—migrant communities were seeking to root themselves against forces that would uproot them. And the collective income-sharing structures that they created helped form niches of more egalitarian resource distribution even as they grappled with how to fit those niches into the larger system of racial capitalism operating around them.

Reintegrating the Disintegrated Family

Perhaps one of the most distinct set of community-led projects stemmed from the uniquely female membership of CAFAMI, a membership that was also made up of the family members of migrants. In addition to campaigns for state resources and organizing around local income streams, the women of CAFAMI explicitly sought to repair familial bonds that had "disintegrated" (in Gabriella's words) due to migration. Like Gabriella, most women joined CAFAMI largely as a way to help them navigate the pain of family separation and loss. One of the projects born from this desire to heal the wounds of separation was a documentary about everyday life in Tetlanohcan.

Irena was one of the leaders of the documentary project. Her husband, Efraím, had left for his most recent trip to the United States in 2007 and had not returned because the enforcement dynamics in the United States would make a return trip north too costly and dangerous. Efraim preferred to "stand it" in the United States until he felt he could invest appropriately for his family. This meant that Irena had been left with the task of being both mother and father to their three children and of filling the gaps in economic resources when Efraím's remittances did not cover all the bills. She was deeply involved with the economic projects, but the project she talked about most was the documentary. "We recorded the streets, traditions, carnival, school, and school parades," she said. The project was part of the reason that Irena joined CAFAMI: it was a way to "connect with Efraím and miss him a little less." Thus, by bringing the life in the town to Efraím, she was seeking to rebuild the family bonds that had frayed due to migration. In the process, Irena also built a deeper connection to her surrounding community. "I am not from Tetlanohcan," she explained. "So, for me, joining meant I could meet other women, talk to them. It is the only thing I do outside the house."

The other project that grew out of the entrenchment of family separation brought about by ongoing divestment and increasing investment in U.S. immigration enforcement was the Theater of the Oppressed workshops described by Celia. The workshops allow women to identify issues that are particularly pressing for them and to explore these issues collectively through the process of producing a play. As Celia explained, "A teacher from the U.S. came to talk about immigration, how people cross the border, and then asked us to talk about our experiences. We were interviewed on what we thought about migration." The responses were developed into a show, including movement and spoken lines, that told the story of how migrant family members were dealing with the absence of their fathers, husbands, sons, and others. Celia joined the production because it meant that she might be able to see her two sons. "I knew that another group had gone to the United States, and I wanted that opportunity as well," she explained. Celia was referring to a group of women that CAFAMI had organized to visit the United States in 2008. The group put together a carnival of different food products and Nahuatl dances and songs to be performed at certain venues in the United States. They obtained visas under a program designed for "culturally unique" performances.[24]

For Gabriela, who was only sixteen when she worked with the group on La Casa Rosa, the journey meant the end of a fourteen-year separation from her siblings. "It was a start," she said, "but one trip cannot erase the wounds of all these years." Her siblings, who had last seen Gabriela when she was a baby, were consumed by the need to work and had little time to spend with her.

"My sister [who worked as a server]," she sighed, "only came home to eat or sleep. Otherwise, she was working." And her youngest brother "does a double shift every day" and uses all of his time away from work to take care of his daughter who was born in the United States. Through these observations, Gabriela began to understand how entrenched migration had become for her siblings and her family who depended on their earnings and how much effort it would take to truly rebuild bonds with her siblings.

Celia had a similarly complex set of emotions at seeing her sons. She was grateful to have been able to spend Christmas with them, but she said, "There is no life there." "It was very impactful for me," she continued. "I was really happy because I got to see my son, who I had not seen for seven years. But at the same time, it was sad because I saw in reality how they lived. They stay three to a room, and they work all the time." Celia's and Gabriela's experiences reinforced their desire to fight the extractive policies that had dislocated their family members. They saw the connections between dislocation and displacement firsthand, though they would not have used this exact language. And their responses were to reinvigorate efforts to reunite with their families more permanently by organizing for more resources.

Celia and Gabriela's work to bridge the emotional and economic gaps of migration were mirrored throughout the communities profiled. Communities across Mexico are seeking to reverse the entrenched dislocating effects of divestment by fighting for more state resources. For Indigenous communities in particular, this includes fighting for the ability to determine how to use those resources. Similarly, communities are seeking to create local sources of employment that can help prevent the displacement of workers into exploitative industries in the United States, exposing them to risks of surveillance, violence, and detention, and counteract the entrenchment of migration as the only means to economic stability. At the same time, groups like FIOB understand that migration has become so entrenched that no amount of local investment will completely obviate the need to journey north. Thus, they are combining efforts to improve local conditions with efforts to improve working conditions in their displaced destinations and make the journeys north more secure. Finally, families that have been torn apart by migration seek to re-form through programs that rebuild connection and repair emotional harm. Just as migration as extraction is multidimensional and layered, so too are the efforts of communities resisting this vicious cycle. In all of these efforts, migrant communities confront extraction with creativity, resilience, and steadfastness. But it is not the responsibility of migrant communities alone to reckon with the harm that migration as extraction has wrought. In Mexico and in the United States, those that have benefited from migration must account for the benefits they have reaped from these communities in material ways. Moreover, migrant community resistance alone cannot transform migration into an act that is chosen. Transforming migration as extraction into migration as choice requires a fundamental reordering of public policy and corporate practices.

Conclusion

Whether through nascent or mature organizing, migrant communities are confronting migration as extraction with demands and efforts to make migration a choice. In particular, migrant communities are engaged in struggles to redirect resources, create local sustainable sources of income and employment, and repair relationships wrenched apart by migration. Embedded in these struggles are efforts to democratize local decision making and create egalitarian structures that increase the participation of women in particular in leadership positions. In their work, migrant communities have sought more resources from the Mexican state but have theorized the need to address larger dynamics of racial capitalist relations that locate decision-making power in multinational banks and corporations and their allies in the United States and Mexico that profit from the dynamics of migration as extraction. As Gaspar Rivera Salgado, FIOB cofounder, has argued, "People in communities of origin, not banks and corporations, should control the economic development choices."[1] The people profiled in this book are seeking control of economic opportunities from a diverse array of perspectives, whether rooted in Mixtec autoridades and cooperatives, Nahuatl traditional knowledge, or non-Indigenous businesses. Similarly, migrant community organizing includes efforts to counteract economic extraction from their labor in the United States and repair the emotional extraction of family separation caused by U.S. immigration laws and border enforcement measures.

Migrant community organizing in Mexico understandably focuses its efforts on Mexican public and private institutions, with some attention to U.S.-based employer practices and U.S. immigration laws. However, as outlined in the previous chapters, the dislocation and displacement faced by these communities are constructed as much by U.S.-based actors as Mexican ones. As outlined in chapter 1, U.S. and Mexican elites collaborated with international banks to implement policies that depressed the economies in migrant communities, including policies that divested from agricultural supports, education funding, and other social programs and intentionally suppressed wages. People dislocated from their homes by these policies were then driven into exploitative industries in the United States or used as the justification for ever greater expenditures by the U.S. state on immigration enforcement, as detailed in chapter 2. The very people who were dislocated and displaced into exploitative industries were then charged with the responsibility for improving economic conditions in their home communities, as evidenced by chapter 3's analysis of the remittances-to-development agenda. As shown in that chapter, the remittances-to-development agenda benefited U.S. and Mexican financial institutions and Mexican public coffers while entrenching migration as the only strategy available to families for "getting ahead." These intersecting dynamics of dislocation, displacement, and entrenchment, driven by both U.S. and Mexican actors, combined to produce migration as extraction.

Given the deep involvement of U.S. actors in the formation of migration as extraction, actualizing migrant communities' conceptualization of migration as choice will require radical changes to both Mexican and U.S. institutions and policies that facilitate "wealth concentration, dismantling of public services, and . . . manufacturing and disciplining of surplus populations" while simultaneously "consolidat[ing] . . . spatial carcerality through borders and prisons."[2] Specifically, migrant community narratives from Tlaxcaltec, Mixtec, and non-Indigenous communities point to the need to radically alter policies that divest from agricultural supports, education funding, and other social programs, as well as policies that shift responsibility for economic development from the Mexican state onto the backs of migrants and their families. They also point to the need to reconfigure an interrelated set of institutions that profit from migrant exploitation and "spatial carcerality," including U.S. employers who control methods of entering the United States and prefer unauthorized migrants and U.S. state and private institutions that profit from the criminalization of migration, militarized migration management, and detention and deportation.

Two frameworks—abolition and reparations—offer theoretical grounding for these expansive analytics and arguments. Though the migrant communities profiled have not explicitly called for abolition or reparations, these two frameworks are particularly useful for supporting their demands because they both seek to address structural harms and are broad enough to encompass the full scale of dynamics that make up migration as extraction. Particularly for the Indigenous migrant communities, which make up the majority of communities profiled, abolition and reparations offer a means to analyze centuries of extraction that predates but evolves into migration as extraction. Through these frameworks, this conclusion offers a vision for supporting and expanding migrant community efforts to make migration a choice, as well as examples of the kinds of redistributive shifts

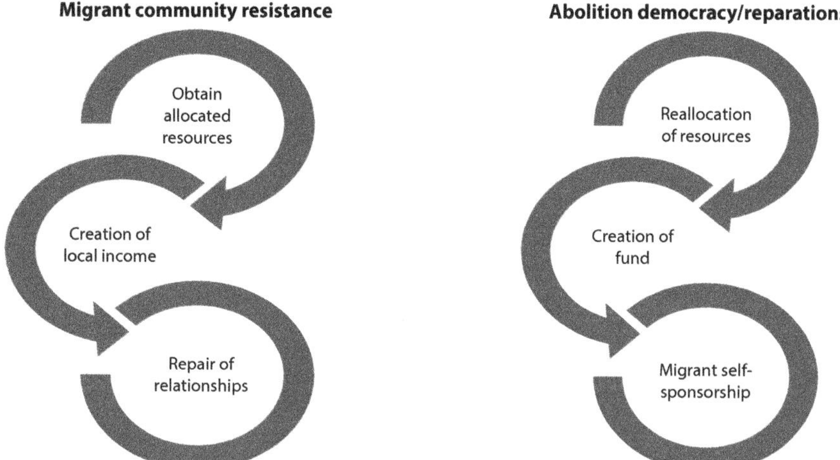

FIGURE 16. Migrant Community Resistance as Abolition Democracy/Reparations.

necessary to fully move from migration as extraction to migration as choice. In particular, it lays out two sets of resource distribution and decision-making shifts that could help fully realize the potential of the new institutions that migrant communities have built. The first set of shifts would require a reversal of extractive policies that underresource migrant communities and overresource the "homeland security state" by fundamentally redistributing resources from extractive policies toward beneficial ones. This redistribution would require increasing the decision-making power that migrant communities have, what levels of funding are necessary to improve material conditions, and how resources are allocated. The second set of changes would need to occur in U.S. migration policy, replacing the extractive policies of employer-controlled displacement of migrants into segregated and exploitative labor markets with a policy that gives potential migrants control over their own movements. This employee-initiated migration process would quite literally make migration more of a choice and contribute to the self-determination of migrant communities. As illustrated in figure 16, the specific policy changes required by each of these shifts are theoretically grounded in the frameworks of abolition and reparations.

MIGRATION AS CHOICE AS ABOLITION DEMOCRACY

Abolition offers a two-step understanding of the need to undo "inevitable and permanent feature[s] of our social lives"[3] that cause harm and the need to replace those features with "new institutions, ideas, and strategies."[4] Migration scholars have recently drawn on abolitionist literature from the slavery, policing and prison contexts to problematize the "inevitable and permanent" militarization of borders,[5] criminalization of migration,[6] detention of migrants,[7] and deportation.[8] While acknowledging that the "build[ing] up . . . of new institutions" is more fundamental to beneficial social change, this literature tends to focus on policies and practices to dismantle rather than alternative, beneficial institutions to support.[9] Migrant community organizing efforts and vision, in contrast, offer concrete examples of what could be invested in both in terms of "re-imagining institutions, ideas, and strategies, and creating new institutions, ideas, and strategies" for replacing migration as extraction with migration as choice.[10] It is these new institutions, ideas, and strategies that are analyzed here as abolitionist with attention to undoing extractive policies as a way to support these initiatives.

The work in migrant communities exemplifies abolition democracy. Coined by W. E. B. Du Bois in the context of the abolition of slavery and further explicated by the leading abolition scholar Angela Davis, "abolition democracy" is the understanding that true abolition of a harmful institution, like slavery, can only be accomplished with the creation of new institutions such as those that "provide [people] with the economic means for their subsistence[,] . . . educational access[,] . . . and political rights."[11] It is no accident that the most robust new institutions, strategies, and ideas stem from Indigenous migrant communities, as those are the communities that feel the greatest impact from policies that have stripped local economies, barred education in local languages, and usurped political structures. Studies of migrant community organizing in Oaxaca have formulated the strategies of these groups as political but have not necessarily focused on the institutions being built through their work.[12] In terms of political rights, one example of the new institutions being built in migrant communities is the reclaiming of historical Mixtec asambleas, or direct democracy forms of governance, in Oaxaca that allow for broad participation by community members in decisions about development priorities. These asambleas have the potential to act as sovereigns, claiming self-determination rights and political power for the Indigenous Mixtec communities on par with what they consider colonial government structures at the national, state, and municipal levels in Mexico. Outside of alternative formal governing structures, Indigenous migrant communities in particular have also built nongovernmental organizations like FIOB and CAFAMI that exert political pressure. These nongovernmental organizations are structured around community-led decision making and have intentionally developed the leadership of women. In Oaxaca, FIOB works in conjunction with asambleas to set priorities and advocate for public resources. CAFAMI operates in areas of Tlaxcala and Puebla that do not have asambleas or other Indigenous sovereign structures but organizes around Nahuatl identity and membership in a migrant family to assert subtler forms of self-determination such as the recapture of language, culture, and resources.

One of the key ways that these institutions exert political pressure is to push for state resources. Efforts like FIOB's to ensure the distribution of resources allocated under Mexico's Tres por Uno (Three for One or 3x1) program or CAFAMI's demands for more state-funded job creation are rooted in migrant communities' understanding that they have rights to functional infrastructure; to accessible education, housing, and health care; and to earn a sustainable living. Even the less formally organized demands of returned migrants in Tabasco call on the Mexican state to invest in infrastructure to support community-run businesses. These demands, similar to demands from Oaxaca's asambleas, are assertions of self-determination, demanding a voice in decisions about how resources are allocated and what levels of funding are necessary to make migration a choice. And like the institutions formed by migrants in other states, migrant communities in Tabasco could benefit from contributions by both Mexican and U.S. actors implicated in their migration dynamics.

Through these new institutions, community members are also creating the "economic means for subsistence" from locally available materials that do not require migration. In Oaxaca, Tlaxcala, and Puebla, workers' cooperatives are creating economic opportunities rooted in Indigenous knowledge and practices and resisting both the racial capitalist wealth accumulation that harms all communities and the colonial domination of Indigenous peoples in particular. Agricultural cooperatives in Oaxaca are returning to Mixtec farming methods that are organic and sustainable and carving out new markets for these methods. In the same region, women's cooperatives are turning Triqui crafts into profit-sharing enterprises. In Tlaxcala, CAFAMI's notion of "creating an economy from the local," draws on Nahuatl knowledge of herbal medicines to build up local enterprises like Herbalini. In Tabasco, the efforts are still in formation and are not associated with particular Indigenous groups. But even in the absence of formal institutions or Indigenous identity, returned migrants here are seeking to recover the local fishing industry decimated by decades of environmental devastation. These projects are directly confronting migration as extraction with programs to allow community members to thrive economically at home.

Migrant communities are also building abolition democracy through the formulation of important new rights, such as the right not to migrate, which challenges the normalization of migration and exposes its constructed nature. In this discourse, the right not to migrate is *not* articulated as the elimination of migration; rather it calls for making migration a true choice, one that occurs in conditions of sufficiency rather than scarcity. Migrant communities understand that some migration may be necessary indefinitely. For this reason, they also challenge the exploitation made possible by employer control over their movement (if authorized) and working conditions (whether authorized or not). Finally, they challenge the harms of protracted family separation, which is created by laws illegalizing migration and requiring illicit, expensive, and dangerous journeys north. CAFAMI in particular has established a project that simultaneously allows its members to build community with each other, practice the Nahuatl language and culture, and mend familial relationships torn apart by migration. Together, this formulation of rights, demands for state funding, and creation of alternative institutions and strategies for economic sustenance evidence a robust articulation of abolition democracy, even in the absence of explicit reference to this term. To support these efforts, the harmful institutions detailed in preceding chapters could be dismantled, allowing for a reallocation of resources and a shift to more worker-controlled migration options.

Replacing Dislocation and Carceral Displacement with an Abolitionist Redistribution of Resources

The agricultural and craft cooperatives in Oaxaca, the herbal medicines enterprise in Tlaxcala, and the businesses in Tabasco are all examples of endeavors that have potential but whose potential is constrained by policies that make people in these communities "surplus" through reduced funding for social programs and abandonment of job creation and infrastructure and then "discipline" their labor as migrants through exploitation and incarceration. In order to fully realize the potential of the various efforts of migrant community organizing, these constraints—imposed by various policies assumed legitimate—must be examined and reversed.

As chapter 1 details, divestment from small farms, advocated by an interrelated set of U.S., Mexican, and international banking elites, dislocated people like Don Pablo, Don Santos, Elfego, Isaís, and Luna who could no longer earn a living from their own land and displaced them into low-paid, highly exploited farm labor. The maquilization of the Mexican economy, pushed by the same set of U.S., Mexican, and international actors, replaced local industries like the Tlaxcaltec textile industry with U.S.-owned maquiladoras, turning artisans like Irena and Efraím into low-paid assembly line workers with little job security. The maquiladora industry was so unstable that it eventually displaced people like Efraím into menial jobs in the United States necessary to the U.S. economy. And all over Mexico, cuts in social spending, including education and health care, displaced people like Isaís, Elfego, Don Santos, Serena, and Elias into U.S.-based agribusiness, food processing, and service work to pay for basic education for their children.

Even as the harms of this economic restructuring became evident to both Mexican and U.S. officials, both governments doubled down on neoliberalism, continuing to adhere to economic austerity and individual responsibility as a means for solving the crises these policies had created. Chapter 3 documents the various ways in which proposed solutions to the crises created by neoliberal economic restructuring were fashioned to entrench the economic abandonment of the state and shift responsibility for development onto marginalized communities. The cuts in education spending, for example, were entrenched by defederalizing education spending and incentivizing private education over the development of public schools. Migrants like Isaís, Rodolfo, Elfego, and Elias filled the gap in public education funding with their own funding from earnings in the United States.

This led to some socioeconomic mobility, as Isaís's, Rodolfo's, and Elias's children were able to make careers in Mexico. But as austerity measures were entrenched, even migrant earnings could not offset education gaps. Elfego's eldest son, Jaime, had to migrate after completing secundaria. Similarly, in Tlaxcala, where Isaís's and Rodolfo's children attended school, and Soyataco, Tabasco, where Elias's children graduated, education was not made more accessible to the community at large. Rather, education spending continued to be cut and new schools were structured as semiprivate, transferring education financing on already burdened families. Thus, out-migration continued to rise in efforts to offset the entrenchment of economic abandonment.

In agriculture, the withdrawal of public support was even more stark and affected Indigenous and non-Indigenous communities alike. Just a short time after the IMF required cuts to agricultural price supports and subsidies took hold, migrants like Don Remedio in Soyataco, Tabasco, and Don Santos in the Mixteca region of Oaxaca found it hard to profit from the land they managed to purchase with their U.S.-based earnings. By the 1990s, changes to soil, rainfall, and air quality brought on by pollution and climate change combined with the lack of state support for irrigation and soil enrichment made smallholder farming next to impossible. And by the time small farmers like Isaís sought to buy land in Sanctorum in the 2000s, price supports and subsidies had been eliminated and lines of credit privatized, resulting in high interest rates. This entrenched the need for some farmers, like Isaís, to continue to sell their labor in the U.S. and Canadian markets, both hungry for agricultural workers. Moreover, the Mexican government's 3x1 program required a large contribution from migrant "hometown associations," but the public matching funds for these contributions paled in comparison to migrant remittances. Though it is not possible to quantify all of the divestments and redistributions of resources, an analysis of public records shows that the equivalent of US$38 billion was withdrawn from agricultural supports and education financing alone between 1980 and 2021.[13]

The enormous cuts in social spending are correlated with an enormous rise in public expenditures and private profits from U.S. border and interior immigration control measures, including militarized border infrastructures (walls, checkpoints, surveillance equipment, and detention facilities), border enforcement personnel, criminalization of unlawful entry, and detention and law enforcement resources directed at people in the interior of the country. This wide array of policies and practices are so enmeshed with U.S. state building that they have been dubbed the "homeland security state" by the political scientist Alfonso González.[14] As shown in chapter 2, this homeland security state, ostensibly designed to prevent entry and compel expulsion, both facilitates the entry and discipline of migrant workers and aids in the wealth accumulation of industries that produce the infrastructure of immigration control. Private industries that build walls, detention centers, planes, cameras, drones, and other monitoring equipment join with public agencies that exploit racialized depictions of Mexican and other migrants as criminals to inflate public budgets and assure private profit. These joint private-public efforts have resulted in a record-setting $26 billion budget for Customs and Border Protection and $8.3 billion for Immigration Customs and Enforcement in 2021,[15] with about a fifth of these expenditures contributing to private profits for companies like Boeing, IBM, Lockheed Martin, and CoreCivic.[16] Additional funds have been directed at co-opting large parts of the Mexican security apparatus to deter migrants from the rest of the western hemisphere from entering the United States. Under the auspices of *Plan Sur* and the Mérida Initiative, the United States has allocated close to $5 billion to this "transnational migration deterrence,"[17] bringing the total allocations for this combined Mexico-U.S. migration control regime to almost $40 billion in 2021.[18]

In order to reverse the harms of militarized migration control and remove the constraints imposed on migrant community efforts to invest in sustainable development, the full homeland security state must be dismantled and the structural gaps that dislocate people from their homes must be filled. In other words, to fulfill migrant community efforts to make migration a choice, the harmful policies that fostered migration as extraction must be abolished and replaced with resources directed at institutions that can help build toward abolition democracy. Dismantling the U.S. homeland security state would potentially free up $40 billion that could be invested in infrastructure, education, health care, and job creation. A shift in priorities of the Mexican government would potentially recoup another $38 billion in social spending lost in the decades of policies of economic abandonment. These massive shifts may not be immediately politically feasible, but political realities can change as groups begin to uncover the ways in which the status quo normalizes the dismantling of public services and the manufacturing of surplus populations who are then used to justify excessive immigration controls and subjected to unchecked labor exploitation. The experiences in migrant communities bring the harms of these normalized policies into sharp relief and, if heard, may contribute to changing political winds that support rather than thwart their efforts at sustainable development and political freedom.

Once the conceptual shift is made toward investing in resources for endeavors grounded in improving local economies and keeping intact familial relationships, it becomes necessary to consider the actors that will best put these resources to use for migrant communities. Alongside the harms of policies of divestment and displacement are the harms embedded in state action itself, including the colonization of Indigenous peoples, the well-documented political corruption in Mexico,[19] and the tendency to use available funds to bolster foreign investment rather than investment in communities.[20] U.S. actors have similarly misdirected efforts aimed at addressing the "root causes" of migration at law enforcement strategies rather than economic development projects. These programs do not send aid to Mexico but rather to Central America. From 2014 to 2016, the U.S. "root causes" strategy distributed a total of $1.5 billion to the governments of El Salvador, Guatemala, and Honduras. The majority of that funding goes to control narcotics trafficking and "regional security initiatives" such as support for the return of failed *mano dura* (iron fist) policies in El Salvador to crack down on transnational gangs. Given the unreliable actions of the U.S. and Mexican states, it is critical to ensure that alternative institutions, like asambleas or nongovernmental organizations, are able to access any funds redirected from migration deterrence and reinvested in social programs directly and independently of the Mexican government. It is equally important that the distribution of funds is controlled in a democratic manner.

One mechanism for redirecting some portion of the almost $80 billion invested in the homeland security state and recouped from divested social programs is through a fund along the lines of the "loss and damage" fund recently established in the context of climate change to compensate nations facing the brunt of climate disasters with funds from nations that contributed most to climate changing emissions.[21] Rather than set up the fund as a kind of foreign aid from the U.S. government that would be distributed to state actors in Mexico, this fund would require a trusted third party to hold and distribute contributions from both private and public actors and would need to allow direct democracy groups like the asambleas in Oaxaca or FIOB or CAFAMI to access these disbursements for projects that migrant communities have prioritized but not yet realized in their efforts to make migration a choice. A third party is critical to ensuring that Indigenous groups like the Mixtec and Tlaxcaltec are included in the process and do not face continued exclusion and discrimination from Mexican state actors. Migrant community-led institutions like FIOB and CAFAMI could then leverage the public and private funds redirected from extractive enforcement policies and refurbished from lost social spending to continue the work of repairing the damage wrought by decades of migration as extraction and more effectively build toward migration as choice.

Replacing Displacement into Exploitative Industries
with Self-Determined Migration

Part of what is contemplated by migration as choice is the understanding that, even with appropriate support, migration itself will not totally cease to be a strategy. Thus, migration as choice is not a call for no migration but rather the ability of migrant community members to assert more control over whether to migrate at all, and if the migration option is exercised, control over the conditions of their movement north and their living conditions once in their now-chosen destinations. Increasing migrants' self-determination over these conditions of migration is abolitionist in the sense that it would require fundamental reconfiguration of immigration laws that are currently structured to benefit U.S. employers and carceral actors. Under the existing immigration law system in the United States, lawfully migrating for the kinds of work done by people like Serena, Luna, Elias, and Efraím requires the sponsorship of an employer in the United States.[22] This places the control over who migrates and for what length of time in the hands of corporate actors. Employers, in turn, seek out Mexican and other immigrant workers, authorized and not, for their perceived subservience and vulnerability to deportation. Thus, it is not so much that migrants like Elfego, Efraím, and Serena are doing work that no U.S.-based workers will do. Rather, they are doing work that U.S. employers *prefer they do* in markets that have been structured, with the help of U.S. policy, to bring in a labor pool that can be underpaid and controlled by the threat of deportation or the inability to return as an authorized migrant. For authorized and unauthorized migrants alike, employer control over who migrates or who is hired facilitates abusive working conditions. It also leads to retaliation. Authorized workers who complain are not allowed to return, and unauthorized workers who complain are threatened with deportation. Moreover, where employers exercise a preference for unauthorized workers, those workers face surveillance, arrest, and even criminal penalties for violating laws barring entry without permission while employers face little to no consequence for their violation of workplace laws.

In order to shift from this extractive system to one that supports migration as choice, the laws privileging employer preference and structures of exclusion would need to be reformulated as laws that allow workers to control their movement through deregulated borders along the lines of what the legal scholar Jennifer Gordon conceptualized as "transnational labor citizenship."[23] Under Gordon's analysis, immigration status would be tied to "membership in organizations of transnational workers."[24] This reformulation of migration would benefit some Indigenous migrant communities, like those in Oaxaca, that have organized transnationally for years. However, as the narratives from Tlaxcala, Puebla, and Tabasco illustrate, many migrants are not part of these organizations prior to migrating for the first time. Another, perhaps more inclusive way to accomplish worker control could be through a change in the law to allow migrant workers to sponsor themselves. Self-sponsorship is an existing mechanism under U.S. immigration laws but is reserved for workers who have "extraordinary ability" or "critical skills . . . which are not of a general nature."[25] These categories privilege well-resourced workers in professionalized occupations, often from the capitalist elite classes in their home countries. Self-sponsorship reinforces the privilege these workers already have that allows them to move relatively freely to the United States and escape the many barriers to entry for other workers and even family members of U.S. citizens. Moreover, the ability to self-sponsor bypasses ostensible protections for U.S. workers, implying that these elites, and the skills that they bring, are inherently valuable.

In contrast, the so-called unskilled work of migrants like Elfego, Serena, and others is devalued by current immigration rules and placed under employer control. Unskilled work, according to U.S. immigration laws, includes agricultural, food processing, and service industry work,[26] exactly the work performed by most of the migrants profiled. These workers must wait for employers in the United States to sponsor them for an H-2A, H-2B, or equivalent visa in order to enter the United States. In order to obtain permission from the U.S. government to sponsor individuals, employers must first attest that there are no workers in the United States who are "able, willing, qualified and available" for the same position.[27] However, these self-attestations are routinely approved without clear evidence that the employer sought out U.S. workers and are allowed at abusively low pay rates. Thus, the visa structure supports employers in the creation of what the workplace law scholar Leticia Saucedo has called "brown collar workplaces," in which high numbers of authorized and unauthorized migrant workers are funneled into the least desirable and most exploitative work.[28] It is not accidental that the very labor markets for which H-2A and H-2B visas are allowed are dominated by unauthorized migrant labor. Moreover, the visas only allow for temporary entry, meaning employers are in control of not only the initial ability to enter but subsequent entries as well and can "blacklist" employees that advocate for better working conditions while in the United States.[29] This employer control over long-term worker mobility reinforces worker subordination in these industries.

Shifting from an employer-sponsored system to a migrant self-sponsorship system would both recognize the dependence of the U.S. industries on migrant labor and better position these workers to control and improve the conditions in which they move and labor. To further protect workers from employer abuse, the new visa holders must be given the power to change employers inside the United States. Known in immigration law as "portability," the ability to change jobs within the same field is already a feature of visas allocated for work considered "professional."[30] Though self-sponsorship and portability may not be able to reverse all of the extractive relationships giving rise to worker subordination, it would provide a foundation for undoing key aspects of that subordination that are facilitated by the law. In a self-sponsorship system that accompanies the deregulation of border crossing, migrants would no longer have to go into debt to pay coyotes and traverse dangerous territory to reach their places of work. They would instead be able to arrive directly at U.S. ports of entry with visas. They would also be able to travel back and forth, relieving the enormous bouts of family separation that they and their families must now endure. In the United States, they would also have more power to confront employers who were engaging in exploitative practices and improve working conditions alongside U.S.-based workers, perhaps creating conditions for a wider and more powerful transnational labor movement. Moreover, worker control would constrain the ability of employers to blacklist workers who advocate for better working conditions while in the United States.[31] Extending portability to agricultural and other low-wage workers would place more power in the hands of workers to leave particularly exploitative employers and perhaps facilitate industry-wide improvements in working conditions. Thus, migrant self-sponsorship could not only actualize migration as choice, but in combination with the dismantling of the homeland security state and a redistribution of funds, it could lead to improved conditions for migrant communities along the lines contemplated by abolition democracy.

MIGRATION AS CHOICE AS REPARATIONS

Another lens through which to view the reallocation of resources and control over movement is the framework of reparations. In his seminal work on the abolition of slavery, W. E. B. Du Bois connected the concepts of abolition democracy, which identified the institutions that needed to be built and invested in to completely abolish slavery, to reparation as one of the mechanisms through which to make communities whole by securing resources from institutions that have done harm.[32] Reparation is distinguishable from abolition in its focus on compensating individuals or collectives of individuals rather than a focus on building and investing in particular kinds of alternative institutions. In the context of the migrant communities profiled, reparations could therefore theoretically offer redress for individuals like those in Tabasco who have not yet built alternative institutions, as well as offer resources for the institutions that have been built in Oaxaca, Puebla, and Tlaxcala.

Under international law, reparation is a set of legal remedies for past harms that includes restitution, compensation, and/or satisfaction awarded "singly or in combination."[33] Restitution is designed to restore the situation that existed before the harm was inflicted and can include remedies such as "release of persons wrongly detained or the return of property wrongly seized."[34] Compensation addresses financially assessable losses, "including loss of profits," where restitution is inadequate or unavailable.[35] Finally, satisfaction consists of the culpable state's "acknowledgement of the breach, an expression of regret, a formal apology or another appropriate modality."[36] To be eligible for any of the reparations remedies, the harm faced by individuals must rise to the level of a "gross violation of international human rights" or a "serious violation of international humanitarian law."[37] The threshold for these violations is high, making reparations claims in legal venues challenging.

Several claims have been made by Mexicans or Mexican Americans to seek redress for U.S. colonial exploits in Mexico, including for U.S. confiscation of land after the Spanish-American War,[38] U.S. and Mexican government failure to pay out a promised "savings plan" and indentured servitude of braceros,[39] the Trump-era U.S. family separation policy,[40] and the Mexican government's killing of Mexican citizens.[41] Legal scholars have also raised the possibility of bringing reparations claims for Mexican Americans whose land was expropriated when they were wrongfully deported in the 1930s.[42] None of these claims has resulted in a court ordering any of the reparations remedies to date, indicating that a formal legal claim by any of the migrant communities profiled may not result in restitution, compensation, or satisfaction. Even outside of formal legal claims, international actors have been reluctant to frame redistribution of resources as reparations. For example, the loss and damage fund established to distribute resources from the producers of climate change excludes liability or compensation that could be described as reparations.[43] However, even with these steep challenges, a legal claim could have important narrative implications that are part of a larger strategy to redistribute resources and support efforts to build abolition democracy.

Compensating Migrant Communities
through a Reparations Framework

Demands for compensation could be a useful way to identify particular institutions causing harm and argue that these institutions must compensate communities from whom they have extracted wealth. For example, in Chiltepec, Tabasco, multinational companies such as Halliburton, Shell, Exxon, and BP whose oil exploration and refinement decimated the local shrimp and oyster farms could be required to compensate communities that were dislocated by these practices and individuals like Serena. Similarly, the multinational clothing, automobile, and other companies that dislocated populations in Tlaxcala and other parts of Mexico could be required to compensate these communities for the loss of profits from local products such as Indigenous Tlaxcaltec textiles that resulted from policies that choked off investment to local industry in favor of foreign corporate investment. In the public sphere, FIOB's and CAFAMI's calls for the Mexican state to fully fund economic development projects and the health and education budgets could also be framed as claims for compensation of financially assessable resources (to the tune of at least $38 billion) pulled out of migrant communities or restitution of public spending to levels prior to neoliberalization. Though beyond the theoretical frames discussed in this book, Indigenous migrant community claims for compensation could go beyond the harms from neoliberalization to claims stemming from Spanish and early Mexican rule.

The harms caused by exploitative employers and carceral immigration enforcement efforts could also potentially be styled as reparation claims for compensation or at the very least satisfaction. For example, requiring U.S. state support for CAFAMI's efforts to repair the emotional loss of family disintegration, akin to claims made against former president Trump's family separation policy, could be one way of compensating for the harms caused by illegalized migration. Other, more direct claims could be made by individuals who have been subjected to detention, deportation, or exploitative labor practices. Even if these claims do not result in any of the legal remedies contemplated by reparation, they could help ground efforts to redistribute resources from corporate interests to community-based ones.

Self-Determined Migration as Reparations

Beyond financial compensation, the framework of reparations can be understood to include migration itself. Legal scholars have theorized that legalized migration for individuals can act as a form of reparation for harms they have faced from human-produced disasters such as "carbon capitalism,"[44] military invasion,[45] and other forms of destabilization.[46] Carmen Gonzalez has argued that migration as a form of reparation could be well suited to addressing the "the interrelated injustices of climate change and imperial intervention" including economic, political and military interventions that undermine the resilience of the Global South."[47] Relatedly, the international law scholar Tendayi Achiume has argued that migration from former colonized states to the centers of colonial power should be regarded as the "personal pursuit of enhanced self-determination" and therefore beyond the reach of migration controls.[48]

Migration as choice, in particular, its implementation as migrant self-sponsorship, could fit within these articulations of reparations. By moving away from the extractive privileging of employer preference and structures of exclusion which facilitate exploitation, migrant self-sponsorship could offer compensation in the form of stability and greater resources. Moreover, a program of self-sponsored migration could also provide satisfaction if accompanied by acknowledgment of the role played by U.S. policies in migrant dislocation and displacement into exploitative industries. Ultimately, migrant self-sponsorship would play a relatively small role in the larger picture of reparations or abolition democracy, which would require a more holistic redistribution of resources. However, this role could gain in importance as the realities of climate change affect a widening group of migrant communities.

REPLACING EXTRACTION WITH INVESTMENT

Whether through a lens of abolition democracy or reparations or both, migration as choice represents the ongoing work of migrant communities to move toward greater political and economic self-determination. Their work challenges understandings of economic growth, development politics, and the need for immigration enforcement. Making migration as choice a reality requires a radical transformation of the many interwoven policies and practices that make up migration as extraction, as that framework has been laid out in the preceding pages. Those include several existing configurations of both U.S. and Mexican policies that depress the economies in migrant communities, including policies that divest from agricultural supports, education funding, and other social programs and policies that shift responsibility for economic development from the Mexican state onto the backs of migrants and their families. They also include an interrelated set of institutions that profit from migrant exploitation and/or imprisonment, including U.S. employers who control methods of entering the United States and prefer unauthorized migrants and U.S. state and private institutions that profit from a militarized border, the criminalization of unlawful entry, and arrest, detention, and deportation of people in/from the interior of the country.

While these shifts may seem too overwhelming at first glance, migrant community organizing has already contributed to political shifts in Mexico (and the United States) that have redistributed some resources on an impressive scale given the current political and economic constraints. Indigenous migrant communities in particular have built democratic institutions that can be directly supported instead of filtering resource distribution through often-corrupt state actors. And the articulation of migration as choice can be actualized in the form of greater control over the conditions under which individuals migrate, both in terms of control over their legal status and their workplace conditions. As FIOB coordinator, Bernardo Ramirez Bautista, explained, "The right not to migrate is about public policy[,] . . . [which includes] social security including health care, a just salary, and a dwelling. It is [about] vindicating the right to decide what to use [our] land for and to allow [us] to self-govern." And while this is particularly poignant for Indigenous migrant communities who have long been denied self-governance, narratives from Tabasco, where Indigenous identity is not as strong, show that people are coming to the same conclusions about the need to organize at the local level to shift resources. The hard work of effecting public policy change through building institutions and experimenting with new strategies is already being done in migrant communities. What is left is for those efforts to be supported in ways that make migration as choice a reality.

INTRODUCTION

1. Until 2002, the agency responsible for immigration enforcement actions in the interior of the United States was the Immigration and Naturalization Service (INS). INS was reorganized and absorbed into the Department of Homeland Security as part of the Homeland Security Act of 2002. The former internal law enforcement operations of INS were transferred to Immigration Customs and Enforcement (ICE). Elfego never encountered agents from INS or ICE in the United States.

2. The Tlaxcaltec alliance with the Spanish has complex roots in preconquest politics. See Ixtlilxóchitl, *Obras Historicas*, vol. 2: *Historias Chichimeca* [Historical Works, vol. 2, Chichimec Stories] (Mexico City: Editorial Nacional, 1965); Jesús Monjarás-Ruiz, "Panorama general de la guerra entre los aztecas" [Overview of the War between the Aztecs], *Estudios de Cultura Náhuatl* 12 (1976): 241–64; Barry L. Isaac, "The Aztec 'Flowery War': A Geopolitical Explanation," *Journal of Anthropological Research* 39, no. 4 (1983): 415–32.

3. Jonathan Fox and Libby Haight, "Mexican Agricultural Policy: Multiple Goals and Conflicting Interests," in *Subsidizing Inequality: Mexican Corn Policy since NAFTA*, ed. Jonathan Fox and Libbby Haight (Washington, DC: Woodrow Wilson International Center for Scholars, 2010), 11–43.

4. Deborah A. Boehm, *Intimate Migrations: Gender, Family, and Illegality among Transnational Mexicans* (New York: New York University Press, 2012), 47; Katharine M. Donato et al., "A Glass Half Full? Gender in Migration Studies 1," *International Migration Review* 40, no. 1 (2006): 3–26; Pierrette Hondagneu-Sotelo, *Doméstica: Immigrant Workers Cleaning and Caring in the Shadows of Affluence* (Berkeley: University of California Press, 2007).

5. Kelly Lytle Hernández, *City of Inmates: Conquest, Rebellion, and the Rise of Human Caging in Los Angeles, 1771–1965* (Chapel Hill: University of North Carolina Press, 2017); Natalia Molina, *How Race Is Made in America: Immigration, Citizenship, and the Historical Power of Racial Scripts* (Berkeley: University of California Press, 2014), 29–34; Doug Keller,

"Re-Thinking Illegal Entry and Re-Entry," *Loyola University Chicago Law Journal* 44 (Fall 2012): 65–139.

6. Victor J. Oliveira, "Trends in Hired Farm Work Force 1945–1987" (Department of Agriculture, Economic Research Service, April 1989); Cristina Salinas, *Managed Migrations: Growers, Farmworkers, and Border Enforcement in the Twentieth Century* (Austin: University of Texas Press, 2018); Employment and Training Administration, "Findings from the National Agricultural Workers Survey (NAWS) 2019–2020: A Demographic and Employment Profile of United States Farmworkers (Research Report No. 16)" (U.S. Department of Labor, June 3, 2022); Hernández, *City of Inmates*, 138–39; U.S. Government Accounting Office, "Immigration Enforcement: Immigration Related Prosecutions Increase from 2017 to 2018 in Response to U.S. Attorney General's Direction" (Washington, DC, December 2019), https://www.gao.gov/assets/710/702965.pdf.

7. Kelly Lytle Hernández, "How Crossing the US-Mexico Border Became a Crime," The Conversation, April 30, 2017, 101, http://theconversation.com/how-crossing-the-us-mexico-border-became-a-crime-74604; Mae Ngai, *Impossible Subjects: Illegal Aliens and the Making of Modern America—Updated Edition* (Princeton, NJ: Princeton University Press, 2004), 67–71.

8. Luis Eduardo Guarnizo, "The Economics of Transnational Living," *International Migration Review* 37, no. 3 (2003): 666–99.

9. Rodolfo Zamora and Juan Padilla, "Zacatecas, migración y minería: El etractivismo como ilusión del desarrollo" [Zacatecas, Migration, and Mining: Extractivism as an Illusion of Development], in *México en la trampa del financiamiento: El sendero del no desarollo* [Mexico in the Financing Trap: The Path of Non-Development] (Mexico City: Universidad Nacional Autónoma de México, 2013), 169.

10. Leisy J. Abrego, *Sacrificing Families: Navigating Laws, Labor, and Love across Borders* (Stanford: Stanford University Press, 2014); Boehm, *Intimate Migrations*.

11. Abigail Leslie Andrews, *Undocumented Politics: Place, Gender, and the Pathways of Mexican Migrants* (Berkeley: University of California Press, 2018); David Bacon, *The Right to Stay Home: How U.S. Policy Drives Mexican Migration* (Boston: Beacon Press, 2013); Gaspar Rivera Salgado and Jonathan Fox, eds., *Indigenous Mexican Migrants in the United States* (La Jolla: University of California, San Diego, Center for U.S.-Mexican Studies and Center for Comparative Immigration Studies, 2004).

12. Andrews, *Undocumented Politics*; Bacon, *The Right to Stay Home*; Centolia Maldonado Vásquez and Patricia Artía Rodriguez, "'Now We Are Awake': Women's Political Participation in the Oaxacan Indigenous Binational Front," in Fox and Rivera Salgado, *Indigenous Mexican Migrants in the United States*, 1–47; María Cristina Velásquez, "Migrant Communities, Gender and Political Power in Oaxaca," in Fox and Rivera Salgado, *Indigenous Mexican Migrants in the United States*, 1–47.

13. This is akin to what the feminist scholar Veronica Gago describes as *cuerpo-territorio* (body-territory). See Verónica Gago, *La potencia feminista; O el deseo de cambiarlo todo* [The Feminist Power; Or the Desire to Change Everything] (Madrid: Traficantes de Sueños, 2019), 79.

14. Edwin Lopez, "Migration as Resistance to Global Capitalism: From Cause to Action in the Migration of Central American Children to the United States," *Perspectives on Global Development and Technology* 16, no. 1–3 (Summer 2014): 34–59; Tayyub Mahmud,

"Migration, Identity and the Colonial Encounter," *Oregon Law Review* 76 (Fall 1997): 657–59; E. Tendayi Achiume, "Migration as Decolonization," *Stanford Law Review* 71 (2019): 1509–74; Carmen G. Gonzalez, "Migration as Reparation: Climate Change and the Disruption of Borders," *Loyola Law Review* 66 (Summer 2020): 401–44.

15. Achiume, "Migration as Decolonization," 1552.

16. Gonzalez, "Migration as Reparation," 493.

17. Achiume, "Migration as Decolonization," 1547.

18. Gonzalez, "Migration as Reparation," 414.

19. Saskia Sassen, *The Mobility of Labor and Capital: A Study in International Investment and Labor Flow* (Cambridge: Cambridge University Press, 1988); Douglas Massey, Jorge Durand, and Nolan J. Malone, *Beyond Smoke and Mirrors: Mexican Immigration in an Era of Economic Integration* (New York: Russell Sage Foundation, 2002); Gilbert G. González and Raúl Fernández, *A Century of Chicano History: Empire, Nations and Migration* (New York: Routledge, 2003).

20. Kelly Lytle Hernández, *Migra! A History of the U.S. Border Patrol* (Berkeley: University of California Press, 2010), 29, 55–57, 72; S. Deborah Kang, *The INS on the Line: Making Immigration Law on the US-Mexico Border, 1917–1954* (New York: Oxford University Press, 2017), 20–35; Joseph Nevins, *Operation Gatekeeper: The Rise of the "Illegal Alien" and the Making of the U.S.-Mexico Boundary* (New York: Routledge, 2002), 28, 35–36; Patrick Ettinger, *Imaginary Lines: Border Enforcement and the Origins of Undocumented Immigration 1882–1930* (Austin: University of Texas Press, 2009), 121–22; Ngai, *Impossible Subjects*; Kitty Calavita, *Inside the State: The Bracero Program, Immigration and the I.N.S.* (New York: Routledge, 1992); Timothy J. Dunn, *The Militarization of the U.S.-Mexico Border 1978–1992: Low Intensity Conflict Doctrine Comes Home* (Austin: Center for Mexican American Studies, University of Texas at Austin, 1996), 17.

21. Ngai, *Impossible Subjects*; Calavita, *Inside the State*.

22. Yolanda Vázquez, "Constructing Crimmigration: Latino Subordination in a 'Post-Racial' World," *Ohio State Law Journal* 76 (2015): 599–657; Kevin Johnson, "The Case against Race Profiling in Immigration Enforcement," *Washington University Law Quarterly* 78 (2000): 680–735; Keller, "Re-Thinking Illegal Entry and Re-Entry"; Tanya Maria Golash-Boza, *Deported: Immigrant Policing, Disposable Labor, and Global Capitalism* (New York: New York University Press, 2015); Nicholas P. De Genova, "Migrant 'Illegality' and Deportability in Everyday Life," *Annual Review of Anthropology* 31 (2002): 419–47.

23. Raúl Delgado Wise and Oscar Mañan Garcia, "Migración México–Estados Unidos e Integración Económica" [Mexico-U.S. Migration and Economic Integration], *Política y Cultura* 23 (n.d.): 9–23; Raúl Delgado Wise and Humberto Márquez Covarrubias, "Migration and Development in Mexico: Toward a New Analytical Approach," *Journal of Latino/Latin American Studies* 2, no. 3 (April 2007): 101–19; Raúl Delgado Wise and Humberto Márquez Covarrubias, "Capitalist Restructuring, Development and Labour Migration: The Mexico-US Case," *Third World Quarterly* 29, no. 7 (2008): 1359–74; Zamora and Padilla, "Zacatecas, migración y minería."

24. Cedric J. Robinson, *Black Marxism: The Making of the Black Radical Tradition* (repr. Chapel Hill: University of North Carolina Press, 2000).

25. Robinson, *Black Marxism*, 59.

26. Alfonso Gonzales, *Reform without Justice: Latino Migrant Politics and the Homeland Security State* (Oxford: Oxford University Press, 2013), 13; Nicholas De Genova, "The Production of Culprits: From Deportability to Detainability in the Aftermath of 'Homeland Security,'" *Citizenship Studies* 11, no. 5 (November 1, 2007): 421–48, https://doi.org/10.1080/13621020701605735.

27. Saskia Sassen, *Expulsions: Brutality and Complexity in the Global Economy* (Cambridge, MA: Harvard University Press, 2014); Golash-Boza, *Deported*; Jamie Longazel and Miranda Cady Hallett, *Migration and Mortality: Social Death, Dispossession, and Survival in the Americas* (Philadelphia: Temple University Press, 2021); Cecilia Menjívar and Leisy Abrego, "Legal Violence: Immigration Law and the Lives of Central American Immigrants," *American Journal of Sociology* 117, no. 5 (2012): 1380–1421.

28. González and Fernández, *A Century of Chicano History*.

29. Raúl Delgado Wise and Henry Veltmeyer, *Agrarian Change, Migration and Development*, Agrarian Change and Peasant Studies (Black Point, Nova Scotia: Fernwood Publishing, 2016), 124–34; González and Fernández, *A Century of Chicano History*, 124–39, 182.

30. Gago, *La potencia feminista*; Zamora and Padilla, "Zacatecas, migración y minería"; Mina Lorena Navarro, "Luchas por lo común contra el renovado cercamiento de bienes naturales en México" [Fight for the Commons against the Renewed Enclosure of Natural Resources in Mexico], *Bajo el Volcán*, no. 21 (2013).

31. Navarro, "Luchas por lo común," 163–64.

32. Gago, *La potencia feminista*, 78.

33. Zamora and Padilla, "Zacatecas, migración y minería," 159.

34. Zamora and Padilla, "Zacatecas, migración y minería," 169.

35. Abrego, *Sacrificing Families*; Boehm, *Intimate Migrations*.

36. Delgado Wise and Veltmeyer, *Agrarian Change, Migration and Development*; Stephen Castles and Raúl Delgado Wise, eds., *Migration and Development: Perspectives from the South* (Geneva: International Organization for Migration, 2008).

37. Gilbert G. González and Raúl Fernández, "Empire and the Origins of Twentieth-Century Migration from Mexico to the United States," *Pacific Historical Review* 71, no. 1 (2002): 19–57; González and Fernández, *A Century of Chicano History*.

38. González and Fernández, "Empire and the Origins of Twentieth-Century Migration from Mexico to the United States," 41; Miguel Tinker Salas, *In the Shadow of the Eagles: Sonora and the Transformation of the Border during the Porfiriato* (Berkeley: University of California Press, 1997), 102–26, 176–200.

39. Arthur Corwin, *Immigrants—and Immigrants: Perspectives on Mexican Labor Migration to the United States* (Westport, CT: Greenwood Press, 1978), 178–79.

40. David G. Gutiérrez, *Walls and Mirrors: Mexican Americans, Mexican Immigrants, and the Politics of Ethnicity* (Berkeley: University of California Press, 1995), 46–47; Molina, *How Race Is Made in America*, 29; Ettinger, *Imaginary Lines*, 161.

41. Dunn, *Militarization of the U.S.-Mexico Border*; Kevin R. Johnson, "Race, the Immigration Laws and Domestic Race Relations: A 'Magic Mirror' into the Heart of Darkness," *Indiana Law Journal* 73 (1998): 1136–40; Ngai, *Impossible Subjects*; Vázquez, "Constructing Crimmigration," 617–22.

42. Adam Goodman, *The Deportation Machine: America's Long History of Expelling Immigrants* (Princeton, NJ: Princeton University Press, 2020), 46.

43. Alexandra Délano, *Mexico and Its Diaspora in the United States: Policies of Emigration since 1848* (Cambridge: Cambridge University Press, 2011), 88–90.

44. Délano, *Mexico and Its Diaspora in the United States*, 98.

45. Manuel García y Griego and Monica Verea, *Mexico y Estados Unidos frente a la migración de los indocumentados* [Mexico and the United States versus the Migration of the Undocumented] (Mexico City: UNAM/Porrúa, 1988).

46. De Genova, "The Production of Culprits."

47. Gonzales, *Reform without Justice*, 13.

48. Castles and Delgado Wise, *Migration and Development*; Delgado Wise and Veltmeyer, *Agrarian Change, Migration and Development*.

49. Raúl Delgado Wise and Humberto Marquez Covarrubias, "The Mexico-United States Migratory System: Dilemmas of Regional Integration, Development and Emigration," in Castles and Delgado Wise, *Migration and Development*, 129.

50. Clare Ribando Seelke, "Mexico: Background and U.S. Relations" (Congressional Research Service, Washington, DC, December 2020), 12.

51. Harald Bauder, "The Possibilities of Open and No Borders," *Social Justice* 39, no. 4 (2012): 86.

52. The most common legal claims my clinic made were those for cancellation of removal (8 U.S.C. §1229b), asylum (8 U.S.C. §1208), and adjustment of status (8 U.S.C. 1255). Asylum claims explicitly require a showing of noneconomic harm (rising to the level of persecution), but often cancellation and adjustment claims require arguments about harm to offset any negative factors such as a criminal history. Even in those claims, legal rules favored a showing of noneconomic harm.

53. Many Indigenous groups in Mexico view themselves as separate ethnic groups, and for many, Spanish is a second language. Of the groups interviewed for this project, this view was most prominent among the Mixtec of Oaxaca. Though I did not need to use an interpreter for any of the interviews, I did need interpretation of community meetings, which were conducted in *mixteca baja*.

54. This is in part due to the gendered pattern of migration that seems to have emerged at the turn of the twenty-first century.

55. Laila Hlass and Lindsay Harris, "Critical Interviewing," *Utah Law Review* 3 (October 1, 2021), https://doi.org/10.26054/0d-8c1z-7z3s.

1. DISLOCATION

1. Francisco Alba, "Mexico's International Migration as a Manifestation of Its Development Pattern," *International Migration Review* 14, no. 4 (1978): 503–13; Saskia Sassen, *The Mobility of Labor and Capital: A Study in International Investment and Labor Flow* (Cambridge: Cambridge University Press, 1988); Alejandro Portes, "Neoliberalism and the Sociology of Development: Emerging Trends and Unanticipated Facts," *Population and Development Review* 23, no. 2 (1997): 229–59; Douglas S. Massey, Jorge Durand, and Nolan Malone, *Beyond Smoke and Mirrors: Mexican Immigration in an Era of Economic Integration* (New York: Russell Sage Foundation, 2002); Armando Bartra, *Cosechas de ira: Economía política de la contrarreforma agraria* [Harvest of Going: The Political Economy of the Agragrian Counterreform] (Mexico City: Itaca/Instituto Maya, 2003); Gilbert G.

González and Raúl Fernández, *A Century of Chicano History: Empire, Nations and Migration* (New York: Routledge, 2003); Raúl Delgado Wise and Humberto Márquez Covarrubias, "Capitalist Restructuring, Development and Labour Migration: The Mexico-US Case," *Third World Quarterly* 29, no. 7 (2008): 1359–74; Stephen Castles and Raúl Delgado Wise, eds., *Migration and Development: Perspectives from the South* (Geneva: International Organization for Migration, 2008); Bill Ong Hing, *Ethical Borders: NAFTA, Globalization, and Mexican Migration* (Philadelphia: Temple University Press, 2010); Gerald López, "Don't We Like Them Illegal?," *UC Davis Law Review* 45 (July 2012): 1711–1816; Tanya Maria Golash-Boza, *Deported: Immigrant Policing, Disposable Labor, and Global Capitalism* (New York: New York University Press, 2015).

2. González and Fernández, *A Century of Chicano History*; Gilbert G. González and Raúl Fernández, "Empire and the Origins of Twentieth-Century Migration from Mexico to the United States," *Pacific Historical Review* 71, no. 1 (2002): 19–57.

3. Delgado Wise and Márquez Covarrubias, "Capitalist Restructuring, Development and Labour Migration," 1360.

4. Golash-Boza, *Deported*, 2–5.

5. Golash-Boza, *Deported*, 16.

6. Instituto Nacional de Estadística y Geografía (INEGI), "Población de 3 años y mas por municipio, sexo y grupo quinquenales de edad según condición de habla indígena y de habla española" [Population 3 Years of Age and Older by City, Sex, and Five-Year Age Group according to Indigenous-Speaking and Spanish-Speaking Status], 2010, https://www.inegi .org.mx/contenidos/programas/ccpv/2010/tabulados/Basico/05_01B_MUNICIPAL_27.pdf.

7. Instituto Nacional de Estadística y Geografía (INEGI), "Información por entidad: Número de habitantes: Oaxaca" [Information by State: Population: Oaxaca], 2010, http:// cuentame.inegi.org.mx/monografias/informacion/oax/poblacion/default.aspx?tema =me&e=20. But note that this number may be an undercount as there are persons who identify as Indigenous but do not speak an Indigenous language.

8. José Aurelio Granados Alcantar and María Félix Quezada Ramírez, "Tendencias de la migración interna de la población indígena en México, 1990–2015 / Trends in Internal Migration among the Indigenous Population in Mexico, 1990–2015," *Estudios Demográficos y Urbanos* 33, no. 2 (2018): 337, table 1.

9. Juan Maldonado Montalvo and Adrián González Romo, "Factores determinantes en la migración de las familias indígena de San Fransisco de Tetlanohcan y sus conseqencias implicitas" [Determining Factors in the Migration of Indigenous Families from San Fransisco de Tetlanohcan and Their Implicit Consequences], in *La migración de Tlaxcaltecas en Estados Unidos y Canadá: Panorama actual y perspectivas* [Migration of Tlaxcaltecs in the United States and Canada: Contemporary Outlook and Perspectives], ed. Raúl Jimenez Guillén and Adrián González Romo (San Pablo Apetatitlán: El Colegio de Tlaxcala, 2008), 212.

10. Instituto Nacional de Estadística y Geografía (INEGI), "Encuesta nacional de dinámica demográfica 2009 Microdatos" [National Survey of Demographic Dynamics Microdata Tables 2009], 2010, 81, https://www.inegi.org.mx/programas/enadid/2009/default .html#Microdatos.

11. Instituto Nacional de Estadística y Geografía, "Encuesta nacional de dinámica demográfica 2009 Microdatos," 201.

12. Centro de Información Estadística y Documental para el Desarrollo, "Carpeta regional: Mixteca información estadística y geografía básica" [Regional Folder: Mixteca Basic Statistical and Geographical Information], 2011, 23.

13. Secretaría de Desarollo Social, "Catálogo de localidades—Tlaxcala" [Catalog of Localities—Tlaxcala], 2010, http://www.microrregiones.gob.mx/catloc/Default.aspx?tipo =clave&campo=mun&valor=29.

14. Secretaría de Desarollo Social, "Catálogo de localidades—Tlaxcala."

15. Instituto Nactional de Estadística y Geografía, "Encuesta nacional de dinámica demográfica 2009 Microdatos."

16. Statistics on Tabasco were taken from INEGI; available online at http://www.micror regiones.gob.mx/catloc/LocdeMun.aspx?tipo=clave&campo=loc&ent=27&mun=010.

17. Jaime Santiago Méndez, "10 de los municipios más pobres según la SEDESOL, son de la Mixteca" [10 of the Poorest Municipalities in the SEDESOL Are in the Mixteca], August 15, 2009.

18. Michael Kearney, *Changing Fields of Anthropology: From Local to Global* (Lanham, MD: Rowman & Littlefield, 2004), 195.

19. Enrique Astorga Lira and Simon Commander, "Agricultural Commercialisation and the Growth of a Migrant Labour Market in Mexico," *International Labour Review* 128, no. 6 (1989): 771.

20. Gary Thompson, Ricardo Amon, and Philip L. Martin, "Agricultural Development and Emigration: Rhetoric and Reality," *International Migration Review* 20, no. 3 (1986): 577.

21. Astorga Lira and Commander, "Agricultural Commercialisation and the Growth of a Migrant Labour Market," 775.

22. Christine Bolling and Constanza Valdes, "The U.S. Presence in Mexico's Agribusiness," Foreign Agricultural Economic Report (Economic Research Service, Washington, DC, 1994), 4.

23. Carol Zabin and Sallie Hughes, "Economic Integration and Labor Flows: Stage Migration in Farm Labor Markets in Mexico and the United States," *International Migration Review* 29, no. 2 (1995): 401; Thompson, Amon, and Martin, "Agricultural Development and Emigration," 588.

24. Andreas F. Lowenfeld, "The International Monetary System: A Look Back over Seven Decades," *Journal of International Economic Law* 1, no. 5–6 (2010): 13–14.

25. Lowenfeld, "International Monetary System," 14.

26. Lowenfeld, "International Monetary System," 14.

27. Carlos Heredia and Mary Purcell, "Structural Adjustment in Mexico," last modified 1995, http://www.hartford-hwp.com/archives/46/013.html.

28. Lowenfeld, "International Monetary System," 6.

29. Lowenfeld, "International Monetary System," 6; Ngaire Woods, *The Globalizers: the IMF, the World Bank, and Their Borrowers* (Ithaca, NY: Cornell University Press, 2006), 65–83.

30. Ngaire Woods, "The United States and the International Financial Institutions: Power and Influence within the World Bank and the IMF," in *US Hegemony and International Organizations,* ed. Rosemary Foot, Neil McFarlane, and Michael Mastanduno (Oxford: Oxford University Press, 2003), 94 ("The IMF *is* the United States"; emphasis in original); Woods, *The Globalizers,* 15; Axel Dreher and Nathan M. Jensen, "Independent

Actor or Agent? An Empirical Analysis of the Impact of U.S. Interests on the International Monetary Fund Conditions," *Journal of Law and Economics* 50 (2008): 105, 111; Lowenfeld, "International Monetary System," 6.

31. Marilyn Gates, *In Default: Peasants, the Debt Crisis, and the Agricultural Challenge in Mexico*, (Boulder, CO: Westview Press,1993), 8.

32. See Minutes of IMF Executive Board Meeting, July 30, 1984, IMF Doc # EMB 84/117 at p. 42. Library of Congress.

33. Mexico, Letter of Intent, July 22, 1986, from Gustavo Petricioli, Secretary of Finance and Public Credit of Mexico, to Jacques de Larosiere, Managing Director, International Monetary Fund, Repository no. 95934, vol. 1, pp. 4–5. The reduction in the number of public entities between 1982 and 1986 was startling. In 1982, there were some 1,155 public entities in Mexico. Four years later, that number was reduced by nearly half, leaving only 697 public entities by the middle of 1986 (p. 5, par. 10). CONASUPO was specifically mentioned, and the Mexican government indicated that it had been reorganized and its subsidies "rationed." The letter also indicated that preferential lending by development banks and official trust funds would be limited to individuals "involved in high priority activities" (p. 6). The letter also indicates that the government will continue to liberalize trade and move toward an export growth model (p. 8). Throughout the letter, reference is made to the devaluation in oil prices and the effect it had on the Mexican government's ability to service its debt (see esp. pp. 9–11, par. 20).

34. Diana Alarcón González, *Changes in the Distribution of Income in Mexico and Trade Liberalization* (Tijuana: El Colegio de la Frontera Norte, 1994), 75.

35. Nora Lustig, *Mexico: The Remaking of an Economy*, 2nd ed. (Washington, DC: Brookings Institution Press, 1998), 205–8.

36. Lustig, *Mexico*, 74–75.

37. Mexico, Letter of Intent, March 24, 1985, at p. 2 (on file with author); George A. Collier and Elizabeth Lowry Quaratiello, *Basta! Land and the Zapatista Rebellion* (Oakland, CA: First Food Banks, 2005), 88.

38. Thomas J. Kelly, "Neoliberal Reforms and Rural Poverty," *Latin American Perspectives* 28, no. 3 (2001): 90.

39. Antonio Yúnez-Naude and Fernando Barceinas Paredes, "The Reshaping of Agricultural Policy in Mexico," in *Changing Structure of Mexico*, 2nd ed., ed. Laura Randall (New York: Routledge, 2006), 223, https://doi.org/10.4324/9781315705859-23.

40. Kelly, "Neoliberal Reforms and Rural Poverty," 90.

41. Kelly, "Neoliberal Reforms and Rural Poverty," 90.

42. Darcy Victor Tetreault, "Alternative Pathways out of Rural Poverty in Mexico," *Revista Europea de Estudios Latinoamericanos y del Caribe / European Review of Latin American and Caribbean Studies*, no. 88 (2010): 81.

43. Duncan Green, *Silent Revolution: The Rise and Crisis of Market Economics in Latin America*, 2nd ed. (New York: New York University Press, 2003), 98.

44. Gerardo Otero, *Neoliberalism Revisited: Economic Restructuring and Mexico's Political Future* (New York: Routledge, 2018).

45. Laura G. Dávila Larránga, "How Does Propsera Work? Best Practices in the Implementation of Conditional Cash Transfer Programs in Latin America and the Caribbean," last modified April 2016, https://publications.iadb.org/publications/english/document/How

-does-Prospera-Work-Best-Practices-in-the-Implementation-of-Conditional-Cash
-Transfer-Programs-in-Latin-America-and-the-Caribbean.pdf.

46. Miguel Niño-Zarazúa, "Mexico's Progreso-Oportunidades and the Emergence of Social Assistance in Latin America," Munich Personal RePec Archive Paper No. 29639, https://mpra.ub.uni-muenchen.de/29639/, posted March 2011.

47. Niño-Zarazúa, "Mexico's Progreso-Oportunidades."

48. Niño-Zarazúa, "Mexico's Progreso-Oportunidades."

49. Mark Weisbrot, Lara Merling, Vitor Mello, Stephan Lefebvre, and Joseph Sammut, "Did NAFTA Help Mexico? An Update after 23 Years," last modified March 2017, https://cepr.net/images/stories/reports/nafta-mexico-update-2017–03.pdf?v=2, 9.

50. Instituto Nacional de Estadística y Geografía Instituto Nacional de Estadística y Geografía (INEG), "Encuesta nacional de la dinámica demográfica 1997: Panorama sociodemográfico. Estados Unidos Mexicanos" [National Survey of Demographic Dynamics: Sociodemographic View 1997. United Mexican States], 71, https://www.inegi.org.mx/app/biblioteca/ficha.html?upc=702825493691; Instituto Nacional de Estadística y Geografía Instituto Nacional de Estadística y Geografía (INEGI), "Modulo sobre migración encuesta nacional de empleo 2002" [Module on Migration National Survey of Employment 2002]; Instituto Nacional de Estadística y Geografía, "Encuesta nacional de dinámica demográfica 2009 microdatos."

51. Consejo Nacional de Población, "Intensidad migratoria a nivel estatal y municipal" [Migration Intensity at the State and Municipal Levels], 2010, 31–32, http://www.conapo.gob.mx/work/models/CONAPO/intensidad_migratoria/pdf/IIM_Estatal_y_Municipal.pdf.

52. Gary Clyde Hufbauer and Jeffrey J. Schott, *NAFTA: An Assessment* (Washington, DC: Peterson Institute for International Economics, 1993); Bolling and Valdes, "The U.S. Presence in Mexico's Agribusiness."

53. Lawrence Douglas Taylor Hansen, "The Origins of the Maquila Industry in Mexico," *Comercio Exterior* 53, no. 11 (n.d.): 12.

54. Mario M. Carrillo Huerta, "The Impact of Maquiladoras on Migration in Mexico," in *The Effects of Receiving Country Policies on Migration Flows*, ed. Sergio Diaz-Briquets and Sidney Weintraub (Boulder, CO: Westview Press, 1991), 75, https://doi.org/10.4324/9780429310393-4.

55. Raúl Vázquez-López, "The Transformation of the Textile and Apparel Sector after NAFTA," *Journal of International Business and Economy* (2014): 89, https://doi.org/10.1007/978-3-030-55265-7_4.

56. Rogelio Ramírez de la O, "Economic Outlook in the 1990s: Mexico," in *U.S-Mexican Industrial Integration: The Road to Free Trade*, ed. Sidney Weintraub, Luis Rubio, and A. D. Jones (Boulder, CO: Westview Press, 1991), 2–32.

57. Jose A. Alonso, "Efectos del TLCAN en la microindustria del vestido en Tlaxcala" [Effects of NAFTA on the Micro-Industry of Clothing in Tlaxcala], *Comercio Exterior* (1997): 107.

58. Judi A. Kessler, "The North American Free Trade Agreement, Emerging Apparel Production Networks, and Industrial Upgrading: The Southern California/Mexico Connection," *Review of International Political Economy* 6, no. 4 (1999): 577–78.

59. Consejo Nacional de Población, "Intensidad migratoria a nivel estatal y municipal," 31–32. Note that this includes all three categories of migrants counted by CONAPO:

emigrants, circular migrants, and return migrants. All three groups left the state of Tlaxcala during this period but are differentiated based on whether they remained in the United States, migrated back and forth, or returned permanently to Tlaxcala.

60. Manuel Pastor and Carol Wise, "State Policy, Distribution, and Neoliberal Reform in Mexico," *Journal of Latin American Studies* 29, no. 2 (1997): 434.

61. Vázquez-López, "The Transformation of the Textile and Apparel Sector after NAFTA," 89.

62. Raúl Delgado Wise and Humberto Márquez Covarrubias, "Migration and Development in Mexico: Toward a New Analytical Approach," *Journal of Latino/Latin American Studies* 2, no. 3 (April 2007): 106, https://doi.org/10.18085/llas.2.3.2545272831756836.

63. Michal Kohout, "The Maquiladora Industry and Migration in Mexico: A Survey of Literature," *Geography Compass* 3, no. 1 (2009): 137, https://doi.org/10.1111/j.1749-8198.2008.00199.x.

64. Kohout, "The Maquiladora Industry and Migration in Mexico," 140.

65. Kohout, "The Maquiladora Industry and Migration in Mexico," 140.

66. Aylin Topal, *Boosting Competitiveness through Decentralization: Subnational Comparison of Local Development in Mexico* (Farnham: Ashgate, 2012), 79.

67. Topal, *Boosting Competitiveness*, 79.

68. Topal, *Boosting Competitiveness*, 80.

69. Interview with Delegado José Luis Sánchez Dominguez of Chiltepec, January 2013.

70. Topal, *Boosting Competitiveness*, 80

71. Mexico, Letter of Intent (on file with author), March 24, 1985, 2–3 (hereafter 1985 LOI). In describing the reforms undertaken, Jesus Silva-Herzog, secretary of finance and public credit, indicated that "particular emphasis was given to the objectives of curbing inflation while reducing reliance on foreign financing" and that "[inflation] is at this time the most serious and pressing problem facing [Mexico]" (indicating that wage deflation would need to be considered as a way to offset inflation). Minutes of International Monetary Fund Executive Board Meeting, March 2, 1984, 84/35, 16 (hereafter Minutes 84/35).

72. Alejandro Álvarez Bejar, "Tribute to Alonso Aguilar Monteverde: Ten Key Policies for Understanding the Neoliberal Transformation of Mexican Capitalism," *Social Justice* 42, no. 1 (2015): 109.

73. Minutes 84/35, 8 (cheering the cooperation of labor unions to keep wage demands down and the resulting effect on inflation).

74. Minutes 84/35, 21, 23–24.

75. 1985 LOI, 7.

76. Timothy A. Canova, "Banking and Financial Reform at the Crossroads of the Neoliberal Contagion," *American University Journal of International Law and Policy* 14 (1999): 1571, 1590–93; Timothy Canova, "Global Finance and the International Monetary Fund's Neoliberal Agenda: The Threat to Employment, Ethnic Identity and Cultural Pluralism of Latina/o Identities," *UC Davis Law Review* 33 (2000): 1547, 1554–55, 1558–59, 1565.

77. See, e.g., Collier and Quaratiello, *Land and the Zapatista Rebellion*, 91–124 (describing the different effects structural adjustment had on the poor and middle class in Zincantán, Chiapas, depending in large part on their access to nonfarm wage labor)

78. Canova, "Neoliberal Contagion," 1590–93; Canova, "Ethnic Identity and Cultural Pluralism," 1554–65; Collier and Quaratiello, *Land and the Zapatista Rebellion*, 116–24.

79. Lustig, *Mexico*, 66–67.

80. Lustig, *Mexico*, 68–69, table 3-2.

81. Lustig, *Mexico*, 68–69, table 3-2.

82. Lustig, *Mexico*, 74.

83. Lustig, *Mexico*, 74.

84. Bejar, "Tribute to Alonso Aguilar Monteverde," 109.

85. Hansen, "The Origins of the Maquila Industry in Mexico," 15.

86. Weisbrot et al., "Did NAFTA Help Mexico?," 11, fig. 7.

87. Weisbrot et al., "Did NAFTA Help Mexico?," 11.

88. Lustig, *Mexico*, 79.

89. Paul Streeten, *First Things First: Meeting Basic Human Needs in the Developing Countries* (Oxford: Oxford University Press, 1981), viii.

90. Inés Castro, "El pragmatismo neoliberal y las desigualdades educativas en América Latina" [Neoliberal Pragmatism and Educational Inequalities in Latin America], *Revista Mexicana de Sociología* 59, no. 3 (1997): 189–205.

91. Lustig, *Mexico*, 89.

92. Eric Roach, "Education in Mexico," *World Education News and Review*, May 23, 2019, https://wenr.wes.org/2019/05/education-in-mexico-2.

93. Pablo Latapí Sarre, *Un siglo de educación en México* [A Century of Education in Mexico] (Mexico City: Fondo de Estudios e Investigaciones Ricardo J. Zevada, Consejo Nacional para la Cultura y las Artes, Fondo de Cultura Económica, 1998), 32–33, 39–40; Alec Ian Gershberg, "Decentralization Process in Mexico and Nicaragua: Legislative vs. Ministry Led Reforms Strategies," *Comparative Education* 35, no. 1 (March 1999): 63–90.

94. Roach, "Education in Mexico."

95. M. Laura Velasco Ortiz, *Mixtec Transnational Identity* (Tucson: University of Arizona Press, 2005), 32.

96. Kearney, *Changing Fields of Anthropology.*

97. Roach, "Education in Mexico."

98. Roach, "Education in Mexico"; Castro, "El pragmatismo neoliberal y las desigualdades educativas en América Latina."

99. "Mojado" is a very derogatory term when used by government officials or outsiders, but here it was used by migrants as a way of reclaiming the derision of undocumented journeys.

100. Emily Ryo, "Deciding to Cross: Norms and Economics of Unauthorized Migration," *American Sociological Review* 78, no. 4 (2013): 578.

2. DISPLACEMENT

1. Yolanda Vázquez, "Constructing Crimmigration: Latino Subordination in a 'Post-Racial' World," *Ohio State Law Journal* 76 (2015): 599–657; Kevin Johnson, "The Case against Race Profiling in Immigration Enforcement," *Washington University Law Quarterly* 78 (2000): 680–735; George J. Sánchez, *Becoming Mexican American: Ethnicity, Culture, and Identity in Chicano Los Angeles, 1900–1945* (New York: Oxford University Press, 1995); Mae Ngai, *Impossible Subjects: Illegal Aliens and the Making of Modern America—Updated Edition* (Princeton, NJ: Princeton University Press, 2004), 6–9; Kelly Lytle Hernández,

Migra! A History of the U.S. Border Patrol (Berkeley: University of California Press, 2010), 10; Joseph Nevins, *Operation Gatekeeper: The Rise of the "Illegal Alien" and the Making of the U.S.-Mexico Boundary* (New York: Routledge, 2002); Nicholas P. De Genova, "Migrant 'Illegality' and Deportability in Everyday Life," *Annual Review of Anthropology* 31 (2002): 419–47.

2. Timothy J. Dunn, *The Militarization of the U.S.-Mexico Border 1978–1992: Low Intensity Conflict Doctrine Comes Home* (Austin: Center for Mexican American Studies, University of Texas at Austin, 1996), 158–60, 189–90; Gilbert G. González, *Guest Workers or Colonized Labor? Mexican Labor Migration to the United States* (Boulder, CO: Paradigm Press, 2013).

3. Tanya Maria Golash-Boza, *Deported: Immigrant Policing, Disposable Labor, and Global Capitalism* (New York: New York University Press, 2015); Harsha Walia, *Border and Rule: Global Migration, Capitalism and the Rise of Racist Nationalism* (Boston: Haymarket Books, 2020); Gargi Bhattacharyya, *Rethinking Racial Capitalism: Questions of Reproduction and Survival* (London: Rowman & Littlefield, 2018).

4. Saskia Sassen, *The Mobility of Labor and Capital: A Study in International Investment and Labor Flow* (Cambridge: Cambridge University Press, 1988); Kitty Calavita, *Inside the State: The Bracero Program, Immigration and the I.N.S.* (New York: Routledge, 1992); Dunn, *Militarization of the U.S.-Mexico Border*; Ngai, *Impossible Subjects*.

5. David G. Gutiérrez, *Walls and Mirrors: Mexican Americans, Mexican Immigrants, and the Politics of Ethnicity* (Berkeley: University of California Press, 1995), 46–47; Natalia Molina, *How Race Is Made in America: Immigration, Citizenship, and the Historical Power of Racial Scripts* (Berkeley: University of California Press, 2014), 29; Patrick Ettinger, *Imaginary Lines: Border Enforcement and the Origins of Undocumented Immigration 1882–1930* (Austin: University of Texas Press, 2009), 161.

6. Manuel Gamio, "The Songs of the Immigrant, Chapter VII," in *Mexican Immigration to the United States: A Study of Human Migration and Adjustment* (Chicago: University of Chicago Press, 1930): 1:86–87.

7. Translation in the original text.

8. Waivers were also granted for work laying railroad ties, another industry that had previously relied on imported Asian labor.

9. Rodolfo Acuña, *Occupied America: The Chicano's Struggle toward Liberation* (San Francisco: Canfield Press, 1972).

10. Acuña, *Occupied America*, 136; Ettinger, *Imaginary Lines*, 161–62; Gutiérrez, *Walls and Mirrors*, 46; Ngai, *Impossible Subjects*, 50–55; Hernandez, *Migra!*, 29–32.

11. Douglas Massey, Jorge Durand, and Nolan J. Malone, *Beyond Smoke and Mirrors: Mexican Immigration in an Era of Economic Integration* (New York: Russell Sage Foundation, 2002), 35.

12. It is important to note that all of the braceros recruited to work in the United States were men and that at this time only 9% of Mexican migrants to the United States were women. Marcela Cerrutti and Magalí Gaudio, "Gender Differences between Mexican Migration to the United States and Paraguayan Migration to Argentina," *Annals of the American Academy of Political and Social Science* 630 (July 2010): 93–113; Massey, Durand, and Malone, *Beyond Smoke and Mirrors*, 36–37.

13. Dunn, *Militarization of the U.S.-Mexico Border*, 14; Calavita, *Inside the State*, 31–32; Ngai, *Impossible Subjects*, 147.

14. Massey, Durand, and Malone, *Beyond Smoke and Mirrors*, 36–37; Deborah Cohen, *Braceros: Migrant Citizens and Transnational Subjects in the Postwar United States and Mexico* (Chapel Hill: University of North Carolina Press, 2011), 209, Calavita, *Inside the State*, 25–26; Ernesto Galarza, *Merchants of Labor: The Mexican Bracero Story* (Charlotte, NC: McNally and Loftin, 1964), 63.

15. Ernesto Galarza, *Strangers in Our Fields* ((Ann Arbor: University of Michigan Press, 1956); González, *Guest Workers or Colonized Labor?*, 85–108.

16. Southern Poverty Law Center, "Close to Slavery: Guestworker Programs in the United States," February 19, 2013, https://www.splcenter.org/20130218/close-slavery-guest worker-programs-united-states.

17. Massey, Durand, and Malone, *Beyond Smoke and Mirrors*, 41.

18. Ngai, *Impossible Subjects*, 256.

19. Douglas S. Massey and Audrey Singer, "New Estimates of Undocumented Mexican Migration and the Probability of Apprehension," *Demography* 32, no. 2 (May 1, 1995): 209, https://doi.org/10.2307/2061740.

20. Massey, Durand, and Malone, *Beyond Smoke and Mirrors*, 41–47; Aviva Chomsky, *Undocumented* (Boston: Beacon Press, 2014). For an in-depth history of congressional debates on applying the quota to Mexico, see Ngai, *Impossible Subjects*, 254–61.

21. Gerald López, "Don't We Like Them Illegal?," *UC Davis Law Review* 45 (July 2012): 1748–49.

22. IRCA also included two new enforcement provisions: an increase in funding for border enforcement efforts and a first-time penalty for employers who hired unauthorized workers. U.S. Congress, Immigration Reform and Control Act of 1986, 99th Cong., 1st sess., sec. 3359, https://www.congress.gov/bill/99th-congress/senate-bill/1200.

23. There was a separate provision that allowed anyone, regardless of occupation, to legalize their status if they could prove that they had continuously resided in the United States since before January 1982 and met other requirements, including payment of fines and back taxes. This separate provision is what is now known as the "amnesty" program.

24. U.S. Congress, Immigration Reform and Control Act of 1986, 99th Cong., 1st sess., sect. 3359, *as further amended by* Immigration Act of 1990 101st Cong., 1st sess., sec. 205(e)(3), https://www.congress.gov/bill/101st-congress/senate-bill/358.

25. Nancy Rytina, "IRCA Legalization Effects: Lawful Permanent Residence and Naturalization through 2001," in *The Effects of Legalization Programs on the United States* (Washington, DC: U.S. Immigration and Naturalization Service Office of Policy and Planning, Statistics Division, 2002), 3, https://www.dhs.gov/sites/default/files/publications /IRCA_Legalization_Effects_2002.pdf.

26. Stanley Mailman, Stephen Yale-Loehr, and Ronald Wada, *Immigration Law and Procedure* (New York: Matthew Bender, 2022), § 20.10.

27. Ruth Ellen Wasem, "Immigration of Agricultural Guest Workers: Policy, Trends, and Legislative Issues" (Congressional Research Service, Washington, DC, August 2001), 5.

28. David J. Bier, "H-2A Visas for Agriculture: The Complex Process for Farmers to Hire Agricultural Guest Workers" (Cato Institute, Immigration Research and Policy Brief, March 10, 2020), https://www.cato.org/publications/immigration-research-policy-brief/h -2a-visas-agriculture-complex-process-farmers-hire.

29. López, "Don't We Like Them Illegal?"

30. Southern Poverty Law Center, "Close to Slavery."

31. Raúl Delgado Wise and Humberto Márquez Covarrubias, "The Mexico–United States Migratory System: Dilemmas of Regional Integration, Development and Emigration," in *Migration and Development: Perspectives from the South*, ed. Stephen Castles and Raúl Delgado Wise (Geneva: International Organization for Migration, 2008), 128.

32. David Bacon, "'Close to Slavery' or Legalization? The Farmworkers' Hard Choice," *American Prospect*, November 25, 2019, https://prospect.org/api/content/b9b94ef0-0f39-11ea-9905-1244d5f7c7c6/.

33. *Federal Register*, "Temporary Changes to Requirements Affecting H-2A Nonimmigrants Due to the COVID-19 National Emergency: Extension of Certain Flexibilities," 85 FR 82291 (2020).

34. Employment and Training Administration, "Adverse Effect Wage Rate Methodology for the Temporary Employment of H-2A Nonimmigrants in Non-Range Occupations in the United States," 85 FR 70445 (2020), https://www.federalregister.gov/documents/2020/11/05/2020-24544/adverse-effect-wage-rate-methodology-for-the-temporary-employment-of-h-2a-nonimmigrants-in-non-range; Daniel Costa, "Trump Administration Looking to Cut the Already Low Wages of H-2A Migrant Farmworkers While Giving Their Bosses a Multibillion-Dollar Bailout," *Economic Policy Institute* (blog), April 20, 2020, https://www.epi.org/blog/trump-administration-reportedly-looking-to-cut-the-already-low-wages-of-h-2a-migrant-farmworkers-while-giving-their-bosses-a-multibillion-dollar-bailout/.

35. David Griffith, "New Immigrants in an Old Industry: Mexican H-2B Workers in the Mid-Atlantic Blue Crab Processing Industry," accessed July 21, 2020, https://migration.ucdavis.edu/cf/more.php?id=148.

36. David Griffith, *American Guestworker: Jamaicans and Mexicans in the U.S. Labor Market* (University Park: Pennsylvania State University Press, 2006), 29–44.

37. Griffith, "New Immigrants in an Old Industry."

38. Griffith, *American Guestworker*.

39. Erika Montoya Zavala, "En búsqueda de mejores salarios y de la Unión Familiar: Jaiberas sinaloenses con visa H-2B en Carolina del Norte: Una solución encontrada o una solución desesperada?" [In Search of the Best Salaries and Family Unity: Sinaloan Crab Cleaners with H-2B Visas in North Carolina: A Solution Found or a Desperate Solution?], *Relaciones* 29, no. 16 (Autumn 2008): 201; Laura Vidal Fernandez, Esperanza Tuñon Pablos, Martha Rojas Weisner, and Ramfis Ayús Reyes, "De paraíso a Carolina del Norte, redes de apoyo y percepciones de la migración a Estados Unidos de mujeres tabasqueñas despulpadoras de jaiba" [From Paraíso to North Carolina, Support Networks and Perceptions of Migration to the United States of Tabascan Women Crab Pulpers], *Migraciones Internacionales* 1, no. 002 (2002): 30.

40. Zavala, "Jaiberas sinolenses," 201.

41. Zavala, "Jaiberas sinolenses," 201.

42. Note that in 2022 the Department of Homeland Security announced that it would make an additional almost 65,000 H-2Bs available to "meet the need of American businesses." See https://www.dhs.gov/news/2022/10/12/dhs-supplement-h-2b-cap-nearly-65000-additional-visas-fiscal-year-2023 (last accessed December 30, 2022).

43. Andorra Bruno, "Immigration of Temporary Lower-Skilled Workers: Current Policy and Related Issues" (Congressional Research Service, Washington, DC, December 2012), appendix C.

44. Department of Homeland Security, "DHS to Supplement H-2B Cap with Nearly 65,000 Additional Visas for Fiscal Year 2023," accessed December 30, 2022, https://www .dhs.gov/news/2022/10/12/dhs-supplement-h-2b-cap-nearly-65000-additional-visas-fiscal -year-2023.

45. Southern Poverty Law Center, "Close to Slavery"; Jessica Garrison, Ken Bensinger, and Jeremy Singer-Vine, "The New American Slavery: Invited to the U.S., Foreign Workers Find a Nightmare," *Buzz Feed News*, accessed December 30, 2022, https://www.buzzfeed news.com/article/jessicagarrison/the-new-american-slavery-invited-to-the-us-foreign -workers-f#.lyREpxV9Kq.

46. See 20 C.F.R. §§ 655.1 to 655.73.

47. Daniel Costa, "The H-2B Temporary Foreign Worker Program: Examining the Effects on American Job Opportunities and Wages" (Economic Policy Institute, 2016), https://www.epi.org/publication/the-h-2b-temporary-foreign-worker-program-examining -the-effects-on-americans-job-opportunities-and-wages/.

48. Costa, "The H-2B Temporary Foreign Worker Program."

49. Griffith, *American Guestworker*.

50. Garrison, Bensinger, and Singer-Vine, "The New American Slavery."

51. Centro de los Derechos del Migrante and Penn State Law Transnational Law Clinic, "Engendering Exploitation: Gender Inequality in U.S. Labor Migration Programs," 2013, https://cdmigrante.org/wp-content/uploads/2018/01/Engendered-Exploita tion.pdf.

52. Centro de los Derechos del Migrante and Penn State Law Transnational Law Clinic, "Engendering Exploitation."

53. Centro de los Derechos del Migrante and Penn State Law Transnational Law Clinic, "Engendering Exploitation."

54. 8 U.S.C.A. § 1324.

55. Andreas, *Border Games*, 9.

56. Hernandez, *Migra!*, 137–38; Calavita, *Inside the State*, 67; Juan Ramon García, *Operation Wetback: The Mass Deportation of Mexican Undocumented Workers in 1954* (Westport, CT: Greenwood Press, 1980), 121, 127; Nevins, *Operation Gatekeeper*, 139–40.

57. Calavita, *Inside the State*, 68.

58. Calavita, *Inside the State*, 69. Note that the H-2A visa was also created this same year as a temporary visa for agricultural workers. Growers did not use the H-2A visa because of the large supply of unauthorized workers with low risk of enforcement and the burdens of paperwork that came with the application process. See Calavita, *Inside the State*, 163.

59. Calavita, *Inside the State*, 70.

60. Richard D. Lyons, "Seldom Active Senate Unit Drew $2-Million in Decade," *New York Times*, September 29, 1975, sec. Archives, https://www.nytimes.com/1975/09/29/archives/new -jersey-pages-seldom-active-senate-unit-drew-2million-in-decade.html.

61. Daniel Tichenor, *Dividing Lines: The Politics of Immigration Control in America* (Princeton, NJ: Princeton University Press, 2002), 253; U.S. Congress, Senate, "Hearings on S. 1200, A Bill to Amend the Immigration and Nationality Act to Effectively Control Unauthorized Immigration to the United States," S. 1200, 99th Cong., 1st sess., pp. 174–95. It must be noted that civil rights groups also opposed employer sanctions based on the fear that verification of eligibility to work would lead to discrimination against Latinos of all immigration statuses. See "Hearings on S. 1200."

62. Philip L. Martin, "Good Intentions Gone Awry: IRCA and U.S. Agriculture," *Annals of the American Academy of Political and Social Science* 534 (July 1994): 47–48; "Hearings on S. 1200," 174–95; U.S. Congress, House. Committee on Agriculture, "Immigration Reform and Control Act of 1983," HR 1510, 98th Cong. Introduced in House, February 17, 1983, https://www.congress.gov/bill/98th-congress/house-bill/1510, 32–33; U.S. Congress, House, "Hearings before the Subcommittee on Immigration, Refugees, and International Law of the Committee on the Judiciary," HR 3080, 99th Cong. 1st sess.,September 9, 1985, p. 12.

63. U.S. Congress, Senate, "Hearings on S. 1200," 180.

64. Tichenor, *Dividing Lines*, 260–61; Martin, "Good Intentions Gone Awry," 48.

65. The one migrant who was asked for paperwork was Don Juan, who is not profiled in this book. In 2010, his employer said that he needed to see a Social Security number in order to rehire Don Juan. Don Juan did not want to obtain a false Social Security card so he found other work that did not require documentation.

66. Wayne A. Cornelius, "Death at the Border: Efficacy and Unintended Consequences of US Immigration Control Policy," *Population and Development Review* 27, no. 4 (2001): 678.

67. Peter Brownell, "The Declining Enforcement of Employer Sanctions" (Migration Policy Institute, September 1, 2005), fig. 3, https://www.migrationpolicy.org/article/declining-enforcement-employer-sanctions.

68. Robert Warren and John Robert Warren, "Unauthorized Immigration to the United States: Annual Estimates and Components of Change by State, 1990 to 2010," *International Migration Review* 47, no. 2 (Summer 2013): 312, table 2; Adam Goodman, *The Deportation Machine: America's Long History of Expelling Immigrants* (Princeton, NJ: Princeton University Press, 2020), 172.

69. Economic Research Service, "U.S. Department of Agriculture Economic Research Service Farm Labor," April 22, 2020, https://www.ers.usda.gov/topics/farm-economy/farm-labor/#size.

70. INS official quoted on the reasons investigations into meatpacking plants in Iowa and Nebraska had not resulted in any deportations, in Cornelius, "Death at the Border."

71. Raquel Aldana, "Of 'Katz' and Aliens: Privacy Expectations and the Immigration Raids," *UC Davis Law Review* 41 (February 2008): 1092; Kevin Johnson, "The Intersection of Race and Class in U.S. Immigration Law and Enforcement," *Law and Contemporary Problems* 72 (Fall 2009): 30.

72. David A. Selden et al., "Criminal Enforcement and I-9 Audits," *HR Simple* (blog), accessed February 23, 2021, https://www.hrsimple.com.

73. Marcy M. Forman, "Worksite Enforcement Strategy" (U.S. Immigration Customs and Enforcement, April 30, 2009), 1, https://www.ice.gov/doclib/foia/dro_policy_memos/worksite_enforcement_strategy4_30_2009.pdf.

74. Andorra Bruno, "Immigration-Related Worksite Enforcement: Performance Measures" (Congressional Research Service, Washington, DC, June 23, 2015), 5, table 1.

75. White House, "Executive Order: Enhancing Public Safety in the Interior of the United States," accessed August 21, 2020, https://www.whitehouse.gov/presidential-actions/executive-order-enhancing-public-safety-interior-united-states/.

76. Sarah Pierce and Jessica Bolter, "Dismantling and Reconstructing the U.S. Immigration System: A Catalog of Changes under the Trump Presidency," accessed May 29, 2024,

https://www.migrationpolicy.org/research/us-immigration-system-changes-trump-presi
dency, 49.

77. Quoted in Ettinger, *Imaginary Lines*, 131.

78. Ettinger, *Imaginary Lines*, 46; emphasis added.

79. Ettinger, *Imaginary Lines*, 46.

80. Ettinger, *Imaginary Lines*, 157.

81. Hernandez, *Migra!*, 72, quoting from "Aliens without Passports Are Turned Back: Stricter Enforcement at Line Ordered to Prevent Illegal Crossings," *Calexico Chronicle*, June 8, 1924.

82. Kelly Lytle Hernández, *City of Inmates: Conquest, Rebellion, and the Rise of Human Caging in Los Angeles, 1771–1965* (Chapel Hill: University of North Carolina Press, 2017), 138–39.

83. Hernandez, *Migra!*, 101; Ngai, *Impossible Subjects*, 67–71.

84. Eric S. Fish, "Race, History, and Immigration Crimes," *Iowa Law Review* 107, no. 1 (April 15, 2021): 1052–1106; Joanna Jacobbi Lydgate, "Assembly-Line Justice: A Review of Operation Streamline," *California Law Review* 98, no. 2 (2010): 481–544.

85. Don Manto became a permanent resident of the United States in 1990 under the Special Agricultural Workers' provision passed as part of IRCA in 1986. Thus, he did not need to migrate without authorization after 1990. When we spoke in 2013, he was back in Santa María Natividad, Oaxaca, for good because he said there was little work in the United States even for those who had "green cards." However, he planned to visit his wife and children who had settled in the United States.

86. Massey and Singer, "New Estimates of Undocumented Mexican Migration and the Probability of Apprehension," 210.

87. Massey and Singer, "New Estimates of Undocumented Mexican Migration and the Probability of Apprehension," 210.

88. Massey and Singer, "New Estimates of Undocumented Mexican Migration and Probability of Apprehension," 210.

89. Massey and Singer, "New Estimates of Undocumented Mexican Migration and Probability of Apprehension," 210.

90. Leonard Chapman, "Illegal Aliens: Time to Call a Halt," *Reader's Digest*, October 1976; Nevins, *Operation Gatekeeper*, 63.

91. Migration Policy Institute, "Immigration Enforcement Spending since IRCA"; American Immigration Council, "The Cost of Immigration Enforcement and Border Security."

92. Todd Miller, "More Than a Wall" (Transnational Institute, Amsterdam, 2019), 31–32, https://www.tni.org/en/publication/more-than-a-wall-0.

93. Todd Miller and Nick Buxton, "Biden's Border Wall" (Transnational Institute, Amsterdam, 2021), 14–18, https://www.tni.org/en/publication/bidens-border.

94. Massey, Durand, and Malone, *Beyond Smoke and Mirrors*, 106–10.

95. U.S. Department of Justice, "Department of Justice Prosecuted a Record-Breaking Number of Immigration-Related Cases in Fiscal Year 2019," *Justice News*, October 17, 2019, https://www.justice.gov/opa/pr/department-justice-prosecuted-record-breaking-number
-immigration-related-cases-fiscal-year.

96. U.S. Department of Justice, "Department of Justice Prosecuted a Record-Breaking Number of Immigration-Related Cases in Fiscal Year 2019."

97. White House, "Executive Order: Border Security and Immigration Enforcement Improvements," accessed May 29, 2024, https://trumpwhitehouse.archives.gov/presidential -actions/executive-order-border-security-immigration-enforcement-improvements/, sec. 13; Maya Srikrishnan, "How San Diego Is Pushing Back against 'Zero Tolerance' at the Border," Voice of San Diego, November, 27, 2018, https://www.voiceofsandiego.org/topics/news /how-san-diego-is-pushing-back-against-zero-tolerance-at-the-border. See also "More Streamlining, More Prisons," Kino Border Initiative, December 18, 2019, https://www.kino borderinitiative.org/more-streamlining-more-prisons.

98. U.S. Department of Justice, "Department of Justice Prosecuted a Record-Breaking Number of Immigration-Related Cases in Fiscal Year 2019."

99. U.S. Government Accounting Office, "Immigration Enforcement: Immigration Related Prosecutions Increase from 2017 to 2018 in Response to U.S. Attorney General's Direction" (Washington, DC, December 2019), 75–76, https://www.gao.gov/assets/710/702965.pdf.

100. Doug Keller, "Re-Thinking Illegal Entry and Re-Entry," *Loyola University Chicago Law Journal* 44 (Fall 2012): 193.

101. Golash-Boza, *Deported*, 145.

102. Massey, Durand, and Malone, *Beyond Smoke and Mirrors*, 93–94; Wayne A. Cornelius and Idean Salehyan, "Does Border Enforcement Deter Unauthorized Immigration? The Case of Mexican Migration to the United States of America," *Regulation and Governance*, no. 1 (2007): 147.

103. Olivia T. Ruiz Marrujo, "Women, Migration and Sexual Violence: Lessons from Mexico's Borders," in *Human Rights Along the U.S.-Mexico Border: Gendered Violence and Insecurity*, ed. Kathleen A. Staudt, Tony Payan, and Z. Anthony Kruszewski (Tucson: University of Arizona Press, 2009), 31.

104. Ruiz Marrujo, "Women, Migration and Sexual Violence," 31.

105. Deborah A. Boehm, *Intimate Migrations: Gender, Family, and Illegality among Transnational Mexicans* (New York: New York University Press, 2012), 92.

106. Rubén Hernández-León, "Conceptualizing the Migration Industry," in *The Migration Industry and Commercialization of International Migration* (Oxford: Routledge, 2012), 33, https://doi.org/10.4324/9780203082737–11.

107. Jeremy Slack and Scott Whiteford, "Violence and Migration on the Arizona-Sonora Border," *Human Organization* 70, no. 1 (2011): 14–16.

108. Simón Pedro Izcara Palacios, "Coyotaje y grupos delictivos en Tamaulipas" [Coyotaje and Criminal Organizations in Tamaulipas], *Latin American Research Review* 47, no. 3 (2012): 46–56.

109. Palacios, "Coyotaje y grupos delictivos en Tamaulipas," 51–54; David Spener, *Clandestine Crossings: Migrants and Coyotes on the Texas-Mexico Border* (Ithaca, NY: Cornell University Press, 2011), 130–34.

110. This figure was given by Don Filadelfo, a man interviewed in Oaxaca who paid this amount to cross through a checkpoint in 2001.

111. Palacios, "Coyotaje y grupos delictivos en Tamaulipas," 46; Slack and Whiteford, "Violence and Migration on the Arizona-Sonora Border," 14–16.

112. Some studies have found that the fees increased 200% between 2004 and 2010. See Palacios, "Coyotaje y grupos delictivos en Tamaulipas," 44.

113. Goodman, *Deportation Machine*, 46.

114. "1,100 Deported Here Since Mid-January," *New York Times*, April 11, 1931, 14.

115. The former is a quote from a *Saturday Evening Post* article and the latter a quote by Dr. Roy L. Garris of Vanderbilt University. Both are documented along with other examples in Acuña, *Occupied America*, 139–40; see also 141–42.

116. Goodman, *Deportation Machine*, 53.

117. Marc Lablonte, "The Current Economic Recession: How Long, How Deep and How Different from the Past?" (Congressional Research Service, Washington, DC, 2002).

118. Calavita, *Inside the State*, 53; Goodman, *Deportation Machine*, 59; García, *Operation Wetback*, 179; Ngai, *Impossible Subjects*, 155.

119. Calavita, *Inside the State*, 56.

120. Angela Y. Davis, *Are Prisons Obsolete?* (New York: Seven Stories Press, 2003); Michelle Alexander, *The New Jim Crow* (New York: New York University Press, 2012).

121. Livia Luan, "Profiting from Enforcement: The Role of Private Prisons in U.S. Immigration Detention" (Migration Policy Institute, Washington, DC, 2018).

3. ENTRENCHMENT

1. CAFAMI is described in more detail in chapter 4.

2. Manuela's father is Don Rodolfo, whose story is found in chapters 1 and 2.

3. Deborah A. Boehm, *Intimate Migrations: Gender, Family, and Illegality among Transnational Mexicans* (New York: New York University Press, 2012), 47.

4. On familial relationships, see Lilia Soto, *Girlhood in the Borderlands: Mexican Teens Caught in the Crossroads of Migration* (New York: New York University Press, 2018); Gabrielle Oliveira, *Motherhood across Borders: Immigrants and Their Children in Mexico and New York* (New York: New York University Press, 2018); Ye Jingzhong, "Left-Behind Children: The Social Price of China's Economic Boom," *Journal of Peasant Studies* 38, no. 3 (July 2011): 613–50, https://doi.org/10.1080/03066150.2011.582946.

On economic consequences, see Douglas S. Massey et al., *Worlds in Motion: Understanding International Migration at the End of the Millennium* (Oxford: Clarendon Press, 1999); Stephen Castles and Raúl Delgado Wise, eds., *Migration and Development: Perspectives from the South* (Geneva: International Organization for Migration, 2008); Roy Germano, *Outsourcing Welfare: How the Money Immigrants Send Home Contributes to Stability in Developing Countries* (Oxford: Oxford University Press, 2018).

5. Leisy J. Abrego, *Sacrificing Families: Navigating Laws, Labor, and Love across Borders* (Stanford: Stanford University Press, 2014).

6. Abrego, *Sacrificing Families*, 11.

7. Rodolfo Zamora and Juan Padilla, "Zacatecas, migración y minería: El extractivismo como ilusión del desarrollo" [Zacatecas, Migration and Mining: Extractivism as an Illusion of Development], in *Mexico en la trampa del financiamiento: El sendero del no desarollo* [Mexico in the Financing Trap: The Path of Non-Development] (Mexico City: Universidad Nacional Autónoma de México, 2013), 165–66.

8. Rúben Hernández, "Crece consumo de drogas en Tlaxcaltecas, narcomenudeo sin ser alarmante" [Drug Consumption Grows among Tlaxcaltecs, Drug Dealing without Being Alarming], *Quadratín Tlaxcala*, February 14, 2018, https://tlaxcala.quadratin.com .mx/principal/crece-consumo-drogas-tlaxcaltecas-narcomenudeo-sin-alarmante/.

9. Mahbub ul Haq, *Reflections on Human Development* (Oxford: Oxford University Press, 1995), 5; Castles and Delgado Wise, *Migration and Development*, 10; John Friedmann, *Empowerment: The Politics of Alternative Development* (Oxford: Blackwell, 1992).

10. Germano, *Outsourcing Welfare*; Prachi Mishra, "Emigration and Wages in Source Countries: Evidence from Mexico," *Journal of Development Economics* 82 (2007): 180–99; Gerardo Esquivel and A. Huerta-Pineda, "Remittances and Poverty in Mexico: A Propensity Score Matching Approach," *Integration and Trade* 27 (January 1, 2007): 1–28; J. Humberto Lopez, Pablo Fajnzylber, and Pablo Acosta, "The Impact of Remittances on Poverty and Human Capital : Evidence from Latin American Household Surveys," World Bank Policy Research Working Papers, 2007; C. B. Keely and B. N. Tran, "Remittances from Labor Migration: Evaluations, Performance and Implications," *International Migration Review* 23, no. 3 (1989): 500–525; Jorge Durand et al., "International Migration and Development in Mexican Communities," *Demography* 33, no. 2 (1996): 249–64.

11. Castles and Delgado Wise, *Migration and Development*, 8, 129. See also Matt Bakker, "Introducing the Remittances-to-Development Agenda: Migration, Remittances, and Development—Three Vignettes," in *Migrating into Financial Markets: How Remittances Became a Development Tool* (Berkeley: University of California Press, 2015), 3–33.

12. Castles and Delgado Wise, *Migration and Development*, 7.

13. Having an autoridad is a signal that the village was organized under the self-governance system of usos y costumbres that has existed since the Spanish colonial era but was made more formal after the Zapatista uprisings in 1994.

14. Ramo 33 was a replacement for the controversial PRONASOL, or Solidaridad, program under President Carlos Salinas. PRONASOL was discontinued due to evidence that the program's benefits had been distributed based on loyalty to Salinas's political party, the Partido Revolucionario Institucional (PRI). Ernesto Zedillo, Salinas's successor, replaced PRONASOL with Ramo 33, which allocated funds to states and municipalities rather than to groups of private citizens. Funds are allocated to states and municipalities on the basis of these entities' poverty index as measured by the number of low-wage workers in a municipality, illiteracy, homes without indoor plumbing, and homes without electricity.

15. Paul Gillingham, *Unrevolutionary Mexico: The Birth of a Strange Dictatorship* (New Haven, CT: Yale University Press, 2021); Stephen D. Morris, *Political Corruption in Mexico: The Impact of Democratization* (Boulder, CO: Lynne Reiner, 2009).

16. Raúl Delgado Wise and Henry Veltmeyer, *Agrarian Change, Migration and Development*, Agrarian Change and Peasant Studies (Black Point, Nova Scotia: Fernwood Publishing, 2016), 133.

17. Secretaría de Desarrollo Social, "Acciones 3x1" [3x1 Actions], last accessed May 31, 2024, https://datos.sedesol.gob.mx/UMR/UMR/oct2015/acciones_3x1_2013.csv.

18. Consejo Nacional de Población, "Intensidad migratoria a nivel estatal y municipal" [Migration Intensity at the State and Municipal Levels]," 2010, 37–38, http://www.conapo .gob.mx/work/models/CONAPO/intensidad_migratoria/pdf/IIM_Estatal_y_Municipal .pdf.

19. Rodolfo García Zamora, "El programa Tres por Uno de remesas colectivas en México: Lecciones y desafíos" [The Three for One Program of Collective Remittances in Mexico: Lessons and Challenges]. *Migraciones Internacionales* 4, no. 1 (2007): 168.

20. Catalina Amuedo-Dorantes and Susan Pozo, "Remittances as Insurance: Evidence from Mexican Immigrants," *Journal of Population Economics* 19, no. 2 (2006): 236.

21. Consejo Nacional de Población, "Anuarion migración y remesas" [Yearbook of Migration and Remittances] (CONAPO, 2019), https://www.gob.mx/cms/uploads/attach ment/file/567288/Anuario_Migracion_y_Remesas_2019_Segunda_Parte.pdf.

22. Consejo Nacional de Población, "Anuarion migración y remesas," 156.

23. Constitution of the United Mexican States, Article 27 (1917). Paragraph 1 of Article 27 states that "ownership of the lands and waters within the boundaries of the national territory is vested originally in the Nation, which has had, and has the right to transfer title thereof to private persons, thereby constituting private property." Paragraph 3 states, in part, "For this purpose necessary measures shall be taken to divide large landed estates; to develop small landed holdings; to establish new centers of population with such lands and waters as may be indispensable to them; to encourage agriculture and to prevent the destruction of natural resources, and to protect property from damage detrimental to society." (A PDF of the 1917 Mexican Constitution is available at the Library of Congress: https://www.loc.gov/item/17021628/.)

24. Constitution of the United Mexican States, Article 27. Paragraph 9-I states, "Only Mexicans by birth or naturalization and Mexican companies have the right to acquire ownership of lands, waters, and their appurtenances, or to obtain concessions for the exploitation of mines or of waters. The State may grant the same right to foreigners, provided they agree before the Ministry of Foreign Relations to consider themselves as nationals in respect to such property, and bind themselves not to invoke the protection of their governments in matters relating thereto; under penalty, in case of noncompliance with this agreement, of forfeiture of the property acquired to the Nation. Under no circumstances may foreigners acquire direct ownership of lands or waters within a zone of one hundred kilometers along the frontiers and of fifty kilometers along the shores of the country."

25. Jonathan Fox and Libby Haight, "Mexican Agricultural Policy: Multiple Goals and Conflicting Interests," in *Subsidizing Inequality: Mexican Corn Policy since NAFTA*, ed. Jonathan Fox and Libbby Haight (Washington, DC: Woodrow Wilson International Center for Scholars, 2010), 1.

26. Thomas J. Kelly, "Neoliberal Reforms and Rural Poverty," *Latin American Perspectives* 28, no. 3 (2001): 90.

27. Nora Lustig, *Mexico: The Remaking of an Economy* (Washington, DC: Brookings Institution Press, 1998), 206. See also Miguel D. Ramirez, "Stabilization and Trade Reform," *Journal of Developing Areas* 27, no. 2 (January 1993): 179 (figures for 1982–89); Miguel D. Ramirez, "The Latest IMF-Sponsored Stabilization Program: Does It Represent a Long-Term Solution for Mexico's Economy?," *Journal of Interamerican Studies and World Affairs* 38, no. 4 (Winter 1996): 132 (figures for 1989–94).

28. S. J. Scherr, *The Oil Syndrome and Agricultural Development: Lessons from Tabasco, Mexico* (New York: Praeger, 1985), 89.

29. Gisele Henriques and Raj Patel, "Agricultural Trade Liberalization and Mexico," Food First, Institute for Food Development Policy (2003), 22; Antonio Yúnez-Naude, "The Dismantling of CONASUPO, a Mexican State Trader in Agriculture," *World Economy* 26, no. 1 (2003): 97–122.

30. Henriques and Patel, "Agricultural Trade Liberalization," 22; Yunez-Naude, "The Dismantling of CONASUPO," 5.

31. See Minutes of International Monetary Fund Executive Board Meeting, July 30, 1984, IMF Doc # EMB 84/117, p. 42.

32. Yúnez-Naude, "The Dismantling of CONASUPO."

33. Marta Ruiz-Arranz et al., "Program Conditionality and Food Security: The Impact of PROGRESA and PROCAMPO Transfers in Rural Mexico," *Economía Journal* 7, no. 2 (August 1, 2006): 253.

34. Fox and Haight, "Mexican Agricultural Policy," 1.

35. Edward J. Taylor, "The New Economics of Labour Migration and the Role of Remittances in the Migration Process," *International Migration* 37, no. 1 (1999): 63–88; Massey et al., *Worlds in Motion*; Tanya Basok, "Migration of Mexican Seasonal Farm Workers to Canada and Development: Obstacles to Productive Investment," *International Migration Review* 34, no. 1 (2000): 79–97; Jesús Aroyo Alejandre, Adriá de Léon Arias, and Basilia Valenzuela Barilla, "Patterns of Migration and Regional Development in the State of Jalisco, Mexico," in *Regional and Sectoral Development in Mexico as Alternatives to Migration*, ed. Sergio Diaz-Briquets and Sidney Weintraub (New York: Routledge, 1991), 47–87; Wayne A. Cornelius, "Labor Migration to the United States: Development Outcomes and Alternatives in Mexican Sending Communities," in Diaz-Briquets and Weintraub, *Regional and Sectoral Deveopment in Mexico as an Alternative to Migration*, 89–131; Douglas S. Massey and Lawrence C. Basem, "Determinants of Savings, Remittances, and Spending Patterns among U.S. Migrants in Four Mexican Communities," *Sociological Inquiry* 62, no. 2 (1992): 185–207; Tanya Basok, "Mexican Seasonal Migration to Canada and Development: A Community-Based Comparison," *International Migration* 41, no. 2 (2003): 3–6; Durand et al., "International Migration and Development in Mexican Communities."

36. Luis Eduardo Guarnizo, "The Economics of Transnational Living," *International Migration Review* 37, no. 3 (2003): 673.

37. Carlos Monoy and Stefan Trines, "Education in Mexico," *World Education News and Reviews* (2019), https://wenr.wes.org/2019/05/education-in-mexico-2.

38. Guarnizo, "The Economics of Transnational Living," 687.

39. Raúl Delgado Wise and Humberto Márquez Covarrubias, "The Mexico–United States Migratory System: Dilemmas of Regional Integration, Development and Emigration," in *Migration and Development: Perspectives from the South*, ed. Stephen Castles and Raúl Delgado Wise (Geneva: International Organization for Migration, 2008), 129.

40. Clare Ribando Seelke, "Mexico: Background and U.S. Relations" (Congressional Research Service, Washington, DC, December 2020), 12.

41. Raúl Delgado Wise and Humberto Márquez Covarrubias, "Migration and Development in Mexico: Toward a New Analytical Approach," *Journal of Latino/Latin American Studies* 2, no. 3 (April 2007): 108.

42. Guarnizo, "The Economics of Transnational Living," 688.

43. Saskia Sassen, *The Mobility of Labor and Capital: A Study in International Investment and Labor Flow* (Cambridge: Cambridge University Press, 1988).

44. Raúl Delgado Wise, "Migration and Imperialism: The Mexican Workforce in the Context of NAFTA," *Latin American Perspectives* 33, no. 147 (2006): 39–40.

45. Manuel Orozco, "Globalization and Migration: The Impact of Family Remittances in Latin America," *Latin American Politics and Society* 44, no. 2 (2002): 52.

46. See *In re Mexico Money Transfer Litigation*, 164 F. Supp. 2d 1002 (N.D. Ill. 2000).

47. Delgado Wise and Márquez Covarrubias, "The Mexico–United States Migratory System."

48. Guarnizo, "The Economics of Transnational Living," 688.

49. Delgado Wise and Márquez Covarrubias, "The Mexico–United States Migratory System," 128.

4. RESISTANCE

1. Augusto Boal, *Theater of the Oppressed* (London: Pluto Press, 2000). In *Theater of the Oppressed*, the Brazilian playwright describes an aesthetic method by which participants describe their own realities and critiques of that reality and represent that in performance. Boal further describes six different "theaters of the oppressed," all of which use the participant-actor model but have different performance methods. CAFAMI uses what is known as Rainbow of Desire techniques described by Boal in *The Rainbow of Desire* (London: Routledge, 2013).

2. The H-2B visa allows a limited number of "temporary" workers into the United States to perform nonagricultural work. See 8 U.S.C. §1101(a)(15)(H)(ii).

3. Deborah A. Boehm, *Intimate Migrations: Gender, Family, and Illegality among Transnational Mexicans* (New York: New York University Press, 2012), 72.

4. María Cristina Velásquez, "Migrant Communities, Gender and Political Power in Oaxaca," in *Indigenous Mexican Migrants in the United States*, ed. Jonathon Fox and Gaspar Rivera Salgado (La Jolla: University of California, San Diego, Center for U.S.-Mexican Studies and Center for Comparative Immigration Studies, 2004), 288.

5. Centolia Maldonado Vásquez and Patricia Artía Rodriguez, "'Now We Are Awake': Women's Political Participation in the Oaxacan Indigenous Binational Front," in Fox and Rivera Salgado, *Indigenous Mexican Migrants in the United States*, 500.

6. The story of women's increased involvement in the autoridad assembly of San Miguel Tlacotepec is told in further detail in Vásquez and Rodriguez, "'Now We Are Awake,'" 498–501.

7. Abigail Leslie Andrews, *Undocumented Politics: Place, Gender, and the Pathways of Mexican Migrants* (Berkeley: University of California Press, 2018).

8. Andrews, *Undocumented Politics*.

9. Rivera Salgado, recorded in David Bacon, *The Right to Stay Home: How U.S. Policy Drives Mexican Migration* (Boston, MA: Beacon Press, 2013), 443–44.

10. Rivera Salgado, recorded in Bacon, *The Right to Stay Home*, 443–44.

11. Roger Nett, "The Civil Right We Are Not Ready For: The Right of Free Movement of People on the Face of the Earth," *Ethics* 81, no. 3 (1971): 212–27; Joseph H. Carens, "Aliens and Citizens: The Case for Open Borders," *Review of Politics* 49, no. 2 (1987): 251–73; Kevin R. Johnson, *Opening the Floodgates: Why America Needs to Rethink Its Borders and Immigration Laws* (New York: New York University Press, 2007).

12. Carens, "Aliens and Citizens"; Johnson, *Opening the Floodgates*.

13. UNORCA would later become part of the Via Campesina (Peasant Way), a global movement launched in 1993 to fight against neoliberal policies on peasants and to argue for what they called food sovereignty.

14. Alejandro Anaya Muñoz, *Autonomia indígena, gobernabilidad y legitimidad en Mexico* [Indigenous Autonomy, Governability, and Legitimacy in Mexico] (Mexico City: Plaza y Valdes, 2006); Horacio Almanza-Alcalde, "Some Actors in the Independent Peasant

Movement," *Revista Vinculando*, May 31, 2005, https://vinculando.org/comerciojusto/fair
_trade/independent_peasant_movement.html.

15. Ramón Vera Herrera and Luis Hernández Navarro, *Acuerdos de San Andrés*
[San Andrés Accords] (Mexico City: Ediciones Era, 1998); Luis Hernández Navarro, "San
Andrés: 20 años después" [San Andrés: 20 Years Later], *El Cotidiano*, 2016, 18; Anaya
Muñoz, *Autonomia indígena*.

16. Michael Kearney and Federico Besserer, "Oaxacan Municipal Governance in a
Transnational Context," in Fox and Rivera Salgado, *Indigenous Mexican Migrants in the
United States*, 451; Allyson Benton, "The Origins of Mexico's Municipal Usos y Costumbres
Regimes: Supporting Local Political Participation or Local Authoritarian Control?," Docu-
mentos de Trabajo de Centro de Investigación y Docencia Económicas, 2011, 36.

17. This does not necessarily mean that usos y costumbres municipalities were more
democratic than the political party system. As Jonathan Fox and Edward Gibson have
found, many of these communities exclude candidates and even voters based on sex,
age, residency and whether or not a person completed a cargo. See Jonathan Fox, "Latin
America's Emerging Local Politics," *Journal of Democracy* 5, no. 2 (1994): 105–16; Edward
L. Gibson, "Boundary Control: Subnational Authoritarianism in Democratic Countries,"
World Politics 58, no. 1 (2005): 101–32. These findings are confirmed by Centolia Maldonado,
a Mixtec woman from Agua Fria, in her unpublished manuscript.

18. Andrews, *Undocumented Politics*, 24, 157.

19. Michael Kearney, "Transnational Oaxacan Indigenous Identity: The Case of Mixtecs
and Zapotecs," *Identities* 7, no. 2 (June 1, 2000): 186–87.

20. Bacon, *The Right to Stay Home*, xii.

21. Ford Foundation, "Mexico and Central America" (2012), https://www.fordfounda
tion.org/media/1605/mexico-brochure-2011.pdf. Accessed July 8, 2021.

22. See chap. 1.

23. See chap. 3.

24. Culturally unique visitors are authorized under U.S. law at 8 U.S.C. §1101(a)(15)(P)(3).
In order to obtain a visa, the visitors must be sponsored by a U.S. entity and must be coming
to the United States temporarily "for the purpose of developing, interpreting, representing,
coaching, or teaching a unique or traditional ethnic, folk, cultural, musical, theatrical, or
artistic performance or presentation." CAFAMI applied for and received temporary visas to
perform a "culturally unique" program in 2008, 2010, and 2012.

CONCLUSION

1. Rivera Salgado, recorded in David Bacon, *The Right to Stay Home: How U.S. Policy
Drives Mexican Migration* (Boston: Beacon Press, 2013), 443–44. This is part of a larger
struggle for self-determination among a broad range of Indigenous communities across
Mexico. See Sergio Segreste Ríos, "Capitulo V: La sistema de usos y costumbres" [Chapter V:
The Uses and Customs System], in *Manual básico de derechos humanos para autoridades
municipales* [Basic Manual of Human Rights for Municipal Authorities] (Mexico City:
Comisión Nacional de los Derechos Humanos, 2019); Alejandro Anaya Muñoz, *Autonomía
indígena, gobernabilidad y legitimidad en Mexico* [Indigenous Autonomy, Governability,
and Legitimacy in Mexico] (Mexico City: Plaza y Valdes, 2006).

2. Harsha Walia, *Border and Rule: Global Migration, Capitalism and the Rise of Racist Nationalism* (Boston: Haymarket Books, 2020), 41–42.

3. Angela Y. Davis, *Are Prisons Obsolete?* (New York: Seven Stories Press, 2003), 1.

4. Angela Y. Davis, *Abolition Democracy: Beyond Empire, Prisons and Torture* (New York: Seven Stories Press, 2005), 20.

5. Joseph H. Carens, "Aliens and Citizens: The Case for Open Borders," *Review of Politics* 49, no. 2 (1987): 251–73; Kevin R. Johnson, *Opening the Floodgates: Why America Needs to Rethink Its Borders and Immigration Laws* (New York: New York University Press, 2007).

6. Eric S. Fish, "Race, History, and Immigration Crimes," *Iowa Law Review* 107, no. 1 (April 15, 2021): 1051–1106.

7. César Cuauhtémoc García Hernández, *Migrating to Prison: America's Obsession with Locking Up Immigrants* (New York: New Press, 2019).

8. Angélica Cházaro, "The End of Deportation," *UCLA Law Review* 68 (2021): 1040.

9. Carens, "Aliens and Citizens"; Johnson, *Opening the Floodgates*, 212; César García Hernández Cuauhtémoc, "Abolishing Immigration Prisons," *Boston College Law Review* 97, no. 1 (2017): 292; Cházaro, "The End of Deportation," 1048; Fish, "Race, History, and Immigration Crimes," 163.

10. Davis, *Abolition Democracy*, 20.

11. Davis, *Abolition Democracy*, 64.

12. Bacon, *The Right to Stay Home*; Abigail Leslie Andrews, *Undocumented Politics: Place, Gender, and the Pathways of Mexican Migrants* (Berkeley: University of California Press, 2018).

13. Instituto Nacional de Estadística y Geografía (INEGI), "Finanzas públicas" [Public Finances] (Mexico City, 2022).

14. Alfonso Gonzales, *Reform without Justice: Latino Migrant Politics and the Homeland Security State* (Oxford: Oxford University Press, 2013).

15. American Immigration Council, "The Cost of Immigration Enforcement and Border Security," January 20, 2021, https://www.americanimmigrationcouncil.org/research /the-cost-of-immigration-enforcement-and-border-security.

16. Todd Miller, "More Than a Wall" (Transnational Institute, Amsterdam, 2019), https://www.tni.org/en/publication/more-than-a-wall-0.

17. Anita Sinha, "Transnational Migration Deterrence," *Boston College Law Review* 63, no. 4 (October 26, 2021): 1295.

18. American Immigration Council, "The Cost of Immigration Enforcement and Border Security"; Clare Ribando Seelke, "Mexico: Evolution of the Mérida Initiative, 2007–2021" (Congressional Research Service, Washington, DC, 2021).

19. Stephen D. Morris, *Political Corruption in Mexico: The Impact of Democratization* (Boulder, CO: Lynne Reiner, 2009); David Hume III, *The Corruption Club: Mexico's Institutional Revolutionary Party* (n.p.: Privately published, 2020).

20. Saskia Sassen, *Expulsions: Brutality and Complexity in the Global Economy* (Cambridge, MA: Harvard University Press, 2014).

21. Angus William Naylor and James Ford, "Vulnerability and Loss and Damage Following the COP27 of the UN Framework Convention on Climate Change," *Regional Environmental Change* 23, no. 1 (2023): 38; Joe Thwaites, "COP28 Climate Fund Pledge Tracker," National Resources Defense Council, *Expert Blog* (blog), December 2, 2023, https://www .nrdc.org/bio/joe-thwaites/cop-28-climate-fund-pledge-tracker.

22. 8 U.S.C.A. §1153(b)(1)(A).

23. Jennifer Gordon, "Transnational Labor Citizenship," *Southern California Law Review* 80 (2007), 503–85.

24. Gordon, "Transnational Labor Citizenship," 509.

25. 8 U.S.C.A. §§ 1101(a)(15)(O).

26. See 8 U.S.C.A. §§ 1101(a)(15)(H).

27. 8 U.S.C.A. §1182(a)(5)(A).

28. Leticia M. Saucedo, "The Employer Preference for the Subservient Worker and the Making of the Brown Collar Workplace," *Ohio State Law Journal* 67, no. 5 (September 5, 2006), 962–1021.

29. Centro de los Derechos del Migrante, "Recruitment Revealed: Fundamental Flaws in the H-2 Temporary Worker Program and Recommendations for Change," 2013, https://cdmigrante.org/wp-content/uploads/2018/02/Recruitment_Revealed.pdf.

30. U.S. Department of Labor, "Fact Sheet #62W: What Is 'Portability' and to Whom Does It Apply?," accessed June 3, 2024, https://www.dol.gov/sites/dolgov/files/WHD/legacy/files/whdfs62W.pdf.

31. Centro de los Derechos del Migrante, "Recruitment Revealed."

32. W. E. B. Du Bois, ed., *Black Reconstruction in America* (New York: Simon and Schuster, 1935).

33. International Law Commission, Report of the International Law Commission on the Work of Its Fifty-Third Session, U.N. Doc. A/56/10, at 94–95 (2001), accessed June 3, 2024, https://legal.un.org/ilc/documentation/english/reports/a_56_10.pdf; United Nations, "Draft Articles on the Responsibility of States for Internationally Wrongful Acts" (2008), Article 34, https://doi.org/10.18356/1b3062be-en.

34. United Nations, "Draft Articles on the Responsibility of States for Internationally Wrongful Acts," Article 35.

35. United Nations, "Draft Articles on the Responsibility of States for Internationally Wrongful Acts," Article 36.

36. United Nations, "Draft Articles on the Responsibility of States for Internationally Wrongful Acts," Article 37.

37. United Nations, "Draft Articles on the Responsibility of States for Internationally Wrongful Acts," Article 15.

38. U.S. Government Accountability Office (GAO), *Treaty of Guadalupe Hidalgo: Findings and Possible Options Regarding Longstanding Community Land Grant Claims in New Mexico* (2004); "Mexican Americans Seek Atonement for Ancestral Lands That Were Taken over Generations," *Turning Point* (ABC News, September 30, 2020), https://abcnews.go.com/US/mexican-americans-seek-atonement-ancestral-lands-generations/story?id=73320792.

39. Ronald Mize, "Reparations for Mexican Braceros: Lessons Learned from Japanese and African American Attempts at Redress," *Cleveland State Law Review* 52, no. 1 (2005): 291–94.

40. "Migrant Families Separated under Trump Face Elusive Quests for Reparations under Biden," May 11, 2022, https://www.cbsnews.com/news/immigration-family-separations-reparations-lawsuits/; "Complaint (Attorney Civil Case Opening)—#1 in Esvin Fernando Arredondo Rodriguez v. United States (C.D. Cal., 2:22-Cv-02845)," April 28, 2022,

https://www.courtlistener.com/docket/63273088/1/esvin-fernando-arredondo-rodriguez
-v-united-states/.

41. Rosa M. Celorio, "The Inter-American Court of Human Rights: Case of González
("Cotton Field") v. Mexico," *International Legal Materials* 49, no. 3 (June 2010): 637–761;
Carson Osberg et al., "Updates from the Regional Human Rights Systems," *Human Rights
Brief* 18 (2011).

42. Eric Ray, "Mexican Repatriation and the Possibility for a Federal Cause of Action:
A Comparative Analysis on Reparations," *University of Miami Inter-American Law Review* 37,
no. 1 (2005): 171.

43. United Nations Framework Convention on Climate Change, "Adoption of the Paris
Agreement," December 12, 2015, Article 8, https://unfccc.int/documents/9064#beg%3E.

44. Carmen G. Gonzalez, "Migration as Reparation: Climate Change and the Disruption of Borders," *Loyola Law Review* 66 (Summer 2020): 401–44.

45. Pooja Dadhania, "State Responsibility for Forced Migration," *Boston College Law
Review* 64, no. 1 (2023).

46. Sarah Sherman-Stokes, "Reparations for Central American Refugees," *Denver Law
Review* 96, no. 1 (2019): 585–634.

47. Gonzalez, "Migration as Reparation," 438.

48. E. Tendayi Achiume, "Migration as Decolonization," *Stanford Law Review* 71 (2019):
1522.

Abrego, Leisy J. *Sacrificing Families: Navigating Laws, Labor, and Love across Borders*. Stanford: Stanford University Press, 2014.

Achiume, E. Tendayi. "Migration as Decolonization." *Stanford Law Review* 71 (2019): 1509–74.

Acuña, Rodolfo. *Occupied America: The Chicanos' Struggle toward Liberation*. San Francisco: Canfield Press, 1972.

Alba, Francisco. "Mexico's International Migration as a Manifestation of Its Development Pattern." *International Migration Review* 14, no. 4 (1978): 503–13.

Alcantar, José Aurelio Granados, and María Félix Quezada Ramírez. "Tendencias de la migración interna de la población indígena en México, 1990–2015 / Trends in Internal Migration among the Indigenous Population in Mexico, 1990–2015." *Estudios Demográficos y Urbanos* 33, no. 2 (2018): 327–64.

Aldana, Raquel. "Of 'Katz' and Aliens: Privacy Expectations and the Immigration Raids." *UC Davis Law Review* 41 (February 2008): 1081–1136.

Alejandre, Jesús Aroyo, Adriá de Léon Arias, and Basilia Valenzuela Barilla. "Patterns of Migration and Regional Development in the State of Jalisco, Mexico." In *Regional and Sectoral Development in Mexico as Alternatives to Migration*, edited by Sergio Diaz-Briquets and Sidney Weintraub, 47–87. New York: Routledge, 1991.

Alexander, Michelle. *The New Jim Crow*. New York: New York University Press, 2012.

Almanza-Alcalde, Horacio. "Some Actors in the Independent Peasant Movement." *Revista Vinculando*, May 31, 2005. https://vinculando.org/comerciojusto/fair_trade/independent_peasant_movement.html.

Alonso, Jose A. "Efectos del TLCAN en la microindustria del vestido en Tlaxcala" [Effects of NAFTA on the Micro-Industry of Clothing in Tlaxcala]. *Comercio Exterior*, 1997. https://scholar.google.com/scholar_lookup?title=Efectos%20del%20TLCAN%20en%20la%20microindustria%20del%20vestido%20de%20Tlaxcala%2C%20M

%C3%A9xico&author=J.%20Alonso&journal=Comercio%20Exterior&volume=47 &issue=2&pages=103-110&publication_year=1997.

American Immigration Council. "The Cost of Immigration Enforcement and Border Security." January 20, 2021. https://www.americanimmigrationcouncil.org/research/the -cost-of-immigration-enforcement-and-border-security.

Amuedo-Dorantes, Catalina, and Susan Pozo. "Remittances as Insurance: Evidence from Mexican Immigrants." *Journal of Population Economics* 19, no. 2 (2006): 227–54.

Anaya Muñoz, Alejandro. *Autonomia indígena, gobernabilidad y legitimidad en Mexico* [Indigenous Autonomy, Governability, and Legitimacy in Mexico]. Mexico City: Plaza y Valdes, 2006.

Andreas, Peter. *Border Games: Policing the U.S. Mexico Divide.* Ithaca, NY: Cornell University Press, 2000.

Andrews, Abigail Leslie. *Undocumented Politics: Place, Gender, and the Pathways of Mexican Migrants.* Berkeley: University of California Press, 2018.

Astorga Lira, Enrique, and Simon Commander. "Agricultural Commercialisation and the Growth of a Migrant Labour Market in Mexico." *International Labour Review* 128, no. 6 (1989): 769–90.

Bacon, David. "'Close to Slavery' or Legalization? The Farmworkers' Hard Choice." *American Prospect*, November 25, 2019. https://prospect.org/api/content/b9b94ef0-0f39-11ea-9905 -1244d5f7c7c6/.

———. *The Right to Stay Home: How U.S. Policy Drives Mexican Migration.* Boston: Beacon Press, 2013.

Bakker, Matt. "Introducing the Remittances-to-Development Agenda: Migration, Remittances, and Development—Three Vignettes." In *Migrating into Financial Markets: How Remittances Became a Development Tool*, 3–33. Berkeley: University of California Press, 2015.

Bartra, Armando. *Cosechas de ira: Economía política de la contrarreforma agraria* [Harvest of Going: The Political Economy of the Agragrian Counterreform]. Mexico City: Itaca/ Instituto Maya, 2003.

Basok, Tanya. "Mexican Seasonal Migration to Canada and Development: A Community-Based Comparison." *International Migration* 41, no. 2 (2003): 3–26.

———. "Migration of Mexican Seasonal Farm Workers to Canada and Development: Obstacles to Productive Investment." *International Migration Review* 34, no. 1 (2000): 79–97.

Bauder, Harald. "The Possibilities of Open and No Borders." *Social Justice* 39, no. 4 (2012): 76–96.

Bejar, Alejandro Álvarez. "Tribute to Alonso Aguilar Monteverde: Ten Key Policies for Understanding the Neoliberal Transformation of Mexican Capitalism." *Social Justice* 42, no. 1 (2015): 107–15.

Benton, Allyson. "The Origins of Mexico's Municipal Usos y Costumbres Regimes: Supporting Local Political Participation or Local Authoritarian Control?" Documentos de Trabajo de Centro de Investigación y Docencia Económicas, 2011. Accessed May 29, 2024. https://repositorio-digital.cide.edu/handle/11651/1345, 36.

Bhattacharyya, Gargi. *Rethinking Racial Capitalism: Questions of Reproduction and Survival.* London: Rowman & Littlefield, 2018.

Bier, David J. "H-2A Visas for Agriculture: The Complex Process for Farmers to Hire Agricultural Guest Workers." Cato Institute, Immigration Research and Policy Brief,

March 10, 2020. https://www.cato.org/publications/immigration-research-policy-brief /h-2a-visas-agriculture-complex-process-farmers-hire.

Boal, Augusto. *The Rainbow of Desire*. London: Routledge, 2013.

———. *Theater of the Oppressed*. London: Pluto Press, 2000.

Boehm, Deborah A. *Intimate Migrations: Gender, Family, and Illegality among Transnational Mexicans*. New York: New York University Press, 2012.

Bolling, Christine, and Constanza Valdes. "The U.S. Presence in Mexico's Agribusiness." Foreign Agricultural Economic Report. Economic Research Service, Washington, DC, 1994.

Brownell, Peter. "The Declining Enforcement of Employer Sanctions." Migration Policy Institute, September 1, 2005. https://www.migrationpolicy.org/article/declining-enforce ment-employer-sanctions.

Bruno, Andorra. "Immigration of Temporary Lower-Skilled Workers: Current Policy and Related Issues." Congressional Research Service, Washington, DC, December 2012, 42.

———. "Immigration-Related Worksite Enforcement: Performance Measures." Congressional Research Service, Washington, DC, June 23, 2015.

Calavita, Kitty. *Inside the State: The Bracero Program, Immigration and the I.N.S.* New York: Routledge, 1992.

Calexico Chronicle. "Aliens without Passports Are Turned Back: Stricter Enforcement at Line Ordered to Prevent Illegal Crossings." June 8, 1924.

Canova, Timothy A. "Banking and Financial Reform at the Crossroads of the Neoliberal Contagion." *American University Journal of International Law and Policy* 14 (1999): 1571, 1590–93.

———. "Global Finance and the International Monetary Fund's Neoliberal Agenda: The Threat to Employment, Ethnic Identity and Cultural Pluralism of Latina/o Identities." *UC Davis Law Review* 33 (2000): 1554–65.

Carens, Joseph H. "Aliens and Citizens: The Case for Open Borders." *Review of Politics* 49, no. 2 (1987): 251–73.

Carrillo Huerta, Mario M. "The Impact of Maquiladoras on Migration in Mexico." In *The Effects of Receiving Country Policies on Migration Flows*, edited by Sergio Diaz-Briquets and Sidney Weintraub, 67–102. Boulder, CO: Westview Press, 1991.

Castles, Stephen, and Raúl Delgado Wise, eds. *Migration and Development: Perspectives from the South*. Geneva: International Organization for Migration, 2008.

Castro, Inés. "El pragmatismo neoliberal y las desigualdades educativas en América Latina" [Neoliberal Pragmatism and the Educational Inequalities in Latin America]. *Revista Mexicana de Sociología* 59, no. 3 (1997): 189–205.

Celorio, Rosa M. "The Inter-American Court of Human Rights: Case of González ('Cotton Field') v. Mexico." *International Legal Materials* 49, no. 3 (June 2010): 637–761.

Centro de Información Éstadistica y Documental para el Desarollo. "Carpeta regional Mixteca" [Regional Folder: Mixteca]. 2011.

Centro de los Derechos del Migrante. "Recruitment Revealed: Fundamental Flaws in the H-2 Temporary Worker Program and Recommendations for Change." 2013. https:// cdmigrante.org/wp-content/uploads/2018/02/Recruitment_Revealed.pdf.

Centro de los Derechos del Migrante and Penn State Law Transnational Law Clinic. "Engendering Exploitation: Gender Inequality in U.S. Labor Migration Programs." 2013. https://cdmigrante.org/wp-content/uploads/2018/01/Engendered-Exploitation.pdf.

Cerrutti, Marcela and Magalí Gaudio, "Gender Differences between Mexican Migration to the United States and Paraguayan Migration to Argentina." *Annals of the American Academy of Political and Social Science* 630 (July 2010): 93–113.

Chacón, Jennifer. "Unsecured Borders: Immigration Restrictions, Crime Control and National Security." *Connecticut Law Review* 39 (July 2007): 1828–90.

Cházaro, Angélica. "The End of Deportation." *UCLA Law Review* 68 (2021): 1040.

Chomsky, Aviva. *Undocumented*. Boston: Beacon Press, 2014.

Cohen, Deborah, *Braceros: Migrant Citizens and Transnational Subjects in the Postwar United States and Mexico*. Chapel Hill University of North Carolina Press, 2011.

Collier, George A., and Elizabeth Lowry Quaratiello. *Basta! Land and the Zapatista Rebellion*. Oakland, CA: First Food Banks, 2005.

"Complaint (Attorney Civil Case Opening)—#1 in Esvin Fernando Arredondo Rodriguez v. United States (C.D. Cal., 2:22-Cv-02845)." April 28, 2022. https://www.courtlistener.com/docket/63273088/1/esvin-fernando-arredondo-rodriguez-v-united-states/.

Consejo Nacional de Población (CONAPO). "Anuario migración y remesas" [Yearbook of Migration and Remittances]. 2019. https://www.gob.mx/cms/uploads/attachment/file/567288/Anuario_Migracion_y_Remesas_2019_Segunda_Parte.pdf.

———. "Índice de marginación por entidad federativa y municipio" [Marginalization Index by State and Municipality]. 1990, 2000, 2010.

———. "Intensidad migratoria a nivel estatal y municipal" [Migration Intensity at the State and Municipal Levels]. 2010. http://www.conapo.gob.mx/work/models/CONAPO/intensidad_migratoria/pdf/IIM_Estatal_y_Municipal.pdf.

Constitution of the United Mexican States. 1917. https://www.loc.gov/item/17021628/.

Cornelius, Wayne A. "Death at the Border: Efficacy and Unintended Consequences of US Immigration Control Policy." *Population and Development Review* 27, no. 4 (2001): 661–85.

———. "Labor Migration to the United States: Development Outcomes and Alternatives in Mexican Sending Communities." In *Regional and Sectoral Deveopment in Mexico as an Alternative to Migration*, edited by Sergio Diaz-Briquets and Sidney Weintraub, 89–131. New York: Routledge, 1991.

Cornelius, Wayne A., and Idean Salehyan. "Does Border Enforcement Deter Unauthorized Immigration? The Case of Mexican Migration to the United States of America." *Regulation and Governance*, no. 1 (2007): 139–53.

Corwin, Arthur. *Immigrants—and Immigrants: Perspectives on Mexican Labor Migration to the United States*. Westport, CT: Greenwood Press, 1978.

Costa, Daniel. "The H-2B Temporary Foreign Worker Program: Examining the Effects on American Job Opportunities and Wages." Economic Policy Institute, 2016. https://www.epi.org/publication/the-h-2b-temporary-foreign-worker-program-examining-the-effects-on-americans-job-opportunities-and-wages/.

———. "Trump Administration Looking to Cut the Already Low Wages of H-2A Migrant Farmworkers While Giving Their Bosses a Multibillion-Dollar Bailout." *Economic Policy Institute* (blog), April 20, 2020. https://www.epi.org/blog/trump-administration-reportedly-looking-to-cut-the-already-low-wages-of-h-2a-migrant-farmworkers-while-giving-their-bosses-a-multibillion-dollar-bailout/.

Dadhania, Pooja. "State Responsibility for Forced Migration." *Boston College Law Review* 64, no. 1 (2023): 746–800.

Dávila Larránga, Laura G. "How Does Propsera Work? Best Practices in the Implementation of Conditional Cash Transfer Programs in Latin America and the Caribbean." Last modified April 2016. https://publications.iadb.org/publications/english/document/How-does-Prospera-Work-Best-Practices-in-the-Implementation-of-Conditional-Cash-Transfer-Programs-in-Latin-America-and-the-Caribbean.pdf.

Davis, Angela Y. *Abolition Democracy: Beyond Empire, Prisons, and Torture*. New York: Seven Stories Press, 2005.

———. *Are Prisons Obsolete?* New York: Seven Stories Press, 2003.

De Genova, Nicholas P. "Migrant 'Illegality' and Deportability in Everyday Life." *Annual Review of Anthropology* 31 (2002): 419–47.

———. "The Production of Culprits: From Deportability to Detainability in the Aftermath of 'Homeland Security.'" *Citizenship Studies* 11, no. 5 (November 1, 2007): 421–48. https://doi.org/10.1080/13621020701605735.

Délano, Alexandra. *Mexico and Its Diaspora in the United States: Policies of Emigration since 1848*. Cambridge: Cambridge University Press, 2011.

Delgado Wise, Raúl. "Migration and Imperialism: The Mexican Workforce in the Context of NAFTA." *Latin American Perspectives* 33, no. 147 (2006): 33–45.

Delgado Wise, Raúl, and Oscar Mañan Garcia. "Migración México–Estados Unidos e integración económica" [Mexico-U.S. Migration and Economic Integration]. *Política y Cultura* 23 (n.d.): 9–23.

Delgado Wise, Raúl, and Humberto Márquez Covarrubias. "Capitalist Restructuring, Development and Labour Migration: The Mexico-US Case." *Third World Quarterly* 29, no. 7 (2008): 1359–74.

———. "The Mexico–United States Migratory System: Dilemmas of Regional Integration, Development and Emigration." In *Migration and Development: Perspectives from the South*, edited by Stephen Castles and Raúl Delgado Wise, 113–42. Geneva: International Organization for Migration, 2008.

———. "Migration and Development in Mexico: Toward a New Analytical Approach." *Journal of Latino/Latin American Studies* 2, no. 3 (April 2007): 101–19.

Delgado Wise, Raúl, and Henry Veltmeyer. *Agrarian Change, Migration and Development*. Agrarian Change and Peasant Studies. Black Point, Nova Scotia: Fernwood Publishing, 2016.

"DHS to Supplement H-2B Cap with Nearly 65,000 Additional Visas for Fiscal Year 2023 | Homeland Security." Accessed December 30, 2022. https://www.dhs.gov/news/2022/10/12/dhs-supplement-h-2b-cap-nearly-65000-additional-visas-fiscal-year-2023.

Donato, Katharine M., Donna Gabaccia, Jennifer Holdaway, Martin Manalansan IV, and Patricia R. Pessar. "A Glass Half Full? Gender in Migration Studies 1." *International Migration Review* 40, no. 1 (2006): 3–26.

Dreher, Axel, and Nathan M. Jensen. "Independent Actor or Agent? An Empirical Analysis of the Impact of U.S. Interests on the International Monetary Fund Conditions." *Journal of Law and Economics* 50 (2008).

Du Bois, W. E. B., ed. *Black Reconstruction in America*. New York: Simon and Schuster, 1935.

Dunn, Timothy J. *The Militarization of the U.S.-Mexico Border 1978–1992: Low Intensity Conflict Doctrine Comes Home*. Austin: Center for Mexican American Studies, University of Texas at Austin, 1996.

Durand, Jorge, William Kandel, Emilio A. Parrado, and Douglas S. Massey. "International Migration and Development in Mexican Communities." *Demography* 33, no. 2 (1996): 249–64.

Economic Research Service. "U.S. Department of Agriculture Economic Research Service Farm Labor." April 22, 2020. https://www.ers.usda.gov/topics/farm-economy/farm-labor /#size.

Employment and Training Administration. "Adverse Effect Wage Rate Methodology for the Temporary Employment of H-2A Nonimmigrants in Non-Range Occupations in the United States." 85 FR 70445 § (2020). https://www.federalregister.gov/documents/2020 /11/05/2020-24544/adverse-effect-wage-rate-methodology-for-the-temporary -employment-of-h-2a-nonimmigrants-in-non-range.

———. "Findings from the National Agricultural Workers Survey (NAWS) 2019–2020: A Demographic and Employment Profile of United States Farmworkers (Research Report No. 16)." U.S. Department of Labor, Washington, DC, June 3, 2022.

Esquivel, Gerardo, and A. Huerta-Pineda. "Remittances and Poverty in Mexico: A Propensity Score Matching Approach." *Integration and Trade* 27 (January 1, 2007): 1–28.

Ettinger, Patrick. *Imaginary Lines: Border Enforcement and the Origins of Undocumented Immigration 1882–1930*. Austin: University of Texas Press, 2009.

Federal Register. "Temporary Changes to Requirements Affecting H-2A Nonimmigrants due to the COVID-19 National Emergency: Extension of Certain Flexibilities." 85 FR 82291 § (2020).

Fernandez, Laura Vidal, Esperanza Tuñon Pablos, Martha Rojas Weisner, and Ramfis Ayús Reyes. "De paraíso a Carolina del Norte, redes de apoyo y percepciones de la migración a Estados Unidos de mujeres tabasqueñas despulpadoras de jaiba" [From Paraíso to North Carolina, Support Networks and Perceptions of Migration to the United States of Tabascan Women Crab Pulpers]. *Migraciones Internacionales* 1, no. 002 (2002): 30.

Fish, Eric S. "Race, History, and Immigration Crimes." *Iowa Law Review* 107, no. 1 (April 15, 2021): 1051–1106.

Ford Foundation. "Mexico and Central America." 2012. https://www.fordfoundation.org /media/1605/mexico-brochure-2011.pdf.

Forman, Marcy M. "Worksite Enforcement Strategy." U.S. Immigration Customs and Enforcement, April 30, 2009. https://www.ice.gov/doclib/foia/dro_policy_memos/worksite _enforcement_strategy4_30_2009.pdf.

Fox, Jonathan. "Latin America's Emerging Local Politics." *Journal of Democracy* 5, no. 2 (1994): 105–16.

Fox, Jonathan, and Libby Haight. "Mexican Agricultural Policy: Multiple Goals and Conflicting Interests." In *Subsidizing Inequality: Mexican Corn Policy since NAFTA*, edited by Jonathan Fox and Libbby Haight, 11–43. Washington, DC: Woodrow Wilson International Center for Scholars, 2010.

Friedmann, John. *Empowerment: The Politics of Alternative Development*. Oxford: Blackwell, 1992.

Gago, Verónica. *La potencia feminista. O el deseo de cambiarlo todo* [The Feminist Power. Or the Desire to Change Everything]. Madrid: Traficantes de Sueños, 2019.

Galarza, Ernesto. *Strangers in Our Fields*. Ann Arbor: University of Michigan Press, 1956.)

Gamio, Manuel. "The Songs of the Immigrant, Chapter VII." In *Mexican Immigration to the United States: A Study of Human Migration and Adjustment*, 1:84–107. Chicago: University of Chicago Press, 1930.

García, Juan Ramon. *Operation Wetback: The Mass Deportation of Mexican Undocumented Workers in 1954.* Westport, CT: Greenwood Press, 1980.

García Hernández, César Cuauhtémoc. "Abolishing Immigration Prisons." *Boston College Law Review* 97, no. 1 (2017), 246–300.

———. *Migrating to Prison: America's Obsession with Locking Up Immigrants.* New York: New Press, 2019.

Garcia y Griego, Manuel, and Monica Verea. *Mexico y Estados Unidos frente a la migración de los indocumentados* [Mexico and the United States versus the Migration of the Undocumented]. Mexico City: UNAM/Porrúa, 1988.

García Zamora, Rodolfo. "El programa Tres por Uno de remesas colectivas en México: Lecciones y desafíos" [The Three for One Program of Collective Remittances in Mexico: Lessons and Challenges]. *Migraciones Internacionales* 4, no. 1 (2007): 8.

Garrison, Jessica, Ken Bensinger, and Jeremy Singer-Vine. "The New American Slavery: Invited to the U.S., Foreign Workers Find a Nightmare." *Buzz Feed News.* Accessed December 30, 2022. https://www.buzzfeednews.com/article/jessicagarrison/the-new-american-slavery-invited-to-the-us-foreign-workers-f#.lyREpxV9Kq.

Gates, Marilyn. *In Default: Peasants, the Debt Crisis, and the Agricultural Challenge in Mexico.* Boulder, CO: Westview Press, 1993.

Germano, Roy. *Outsourcing Welfare: How the Money Immigrants Send Home Contributes to Stability in Developing Countries.* Oxford: Oxford University Press, 2018.

Gershberg, Alec Ian. "Decentralization Process in Mexico and Nicaragua: Legislative vs. Ministry Led Reforms Strategies." *Comparative Education* 35, no. 1 (March 1999): 63–90.

Gibson, Edward L. "Boundary Control: Subnational Authoritarianism in Democratic Countries." *World Politics* 58, no. 1 (2005): 101–32.

Gillingham, Paul. *Unrevolutionary Mexico: The Birth of a Strange Dictatorship.* New Haven, CT: Yale University Press, 2021.

Golash-Boza, Tanya Maria. *Deported: Immigrant Policing, Disposable Labor, and Global Capitalism.* New York: New York University Press, 2015.

Gonzales, Alfonso. *Reform without Justice: Latino Migrant Politics and the Homeland Security State.* Oxford: Oxford University Press, 2013.

Gonzalez, Carmen G. "Migration as Reparation: Climate Change and the Disruption of Borders." *Loyola Law Review* 66 (Summer 2020): 401–44.

González, Diana Alarcón. *Changes in the Distribution of Income in Mexico and Trade Liberalization.* Tijuana: El Colegio de la Frontera Norte, 1994.

González, Gilbert G. *Guest Workers or Colonized Labor? Mexican Labor Migration to the United States.* Boulder, CO: Paradigm Press, 2013.

González, Gilbert G., and Raúl Fernández. *A Century of Chicano History: Empire, Nations and Migration.* New York: Routledge, 2003.

———. "Empire and the Origins of Twentieth-Century Migration from Mexico to the United States." *Pacific Historical Review* 71, no. 1 (2002): 19–57.

Goodman, Adam. *The Deportation Machine: America's Long History of Expelling Immigrants.* Princeton, NJ: Princeton University Press, 2020.

Gordon, Jennifer. "Transnational Labor Citizenship." *Southern California Law Review* 80 (2007): 503–85.

Green, Duncan. *Silent Revolution: The Rise and Crisis of Market Economics in Latin America.* 2nd ed. New York: New York University Press, 2003.

Griffith, David, *American Guestworker: Jamaicans and Mexicans in the U.S. Labor Market.* University Park: Pennsylvania State University Press, 2006.

———. "New Immigrants in an Old Industry: Mexican H-2B Workers in the Mid-Atlantic Blue Crab Processing Industry." Accessed July 21, 2020. https://migration.ucdavis.edu /cf/more.php?id=148.

Guarnizo, Luis Eduardo. "The Economics of Transnational Living." *International Migration Review* 37, no. 3 (2003): 666–99.

Gutiérrez, David G. *Walls and Mirrors: Mexican Americans, Mexican Immigrants, and the Politics of Ethnicity.* Berkeley: University of California Press, 1995.

Hansen, Lawrence Douglas Taylor. "The Origins of the Maquila Industry in Mexico." *Comercio Exterior* 53, no. 11 (n.d.): 16.

Haq, Mahbub ul. *Reflections on Human Development.* Oxford: Oxford University Press, 1995.

Henriques, Gisele, and Raj Patel. "Agricultural Trade Liberalization and Mexico." Food First, Institute for Food Development Policy, 2003.

Heredia, Carlos, and Mary Purcell. "Structural Adjustment in Mexico." Last modified 1995. http://www.hartford-hwp.com/archives/46/013.html.

Hernández, César García Cuauhtémoc. *Migrating to Prison: America's Obsession with Locking Up Immigrants.* New York: New Press, 2019.

Hernández, Kelly Lytle. *City of Inmates: Conquest, Rebellion, and the Rise of Human Caging in Los Angeles, 1771–1965.* Chapel Hill: University of North Carolina Press, 2017.

———. "How Crossing the US-Mexico Border Became a Crime." The Conversation, April 30, 2017. http://theconversation.com/how-crossing-the-us-mexico-border-became-a-crime -74604.

———. *Migra! A History of the U.S. Border Patrol.* Berkeley: University of California Press, 2010.

Hernández, Rúben. "Crece consumo de drogas en Tlaxcaltecas, narcomenudeo sin ser alarmante" [Drug Consumption Grows among Tlaxcaltecs, Drug Dealing without Being Alarming]. *Quadratín Tlaxcala*, February 14, 2018. https://tlaxcala.quadratin.com.mx /principal/crece-consumo-drogas-tlaxcaltecas-narcomenudeo-sin-alarmante/.

Hernández-León, Rubén. "Conceptualizing the Migration Industry." In *The Migration Industry and Commercialization of International Migration*, 42–62. Oxford: Routledge, 2012. https://doi.org/10.4324/9780203082737–11.

Herrera, Ramón Vera, and Luis Hernández Navarro. *Acuerdos de San Andrés* [San Andrés Accords]. Mexico City: Ediciones Era, 1998.

Hing, Bill Ong. *Ethical Borders: NAFTA, Globalization, and Mexican Migration.* Philadelphia: Temple University Press, 2010.

Hlass, Laila, and Lindsay Harris. "Critical Interviewing." *Utah Law Review* 2021, no. 3 (October 1, 2021). https://doi.org/10.26054/od-8c1z-7z3s.

Hondagneu-Sotelo, Pierrette. *Doméstica: Immigrant Workers Cleaning and Caring in the Shadows of Affluence.* Berkeley: University of California Press, 2007.

Hufbauer, Gary Clyde, and Jeffrey J. Schott. *NAFTA: An Assessment.* Washington, DC: Peterson Institute for International Economics, 1993.

Human Rights First. "Punishing Refugees and Migrants: The Trump Administration's Misuse of Criminal Prosecutions." January 2018. https://www.humanrightsfirst.org/sites /default/files/2018-Report-Punishing-Refugees-Migrants.pdf.

Hume III, David. *The Corruption Club: Mexico's Institutional Revolutionary Party*. n.p.: Privately published, 2020.

Instituto Nacional de Estadística y Geografía (INEGI). "ENADID. Encuesta nacional de la dinámica demográfica 1997: Panorama sociodemográfico. Estados Unidos Mexicanos" [National Survey of Demographic Dynamics 1997. United States of Mexico]. 1997. https://www.inegi.org.mx/app/biblioteca/ficha.html?upc=702825493691.

———. "Encuesta nacional de dinámica demográfica 2009 microdatos" [National Survey of Demographic Dynamics Microdata Tables 2009]. 2010. https://www.inegi.org.mx/programas/enadid/2009/default.html#Microdatos.

———. "Finanzas públicas" [Public Finances]. 2022.

———. "Información por entidad: Número de habitantes. Oaxaca" [Infomation by State: Population: Oaxaca]. 2010. http://cuentame.inegi.org.mx/monografias/informacion/oax/poblacion/default.aspx?tema=me&e=20.

———. "Modulo sobre migración: Encuesta nacional de empleo 2002" [Module on Migration: National Survey of Employment 2002]. 2002.

———. "Población de 3 años y mas por municipio, sexo y grupo quinquenales de edad según condición de habla indígena y de habla española" [Population 3 Years of Age and Older by City, Sex, and Five-Year Age Group according to Indigenous-Speaking and Spanish-Speaking Status], 2010, https://www.inegi.org.mx/contenidos/programas/ccpv/2010/tabulados/Basico/05_01B_MUNICIPAL_27.pdf.

———. "Tendencias y características de la migración mexicana a los Estados Unidos" [Tendencies and Characteristics of Mexican Migration to the United States]. 1990, 2000, 2010.

International Law Commission. Report of the International Law Commission on the Work of Its Fifty-Third Session. U.N. Doc. A/56/10. 2001. https://legal.un.org/ilc/documentation/english/reports/a_56_10.pdf.

Isaac, Barry L. "The Aztec 'Flowery War': A Geopolitical Explanation." *Journal of Anthropological Research* 39, no. 4 (1983): 415–32.

Ixtlilxóchitl. *Obras Historicas*. Vol. 2: *Historias Chichimeca* [Historical Works. Vol. 2: Chichimec Stories]. Mexico City: Editorial Nacional, 1965.

Jingzhong, Ye. "Left-Behind Children: The Social Price of China's Economic Boom." *Journal of Peasant Studies* 38, no. 3 (July 2011): 613–50. https://doi.org/10.1080/03066150.2011.582946.

Johnson, Kevin. "The Case against Race Profiling in Immigration Enforcement." *Washington University Law Quarterly* 78 (2000): 680–735.

———. "The Intersection of Race and Class in U.S. Immigration Law and Enforcement." *Law and Contemporary Problems* 72 (Fall 2009): 1–35.

———. *Opening the Floodgates: Why America Needs to Rethink Its Borders and Immigration Laws*. New York: New York University Press Press, 2007.

———. "Race, the Immigration Laws, and Domestic Race Relations: A 'Magic Mirror' into the Heart of Darkness." *Indiana Law Journal* 73 (1998): 1111–59.

Kang, S. Deborah. *The INS on the Line: Making Immigration Law on the US-Mexico Border, 1917–1954*. New York: Oxford University Press, 2017.

Kanstroom, Dan. *Deportation Nation: Outsiders in American History*. Cambridge, MA: Harvard University Press, 2007.

Kanstroom, Daniel. "Criminalizing the Undocumented: Ironic Boundaries of the Post–September 11 'Pale of Law.'" *North Carolina Journal of International Law and Commercial Regulation* 29 (2004): 639–70.

Kearney, Michael. *Changing Fields of Anthropology: From Local to Global.* Lanham, MD: Rowman & Littlefield, 2004.

———. "Transnational Oaxacan Indigenous Identity: The Case of Mixtecs and Zapotecs." *Identities* 7, no. 2 (June 1, 2000): 173–95.

Kearney, Michael, and Federico Besserer. "Oaxacan Municipal Governance in a Transnational Context." In *Indigenous Mexican Migrants in the United States,* edited by Jonathan Fox and Gaspar Rivera Salgado, 449–66. La Jolla: University of California, San Diego, Center for U.S.-Mexican Studies, 2004.

Keely, C. B., and B. N. Tran. "Remittances from Labor Migration: Evaluations, Performance and Implications." *International Migration Review* 23, no. 3 (1989): 500–525.

Keller, Doug. "Re-Thinking Illegal Entry and Re-Entry." *Loyola University Chicago Law Journal* 44 (Fall 2012): 65–139.

Kelly, Thomas J. "Neoliberal Reforms and Rural Poverty." *Latin American Perspectives* 28, no. 3 (2001): 84–103.

Kessler, Judi A. "The North American Free Trade Agreement, Emerging Apparel Production Networks, and Industrial Upgrading: The Southern California/Mexico Connection." *Review of International Political Economy* 6, no. 4 (1999): 565–608.

Kohout, Michal. "The Maquiladora Industry and Migration in Mexico: A Survey of Literature." *Geography Compass* 3, no. 1 (2009): 135–53. https://doi.org/10.1111/j.1749-8198 .2008.00199.x.

Lablonte, Marc. "The Current Economic Recession: How Long, How Deep, and How Different From the Past?" Congressional Research Service, Washington, DC, 2002.

Longazel, Jamie, and Miranda Cady Hallett. *Migration and Mortality: Social Death, Dispossession, and Survival in the Americas.* Philadelphia: Temple University Press, 2021.

Lopez, Edwin. "Migration as Resistance to Global Capitalism: From Cause to Action in the Migration of Central American Children to the United States." *Perspectives on Global Development and Technology* 16, no. 1–3 (Summer 2014): 34–59.

López, Gerald. "Don't We Like Them Illegal?" *UC Davis Law Review* 45 (July 2012): 1711–1816.

Lopez, J. Humberto, Pablo Fajnzylber, and Pablo Acosta. "The Impact of Remittances on Poverty and Human Capital : Evidence from Latin American Household Surveys." World Bank Policy Research Working Papers, 2007.

Lowenfeld, Andreas F. "The International Monetary System: A Look Back over Seven Decades." *Journal of International Economic Law* 1, no. 5–6 (2010): 13–14.

Luan, Livia. "Profiting from Enforcement: The Role of Private Prisons in U.S. Immigration Detention." Migration Policy Institute, Washington, DC, 2018.

Lustig, Nora. *Mexico: The Remaking of an Economy.* Washington, DC: Brookings Institution Press, 1998.

Lydgate, Joanna Jacobbi. "Assembly-Line Justice: A Review of Operation Streamline." *California Law Review* 98, no. 2 (2010): 481–544.

Lyons, Richard D. "Seldom Active Senate Unit Drew $2-Million in Decade." *New York Times,* September 29, 1975, sec. Archives. https://www.nytimes.com/1975/09/29/archives/new -jersey-pages-seldom-active-senate-unit-drew-2million-in-decade.html.

Mahmud, Tayyub. "Migration, Identity, and the Colonial Encounter." *Oregon Law Review* 76 (Fall 1997): 633–90.

Mailman, Stanley, Stephen Yale-Loehr, and Ronald Wada. *Immigration Law and Procedure.* New York: Matthew Bender, 2022.

Maldonado Vásquez, Centolia, and Patricia Artía Rodriguez. "'Now We Are Awake': Women's Political Participation in the Oaxacan Indigenous Binational Front." In *Indigenous Mexican Migrants in the United States*, edited by Jonathan Fox and Gaspar Rivera Salgado, 1–47. La Jolla: University of California, San Diego, Center for U.S.-Mexican Studies and Center for Comparative Immigration Studies, 2004.

Martin, Philip L. "Good Intentions Gone Awry: IRCA and U.S. Agriculture." *Annals of the American Academy of Political and Social Science* 534 (July 1994): 44–57.

Massey, Douglas S., Joaquin Arango, Graeme Hugo, Ali Kouaouci, and Adela Pellegrino. *Worlds in Motion: Understanding International Migration at the End of the Millennium.* Oxford: Clarendon Press, 1999.

Massey, Douglas S., and Lawrence C. Basem. "Determinants of Savings, Remittances, and Spending Patterns among U.S. Migrants in Four Mexican Communities." *Sociological Inquiry* 62, no. 2 (1992): 185–207.

Massey, Douglas S., Jorge Durand, and Nolan Malone. *Beyond Smoke and Mirrors: Mexican Immigration in an Era of Economic Integration.* New York: Russell Sage Foundation, 2002.

Massey, Douglas S., and Audrey Singer. "New Estimates of Undocumented Mexican Migration and Probability of Apprehension." *Demography* 32, no. 2 (May 1995): 203–13. https://doi.org/10.2307/2061740.

Menjívar, Cecilia, and Leisy Abrego. "Legal Violence: Immigration Law and the Lives of Central American Immigrants." *American Journal of Sociology* 117, no. 5 (2012): 1380–1421.

"Mexican Americans Seek Atonement for Ancestral Lands That Were Taken over Generations." *Turning Point*, ABC News, September 30, 2020. https://abcnews.go.com/US /mexican-americans-seek-atonement-ancestral-lands-generations/story?id=73320792.

"Migrant Families Separated under Trump Face Elusive Quests for Reparations under Biden." May 11, 2022. https://www.cbsnews.com/news/immigration-family-separations -reparations-lawsuits/.

Migration Policy Institute. "Immigration Enforcement Spending since IRCA." Migration Policy Institute, Washington, DC, November 2005. https://www.migrationpolicy.org/sites /default/files/publications/FactSheet_Spending.pdf.

Miller, Todd. "More Than a Wall." Transnational Institute, Amsteram, 2019. https://www .tni.org/en/publication/more-than-a-wall-0.

Miller, Todd, and Nick Buxton. "Biden's Border Wall." Amsterdam: Transnational Institute, 2021. https://www.tni.org/en/publication/bidens-border.

Mishra, Prachi. "Emigration and Wages in Source Countries: Evidence from Mexico." *Journal of Development Economics* 82 (2007): 180–99.

Mize, Ronald. "Reparations for Mexican Braceros: Lessons Learned from Japanese and African American Attempts at Redress." *Cleveland State Law Review* 52, no. 1 (2005), 274–95.

Molina, Natalia. *How Race Is Made in America: Immigration, Citizenship, and the Historical Power of Racial Scripts.* Berkeley: University of California Press, 2014.

Monjarás-Ruiz, Jesús. "Panorama general de la guerra entre los Aztecas" [Overview of the War between the Aztecs]. *Estudios de Cultura Náhuatl* 12 (1976): 241–64.

Monoy, Carlos, and Stefan Trines, "Education in Mexico." *World Education News and Reviews*, 2019. https://wenr.wes.org/2019/05/education-in-mexico-2.

Montalvo, Juan Maldonado, and Adrián González Romo. "Factores determinantes en la migración de las familias indígena de San Francisco de Tetlanohcan y sus conseqencias implicitas" [Determining Factors in the Migration of Indigenous Families from San Francisco de Tetlanohcan and Their Implicit Consequences]. In *La migración de Tlaxcaltecas en Estados Unidos y Canadá: Panorama actual y perspectivas* [Migration of Tlaxcaltecs in the United States and Canada: Contemporary Outlook and Perspectives], edited by Raúl Jimenez Guillén and Adrián González Romo, 207–32. San Pablo Apetatitlán: El Colegio de Tlaxcala, 2008.

Morris, Stephen D. *Political Corruption in Mexico The Impact of Democratization*. Boulder, CO: Lynne Rienner, 2009.

Naude, Alejandro Yúnez. "The Dismantling of CONASUPO: A Mexican State Trader in Agriculture." *World Economy* 26, no. 1 (2003): 97–122.

Naude, Alejandro Yúnez, and Fernando Barceinas Paredes. "The Reshaping of Agricultural Policy in Mexico." In *Changing Structure of Mexico*, 2nd ed., edited by Laura Randall. New York: Routledge, 2006.

Navarro, Luis Hernández. "San Andrés: 20 años después" [San Andrés: 20 Years Later]. *El Cotidiano*, 2016, 18.

Navarro, Mina Lorena. "Luchas por lo común contra el renovado cercamiento de bienes naturales en México" [Fight for the Commons against the Renewed Enclosure of Natural Resources in Mexico]. *Bajo el Volcán*, no. 21 (2013).

Naylor, Angus William, and James Ford. "Vulnerability and Loss and Damage Following the COP27 of the UN Framework Convention on Climate Change." *Regional Environmental Change* 23, no. 1 (2023): 38.

Nett, Roger. "The Civil Right We Are Not Ready For: The Right of Free Movement of People on the Face of the Earth." *Ethics* 81, no. 3 (1971): 212–27.

Nevins, Joseph. *Operation Gatekeeper: The Rise of the "Illegal Alien" and the Making of the U.S.-Mexico Boundary*. New York: Routledge, 2002.

Ngai, Mae. *Impossible Subjects: Illegal Aliens and the Making of Modern America—Updated Edition*. Princeton, NJ: Princeton University Press, 2004.

Niño-Zarazúa, Miguel. "Mexico's Progreso-Oportunidades and the Emergence of Social Assistance in Latin America." Munich Personal RePec Archive Paper No. 29639. https:// mpra.ub.uni-muenchen.de/29639/. Posted March 2011.

Oliveira, Gabrielle. *Motherhood across Borders: Immigrants and Their Children in Mexico and New York*. New York: New York University Press, 2018.

Oliveira, Victor J. "Trends in Hired Farm Work Force 1945–1987." U.S. Department of Agriculture, Economic Research Service, April 1989.

Orozco, Manuel. "Globalization and Migration: The Impact of Family Remittances in Latin America." *Latin American Politics and Society* 44, no. 2 (2002): 41–66.

Ortiz, M. Laura Velasco. *Mixtec Transnational Identity*. Tucson: University of Arizona Press, 2005.

Osberg, Carson, Emily Rose Johns, Christopher Tansey, and Michael Becker. "Updates from the Regional Human Rights Systems." *Human Rights Brief* 18 (n.d.): 2011.

Otero, Gerardo. *Neoliberalism Revisited: Economic Restructuring and Mexico's Political Future*. New York: Routledge, 2018.

Palacios, Simón Pedro Izcara. "Coyotaje y grupos delictivos en Tamaulipas" [Coyotaje and Criminal Organizations in Tamaulipas]. *Latin American Research Review* 47, no. 3 (2012): 41–61.

Pastor, Manuel, and Carol Wise. "State Policy, Distribution and Neoliberal Reform in Mexico." *Journal of Latin American Studies* 29, no. 2 (1997): 419–56.

Pierce, Sarah, and Jessica Bolter. "Dismantling and Reconstructing the U.S. Immigration System: A Catalog of Changes under the Trump Presidency." Accessed May 29, 2024. https://www.migrationpolicy.org/research/us-immigration-system-changes-trump -presidency, 126.

Portes, Alejandro. "Neoliberalism and the Sociology of Development: Emerging Trends and Unanticipated Facts." *Population and Development Review* 23, no. 2 (1997): 229–59.

Ramirez, Miguel D., "The Latest IMF-Sponsored Stabilization Program: Does It Represent a Long-Term Solution for Mexico's Economy?" *Journal of Interamerican Studies and World Affairs* 38, no. 4 (Winter 1996): 129–56.

———. "Stabilization and Trade Reform." *Journal of Developing Areas* 27, no. 2 (January 1993): 173–90.

Ramírez de la O, Rogelio. "Economic Outlook in the 1990s: Mexico." In *U.S-Mexican Industrial Integration: The Road to Free Trade*, edited by Sidney Weintraub, Luis Rubio, and A. D. Jones, 2–32. Boulder, CO: Westview Press, 1991.

Ray, Eric. "Mexican Repatriation and the Possibility for a Federal Cause of Action: A Comparative Analysis on Reparations." *University of Miami Inter-American Law Review* 37, no. 1 (2005): 171–95.

Rivera Salgado, Gaspar, and Jonathan Fox, eds. *Indigenous Mexican Migrants in the United States*. La Jolla: University of California, San Diego, Center for U.S.-Mexican Studies and Center for Comparative Immigration Studies, 2004.

Robinson, Cedric J. *Black Marxism: The Making of the Black Radical Tradition*. Reprint. Chapel Hill: University of North Carolina Press, 2000.

Ruiz-Arranz, Marta, Benjamin Davis, Sudhanshu Handa, Marco Stampini, and Paul Winters. "Program Conditionality and Food Security: The Impact of PROGRESA and PROCAMPO Transfers in Rural Mexico." *Economía Journal* 7, no. 2 (August 1, 2006).

Ruiz Marrujo, Olivia T. "Women, Migration, and Sexual Violence: Lessons from Mexico's Borders." In *Human Rights Along the U.S.-Mexico Border: Gendered Violence and Insecurity*, edited by Kathleen A. Staudt, Tony Payan, and Z. Anthony Kruszcwski, 31 47. Tucson: University of Arizona Press, 2009.

Ryo, Emily. "Deciding to Cross: Norms and Economics of Unauthorized Migration." *American Sociological Review* 78, no. 4 (2013): 574–603.

Rytina, Nancy. "IRCA Legalization Effects: Lawful Permanent Residence and Naturalization through 2001." In *The Effects of Legalization Programs on the United States*. Washington, DC: U.S. Immigration and Naturalization Service, Office of Policy and Planning, Statistics Division. 2002. https://www.dhs.gov/sites/default/files/publications /IRCA_Legalization_Effects_2002.pdf.

Salinas, Cristina. *Managed Migrations: Growers, Farmworkers, and Border Enforcement in the Twentieth Century*. Austin: University of Texas Press, 2018.

Sánchez, George J. *Becoming Mexican American: Ethnicity, Culture, and Identity in Chicano Los Angeles, 1900–1945*. New York: Oxford University Press, 1995.

Sarre, Pablo Latapí. *Un siglo de educación en México* [A Century of Education in Mexico]. Mexico City: Fondo de Estudios e Investigaciones Ricardo J. Zevada, Consejo Nacional para la Cultura y las Artes, Fondo de Cultura Económica, 1998.

Sassen, Saskia. *Expulsions: Brutality and Complexity in the Global Economy*. Cambridge, MA: Harvard University Press, 2014.

———. *The Mobility of Labor and Capital: A Study in International Investment and Labor Flow*. Cambridge: Cambridge University Press, 1988.

Saucedo, Leticia M. "The Employer Preference for the Subservient Worker and the Making of the Brown Collar Workplace." *Ohio State Law Journal* 67, no. 5 (September 5, 2006): 962–1021.

Scherr, S. J. *The Oil Syndrome and Agricultural Development: Lessons from Tabasco, Mexico*. New York: Praeger, 1985.

Secretaría de Desarrollo Social. "Acciones 3x1" [3x1 Actions]. Last accessed May 31, 2024. https://datos.sedesol.gob.mx/UMR/UMR/oct2015/acciones_3x1_2013.csv

———. "Católogo de localidades—Tlaxcala" [Catalog of Localities]. 2010. http://www.microrregiones.gob.mx/catloc/Default.aspx?tipo=clave&campo=mun&valor=29.

Seelke, Clare Ribando. "Mexico: Background and U.S. Relations." Congressional Research Service, Washington, DC, December 2020.

———. "Mexico: Evolution of the Mérida Initiative, 2007–2021." Congressional Research Service, Washington, DC, 2021.

Segreste Ríos, Sergio. "Capitulo V: La sistema de usos y costumbres" [Chapter V: The Ways and Customs System]. In *Manual básico de derechos humanos para autoridades municipales* [Basic Manual of Human Rights for Municipal Authorities]. Mexico City: Comisión Nacional de los Derechos Humanos, 2019.

Selden, David A., Heidi Nunn-Gilman, Jennifer L Sellers, Julie A. Pace, and Yijee Jeong. "Criminal Enforcement and I-9 Audits." *HR Simple* (blog). Accessed February 23, 2021. https://www.hrsimple.com.

Sherman-Stokes, Sarah. "Reparations for Central American Refugees." *Denver Law Review* 96, no. 1 (2019): 585–634.

Sinha, Anita. "Transnational Migration Deterrence." *Boston College Law Review* 63, no. 4 (October 26, 2021): 1295.

Slack, Jeremy, and Scott Whiteford. "Violence and Migration on the Arizona-Sonora Border." *Human Organization* 70, no. 1 (2011): 11–21.

Soto, Lilia. *Girlhood in the Borderlands: Mexican Teens Caught in the Crossroads of Migration*. New York: New York University Press, 2018.

Southern Poverty Law Center. "Close to Slavery: Guestworker Programs in the United States." February 19, 2013. https://www.splcenter.org/20130218/close-slavery-guestworker-programs-united-states.

Spener, David. *Clandestine Crossings: Migrants and Coyotes on the Texas-Mexico Border*. Ithaca, NY: Cornell University Press, 2011.

Srikrishnan, Maya. "How San Diego Is Pushing Back against 'Zero Tolerance' at the Border." Voice of San Diego, November, 27, 2018. https://www.voiceofsandiego.org/topics/news/how-san-diego-is-pushing-back-against-zero-tolerance-at-the-border.

Streeten, Paul. *First Things First: Meeting Basic Human Needs in the Developing Countries*. Oxford: Oxford University Press, 1981.

Taylor, Edward J. "The New Economics of Labour Migration and the Role of Remittances in the Migration Process." *International Migration* 37, no. 1 (1999): 63–88.

Tetreault, Darcy Victor. "Alternative Pathways out of Rural Poverty in Mexico." *Revista Europea de Estudios Latinoamericanos y del Caribe / European Review of Latin American and Caribbean Studies*, no. 88 (2010): 77–94.

Thompson, Gary, Ricardo Amon, and Philip L. Martin. "Agricultural Development and Emigration: Rhetoric and Reality." *International Migration Review* 20, no. 3 (1986): 575–97.

Thwaites, Joe. "COP28 Climate Fund Pledge Tracker." National Resources Defense Council. *Expert Blog*, December 2, 2023. https://www.nrdc.org/bio/joe-thwaites/cop-28-climate-fund-pledge-tracker.

Tichenor, Daniel. *Dividing Lines: The Politics of Immigration Control in America*. Princeton, NJ: Princeton University Press, 2002.

Tinker Salas, Miguel. *In the Shadow of the Eagles: Sonora and the Transformation of the Border during the Porfiriato*. Berkeley: University of California Press, 1997.

Topal, Aylin. *Boosting Competitiveness through Decentralization: Subnational Comparison of Local Development in Mexico*. Farnham: Ashgate, 2012.

United Nations. "Draft Articles on the Responsibility of States for Internationally Wrongful Acts." 2008. https://doi.org/10.18356/1b3062be-en.

United Nations Framework Convention on Climate Change. "Adoption of the Paris Agreement." December 12, 2015. https://unfccc.int/documents/9064#beg%3E.

U.S. Congress. House. Committee on Agriculture. "Immigration Reform and Control Act of 1983." HR 1510. 98th Cong. Introduced in House, February 17, 1983. https://www.congress.gov/bill/98th-congress/house-bill/1510.

———. "Hearings before the Subcommittee on Immigration, Refugees, and International Law of the Committee on the Judiciary," HR 3080. 99th Cong. 1st sess., September 9 and 11, 1985.

———. Senate. "Hearings on S. 1200, A Bill to Amend the Immigration and Nationality Act to Effectively Control Unauthorized Immigration to the United States." S 1200. 99th Cong., 1st sess. Introduced in Senate, May 23, 1985.

U.S. Department of Justice. "Department of Justice Prosecuted a Record-Breaking Number of Immigration-Related Cases in Fiscal Year 2019." *Justice News*, October 17, 2019. https://www.justice.gov/opa/pr/department-justice-prosecuted-record-breaking-number-immigration-related-cases-fiscal-year.

U.S. Department of Labor. "Fact Sheet #62W: What Is 'Portability' and to Whom Does It Apply?" Accessed June 3, 2024. https://www.dol.gov/agencies/whd/fact-sheets/62w-H1b-portability#:~:text=The%20portability%20provision%20enables%20an,the%20services%20of%20that%20worker.

U.S. Government Accountability Office (GAO). "Immigration Enforcement: Immigration Related Prosecutions Increase from 2017 to 2018 in Response to U.S. Attorney General's Direction." Washington, DC, December 2019. https://www.gao.gov/assets/710/702965.pdf.

———. *Treaty of Guadalupe Hidalgo: Findings and Possible Options Regarding Longstanding Community Land Grant Claims in New Mexico*. Washington, DC, 2004.

Vázquez, Yolanda. "Constructing Crimmigration: Latino Subordination in a 'Post-Racial' World." *Ohio State Law Journal* 76 (2015): 599–657.

Vázquez-López, Raúl. "The Transformation of the Textile and Apparel Sector after NAFTA." *Journal of International Business and Economy* (2014): 83–112. https://doi.org/10.1007/978-3-030-55265-7_4.

Velásquez, María Cristina. "Migrant Communities, Gender and Political Power in Oaxaca." In *Indigenous Mexican Migrants in the United States*, edited by Jonathan Fox and Gaspar

Rivera Salgado, 1–47. La Jolla: University of California, San Diego, Center for U.S.-Mexican Studies and Center for Comparative Immigration Studies, 2004.

Walia, Harsha. *Border and Rule: Global Migration, Capitalism and the Rise of Racist Nationalism*. Boston: Haymarket Books, 2020.

Warren, Robert, and John Robert Warren. "Unauthorized Immigration to the United States: Annual Estimates and Components of Change by State, 1990 to 2010." *International Migration Review* 47, no. 2 (Summer 2013): 296–329.

Wasem, Ruth Ellen. "Immigration of Agricultural Guest Workers: Policy, Trends, and Legislative Issues." Congressional Research Service, August 2001, 21.

Weisbrot, Mark, Laura Merlling, Victor Mello, Stephen Lefebvre, and Joseph Sammut. "Did NAFTA Help Mexico? An Update after 23 Years." Center for Economic and Policy Research, March 2017.

White House. "Executive Order: Border Security and Immigration Enforcement Improvements." Accessed May 29, 2024 https://trumpwhitehouse.archives.gov/presidential-actions/executive-order-border-security-immigration-enforcement-improvements/,

———. "Executive Order: Enhancing Public Safety in the Interior of the United States." Accessed August 21, 2020. https://www.whitehouse.gov/presidential-actions/executive-order-enhancing-public-safety-interior-united-states/.

Woods, Ngaire. *The Globalizers: the IMF, the World Bank, and Their Borrowers*. Ithaca, NY: Cornell University Press, 2006.

———. "The United States and the International Financial Institutions: Power and Influence within the World Bank and the IMF." In *US Hegemony and International Organizations*, edited by Rosemary Foot, Neil McFarlane, and Michael Mastanduno. Oxford: Oxford University Press, 2003.

Yúnez-Naude, Antonio, and Fernando Barceinas Paredes. "The Reshaping of Agricultural Policy in Mexico." In *Changing Structure of Mexico*, 2nd ed., edited by Laura Randall, 231–53. London: Routledge, 2006. https://doi.org/10.4324/9781315705859-23.

Zabin, Carol, and Sallie Hughes. "Economic Integration and Labor Flows: Stage Migration in Farm Labor Markets in Mexico and the United States." *International Migration Review* 29, no. 2 (1995): 395–422.

Zamora, Rodolfo, and Juan Padilla. "Zacatecas, migración y minería: El extractivismo como ilusión del desarrollo" [Zacatecas, Migration and Mining: Extractivism as an Illusion of Development]. In *Mexico en la trampa del financiamiento: El sendero del no desarollo* [Mexico in the Financing Trap: The Path of Non-Development]. Mexico City: Universidad Nacional Autónoma de México, 2013.

Zavala, Erika Montoya, "En búsqueda de mejores salarios y de la Unión Familiar: Jaiberas sinaloenses con visa H-2B en Carolina del Norte: Una solución encontrada o una solución desesperada?" [In Search of the Best Salaries and Family Unity: Sinaloan Crab Cleaners with H-2B Visas in North Carolina: A Solution Found or a Desperate Solution?]. *Relaciones* 29, no. 16 (Autumn 2008): 201.

abarrotes, 29
abolition, 120–21; migration as choice as abolition democracy, 121–30
Abrego, Leisy, 11, 78
Acevedo, Dolores, 10
Achiume, Tendayi, 8–9, 132
agribusiness, 4, 14–15; Mexican, 59, 86–89; Mexican state support for, 90; United States, 33, 51–63, 89. *See also* agriculture
agriculture, 2, 15; abandonment of Mexican small-producing, 16, 27–28, 32–36, 86–89, 115, 125; corporate interests in, 36, 87–89; distribution of Mexican resources in the sectors of manufacturing and, 90, 106, 115, 117; government co-ops in Mexican, 86–87; irrigation pipes to support local Mexican, 106–7; Mexican, 34, 40, 59, 86–89, 97; Mexican resources allocated to large-scale, 115; Mexican small-producing organic, 97, 123; Mixtec methods of, 123; rain-fed, 81–82; remittance-based investments in, 85, 88; of United States, 48–56; 62, 72–73, wage suppression in, 40, 46. *See also* agribusiness; land; resources
Anderson Clayton, 87
Andrews, Abigail, 100, 105
Arizona, 66, 68
asambleas, 99, 122–23, 127
asylum, 19, 139n52
AT&T, 95

austerity, 28, 34–35, 41, 87, 124–25. *See also* International Monetary Fund (IMF); structural adjustment
autoempleo, 106
autoridades, 82–83, 90, 97, 99, 105, 107–8, 119, 154n13
Aztec Empire, 37

Baja California, 65
bajadores, 70
barrio, 97
Bautista, Bernardo Ramirez, 21, 106, 133
Berkshire, Frank, 63–64
Bhattacharyya, Gargi, 50
Biden, President Joseph, 58
Blease, Senator Coleman Livingston, 64
Boal, Augusto: *Theater of the Oppressed*, 157n1
Boehm, Deborah, 11–12, 98
Boeing, 66, 126
Border Patrol, 1, 17, 63–64; checkpoints of, 65; fortified presence of, 66–69; increases in the funding of the, 66. *See also* enforcement
borders: extraction in United States policies of control of the, 63–69; militarization of, 121–22, 125. *See also* enforcement; Mexico-United States border
Bracero Program, 15–16, 28, 47, 53–54, 59, 92
braceros, 53–54, 73, 88, 130, 146n12.
See also migrants
British Petroleum, 90
Bush, President George W., 58, 62

Founded in 1893,
UNIVERSITY OF CALIFORNIA PRESS
publishes bold, progressive books and journals
on topics in the arts, humanities, social sciences,
and natural sciences—with a focus on social
justice issues—that inspire thought and action
among readers worldwide.

The UC PRESS FOUNDATION
raises funds to uphold the press's vital role
as an independent, nonprofit publisher, and
receives philanthropic support from a wide
range of individuals and institutions—and from
committed readers like you. To learn more, visit
ucpress.edu/supportus.